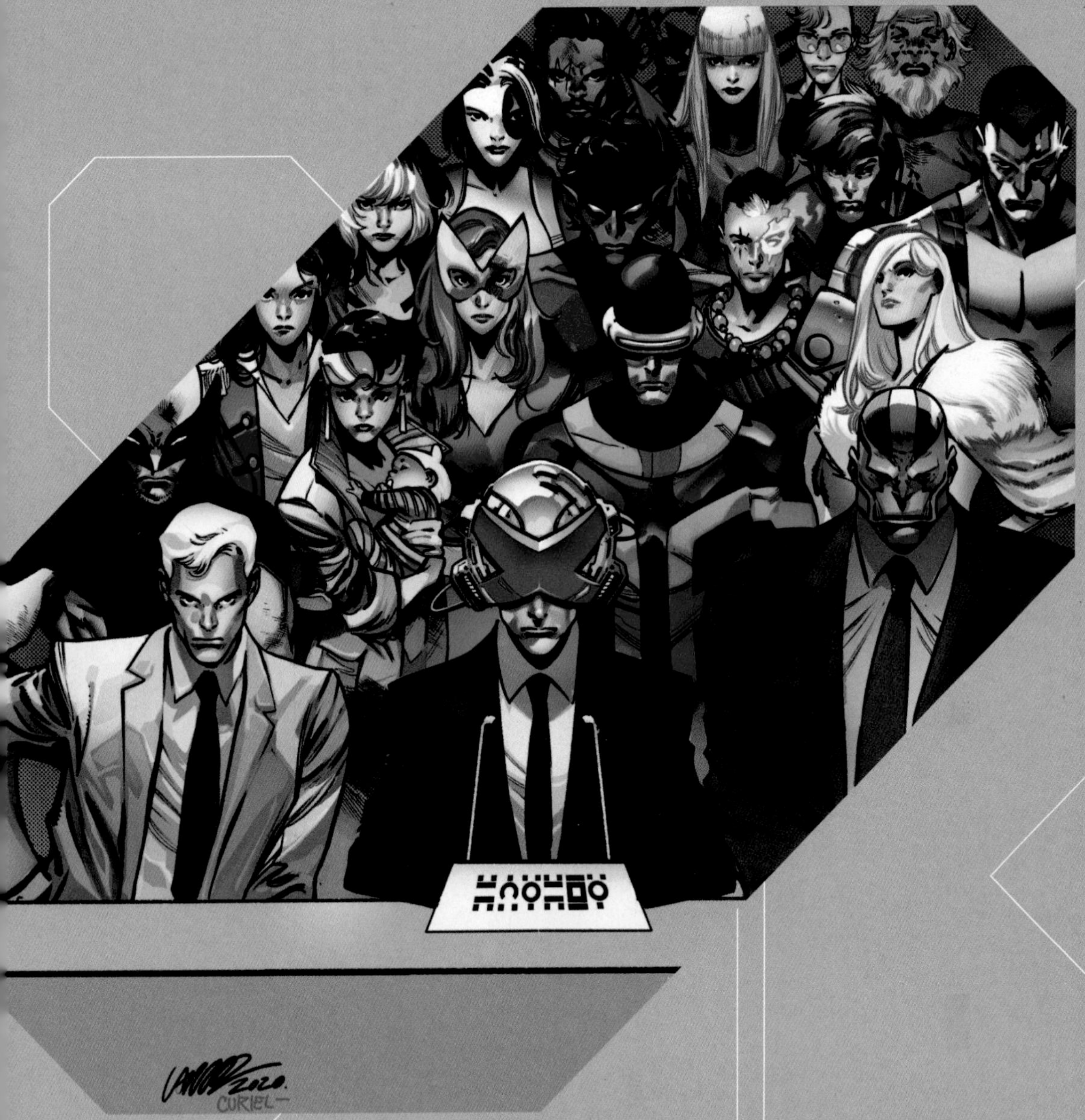
2020.
CURIEL

DAWN OF X VOL. 4. Contains material originally published in magazine form as X-MEN (2019) #4, X-FORCE (2019) #4, MARAUDERS (2019) #4, EXCALIBUR (2019) #4, FALLEN ANGELS (2019) #4 and NEW MUTANTS (2019) #4. First printing 2020. ISBN 978-1-302-92159-0. Published by MARVEL WORLDWIDE, INC., a subsidiary of MARVEL ENTERTAINMENT, LLC. OFFICE OF PUBLICATION: 1290 Avenue of the Americas, New York, NY 10104. © 2020 MARVEL No similarity between any of the names, characters, persons, and/or institutions in this magazine with those of any living or dead person or institution is intended, and any such similarity which may exist is purely coincidental. **Printed in the U.S.A.** KEVIN FEIGE, Chief Creative Officer; DAN BUCKLEY, President, Marvel Entertainment; JOHN NEE, Publisher; JOE QUESADA, EVP & Creative Director; TOM BREVOORT, SVP of Publishing; DAVID BOGART, Associate Publisher & SVP of Talent Affairs; Publishing & Partnership; DAVID GABRIEL, VP of Print & Digital Publishing; JEFF YOUNGQUIST, VP of Production & Special Projects; DAN CARR, Executive Director of Publishing Technology; ALEX MORALES, Director of Publishing Operations; DAN EDINGTON, Managing Editor; SUSAN CRESPI, Production Manager; STAN LEE, Chairman Emeritus. For information regarding advertising in Marvel Comics or on Marvel.com, please contact Vit DeBellis, Custom Solutions & Integrated Advertising Manager, at vdebellis@marvel. com. For Marvel subscription inquiries, please call 888-511-5480. **Manufactured between 1/31/2020 and 3/3/2020 by LSC COMMUNICATIONS INC., KENDALLVILLE, IN, USA.**

10 9 8 7 6 5 4 3 2 1

DAWN OF X

● Volume
04

X-Men created by Stan Lee & Jack Kirby

Writers:	**Jonathan Hickman, Gerry Duggan, Tini Howard, Ed Brisson, Benjamin Percy & Bryan Hill**
Artists:	**Leinil Francis Yu & Gerry Alanguilan; Lucas Werneck; Marcus To; Marco Failla; Joshua Cassara and Szymon Kudranski**
Color Artists:	**Sunny Gho, Federico Blee, Erick Arciniega, Carlos Lopez, Dean White, Guru-eFX & Frank D'Armata**
Letterers:	**VC's Clayton Cowles, Cory Petit, Travis Lanham, Joe Caramanga & Joe Sabino**
Cover Art:	**Leinil Francis Yu & Sunny Gho; Russell Dauterman & Matthew Wilson; Mahmud Asrar & Matthew Wilson; Rod Reis; Dustin Weaver & Edgar Delgado; and David Nakayama**
Head of X:	**Jonathan Hickman**
Design:	**Tom Muller**
Assistant Editors:	**Annalise Bissa & Chris Robinson**
Editor:	**Jordan D. White**
Collection Cover Art:	**Pepe Larraz & David Curiel**
Collection Editor:	**Jennifer Grünwald**
Assistant Managing Editor:	**Maia Loy**
Assistant Managing Editor:	**Lisa Montalbano**
Associate Managing Editor:	**Kateri Woody**
Editor, Special Projects:	**Mark D. Beazley**
VP Production & Special Projects:	**Jeff Youngquist**
SVP Print, Sales & Marketing:	**David Gabriel**
Editor in Chief:	**C.B. Cebulski**

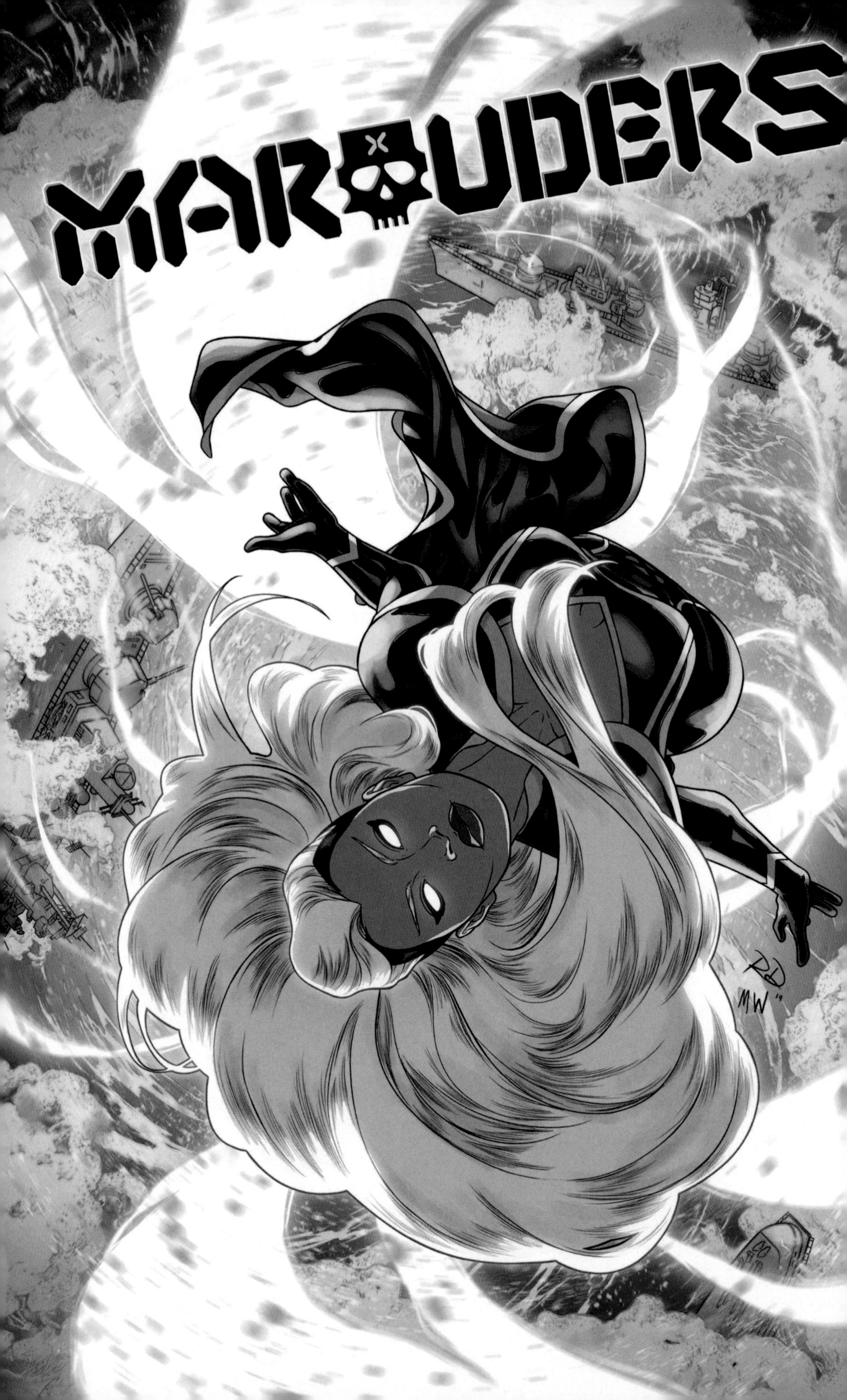
MARAUDERS

[kra_[0.4]
[koa_[0.4]

[kra_[0.X]
[koa_[0.X]

PUBLIC HUMILIATION

Mutants around the world are flocking to the island-nation of Krakoa for safety, security and to be part of the first mutant society.

The Hellfire Trading Company is responsible for distributing Krakoa's pharmaceuticals to friendly nations and smuggling mutants out of unfriendly ones. Conducting the organization's duties across the high seas are Captain Kate Pryde and her crew aboard their vessel, the *Marauder*!

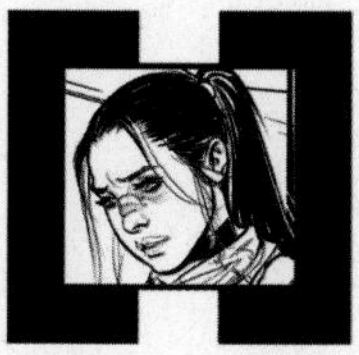

Kate Pryde

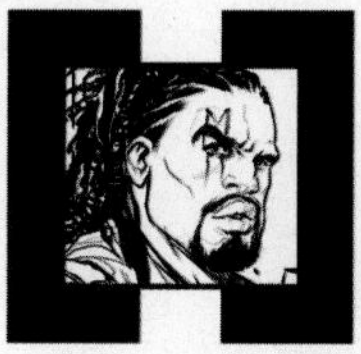

Bishop

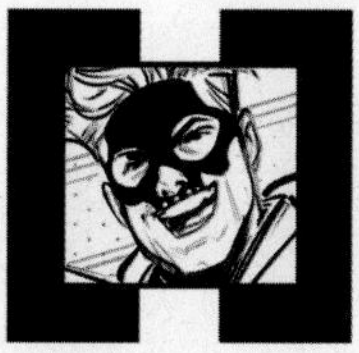

Pyro

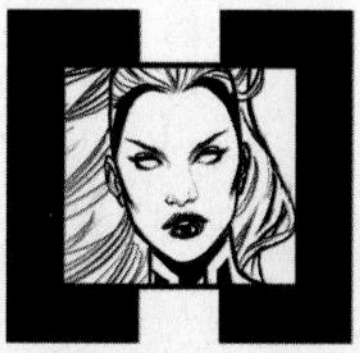

Storm

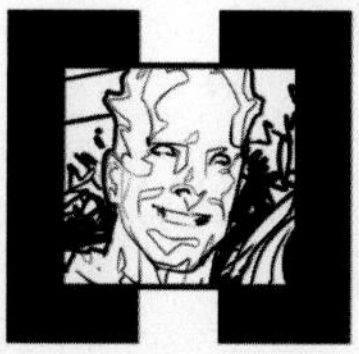

Iceman

[kra_[0.4]...]
[koa_[0.4]...]

[A._Shore_Thing]

[00_mutant_piracy]
[00_sea_shores_X_]

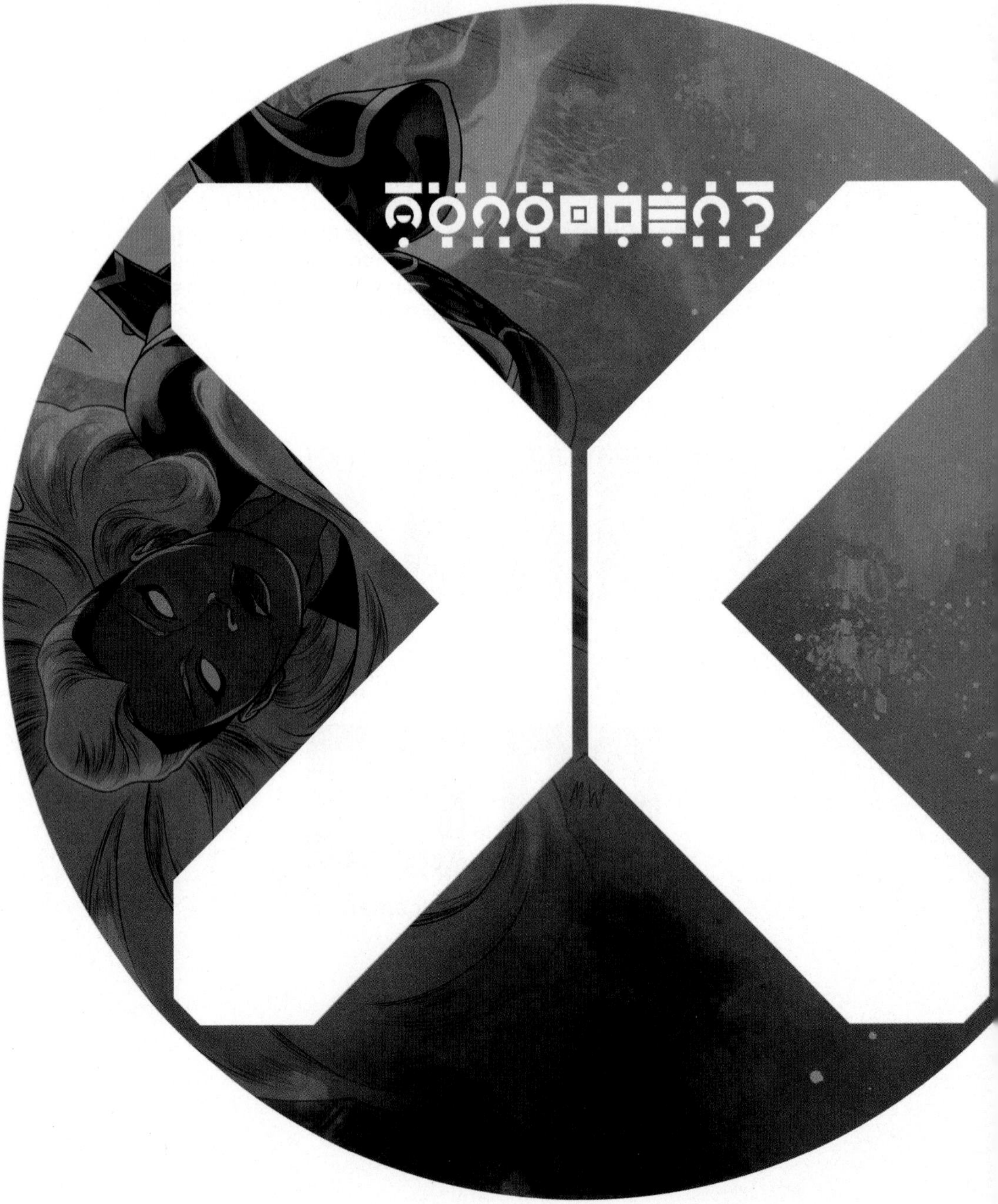

[00_mutant_piracy]
[00_sea_shores_X_]

GERRY DUGGAN..[WRITER]
LUCAS WERNECK...[ARTIST]
FEDERICO BLEE...................................[COLOR ARTIST]
VC's CORY PETIT....................................[LETTERER]
TOM MULLER..[DESIGN]

RUSSELL DAUTERMAN & MATTHEW WILSON......[COVER ARTISTS]

NICK RUSSELL.....................................[PRODUCTION]

JONATHAN HICKMAN...............................[HEAD OF X]
CHRIS ROBINSON........................[ASSISTANT EDITOR]
JORDAN D. WHITE.......................................[EDITOR]
C.B. CEBULSKI.........................[EDITOR IN CHIEF]
JOE QUESADA...................[CHIEF CREATIVE OFFICER]
DAN BUCKLEY.......................................[PRESIDENT]
ALAN FINE..............................[EXECUTIVE PRODUCER]

[04] MARAUDERS

[ISSUE FOUR].............THE RED BISHOP

[00_mutant_piracy]
[00_sea_shores_X_]

[00_00...0]
[00_00...4]

[00_boat__]
[00______]

[00______]

[00______X]

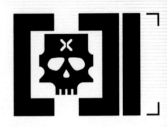

TOP SECRET EYES-ONLY ACCESS

FROM: THE X-DESK
TO: ▮▮▮▮▮▮▮▮
SUBJECT: RE: Krakoa

—

There's at least three Krakoan ships. No registry on any of them. Only two have even been photographed. The yacht with the big cannon extensively, the black military frigate only at a distance, but there's at least a third because delivery of the Krakoan drugs has occurred while both of those ships have been engaged elsewhere. You're gonna have to get the relevant stuff from U.S. NAVY INTEL.

Not much else I can tell you, 'cause I'm on a desk. Not a boat. The United States is going to need to throw bodies at this desk — fast. The human intelligence world is paralyzed. Even friendlies have clammed up. Nobody's talking because nobody knows what they know is currently worth. I hear MI6 hired a hundred bodies for their X-Desk. Must be nice. Maybe I can be recruited by a foreign government.

Oh, there was one interesting thing that happened this week. Emma Frost, White Queen of the Hellfire Trading Company, arrived in Manhattan's fashion district accompanied by a large bald man with four arms named Jumbo Carnation. That's not actually the interesting part; I'll get to that in a minute. Frost and Jumbo ran around the shops all afternoon dropping cash on mostly red and white fabrics. I know this from social media, because I have no bodies on the X-Desk. Where was I? Oh, yeah. Anyway, the interesting part is that Jumbo Carnation died a few years back. I was living in Manhattan at the time, and it made all the papers. Long story short: Jumbo was attacked after he left a club, and it was unclear whether he died in the attack or a drug overdose, or he was attacked and dosed, but the end result was his insides cooked inside his Teflon skin. I had the coroner send over the file. There's no doubt that he died a while back. I know mutant graves have always had a revolving door, but it still struck me as odd that the mutant fashion designer is back. Maybe the mutants are going back in time? But what do I know? I'm on a desk.

If you're still reading, send money and bodies. We're still behind.
▮▮▮▮▮▮▮▮

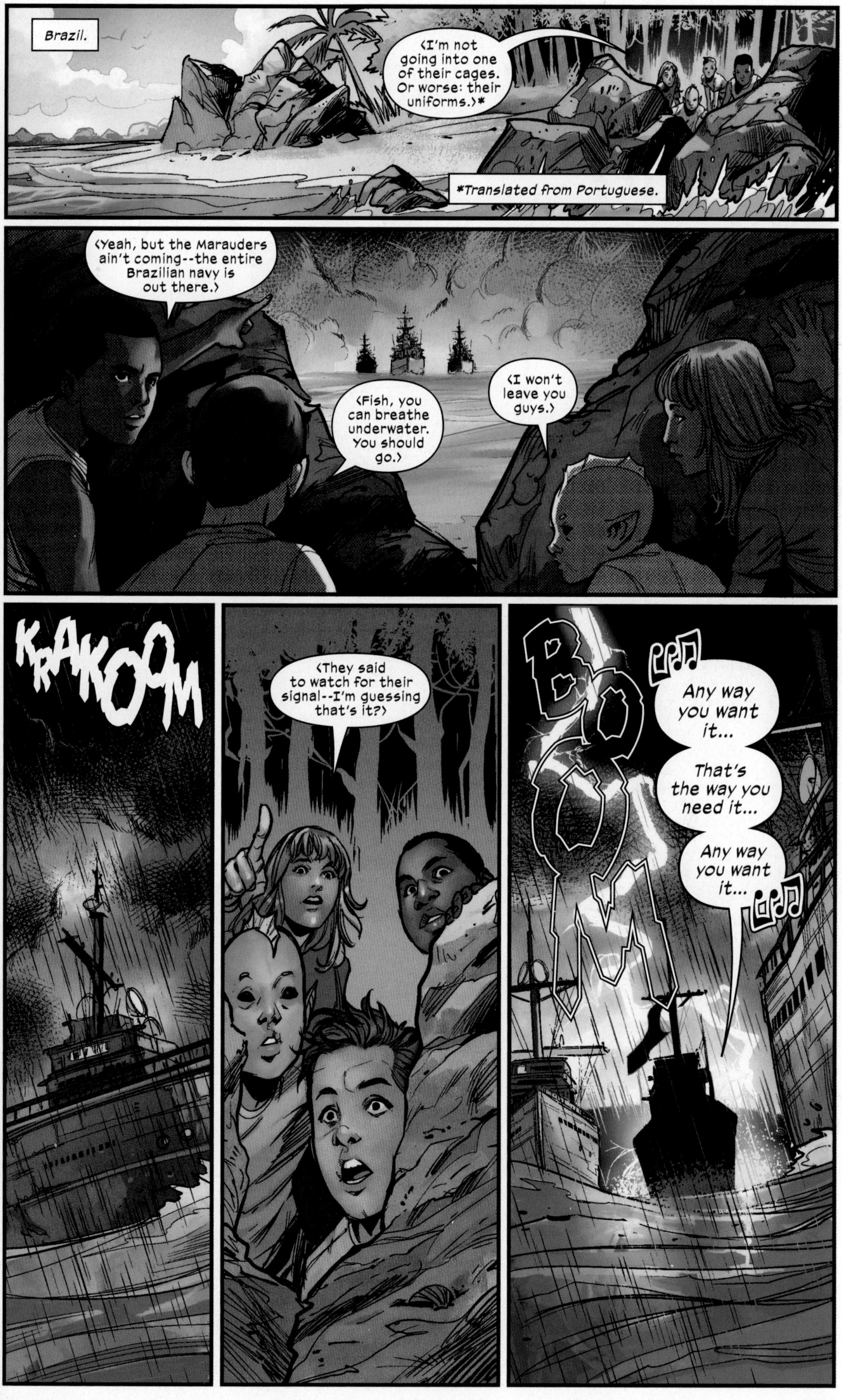
Brazil.
‹I'm not going into one of their cages. Or worse: their uniforms.›*
*Translated from Portuguese.
‹Yeah, but the Marauders ain't coming--the entire Brazilian navy is out there.›
‹Fish, you can breathe underwater. You should go.›
‹I won't leave you guys.›
KRAKOOM
‹They said to watch for their signal--I'm guessing that's it?›
BOOM
Any way you want it...
That's the way you need it...
Any way you want it...

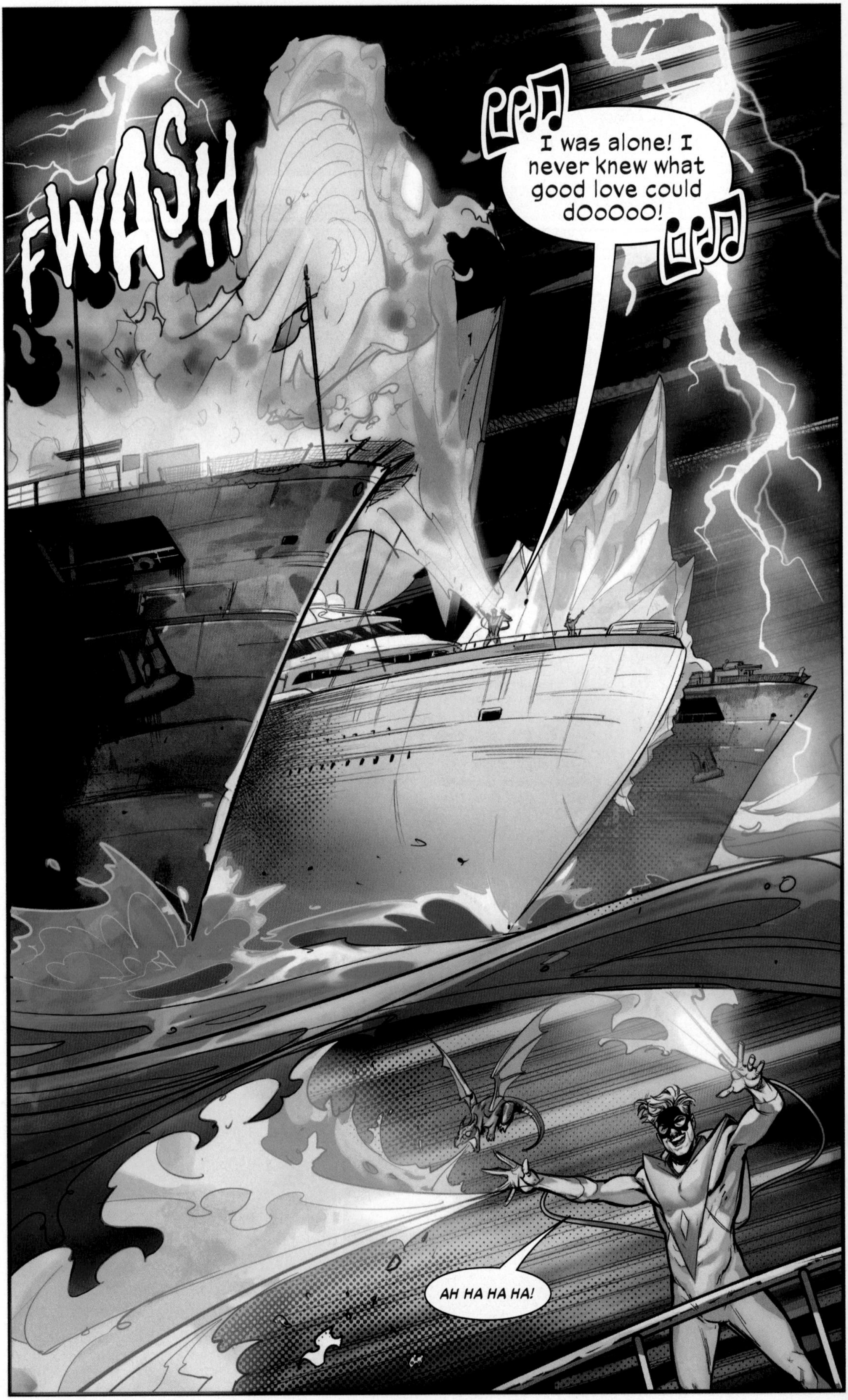
FWASH
I was alone! I never knew what good love could dOoOoO!
AH HA HA HA!

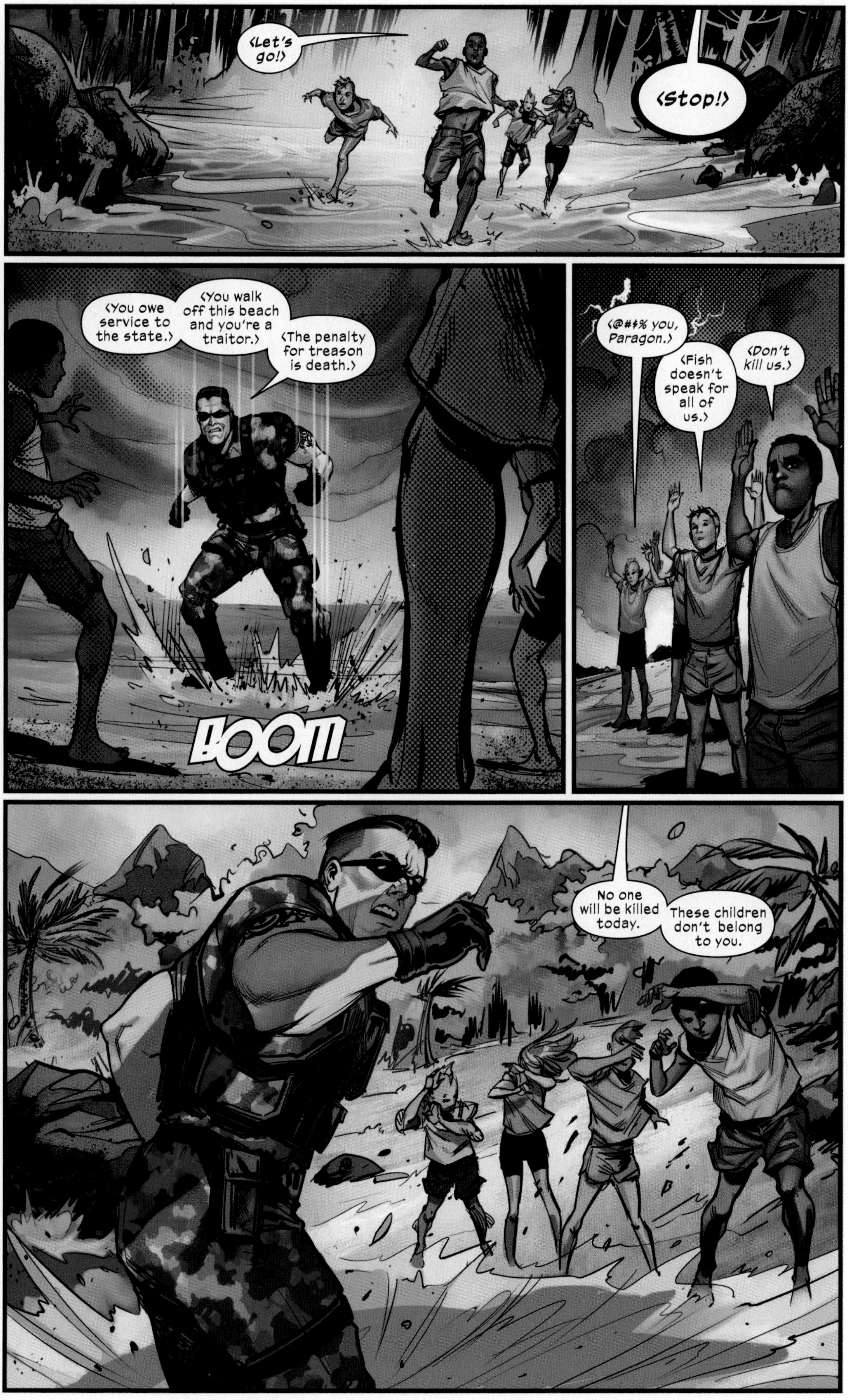
‹Let's go!›
‹Stop!›
‹You owe service to the state.›
‹You walk off this beach and you're a traitor.›
‹The penalty for treason is death.›
BOOM
‹@#$% you, Paragon.›
‹Fish doesn't speak for all of us.›
‹Don't kill us.›
No one will be killed today.
These children don't belong to you.

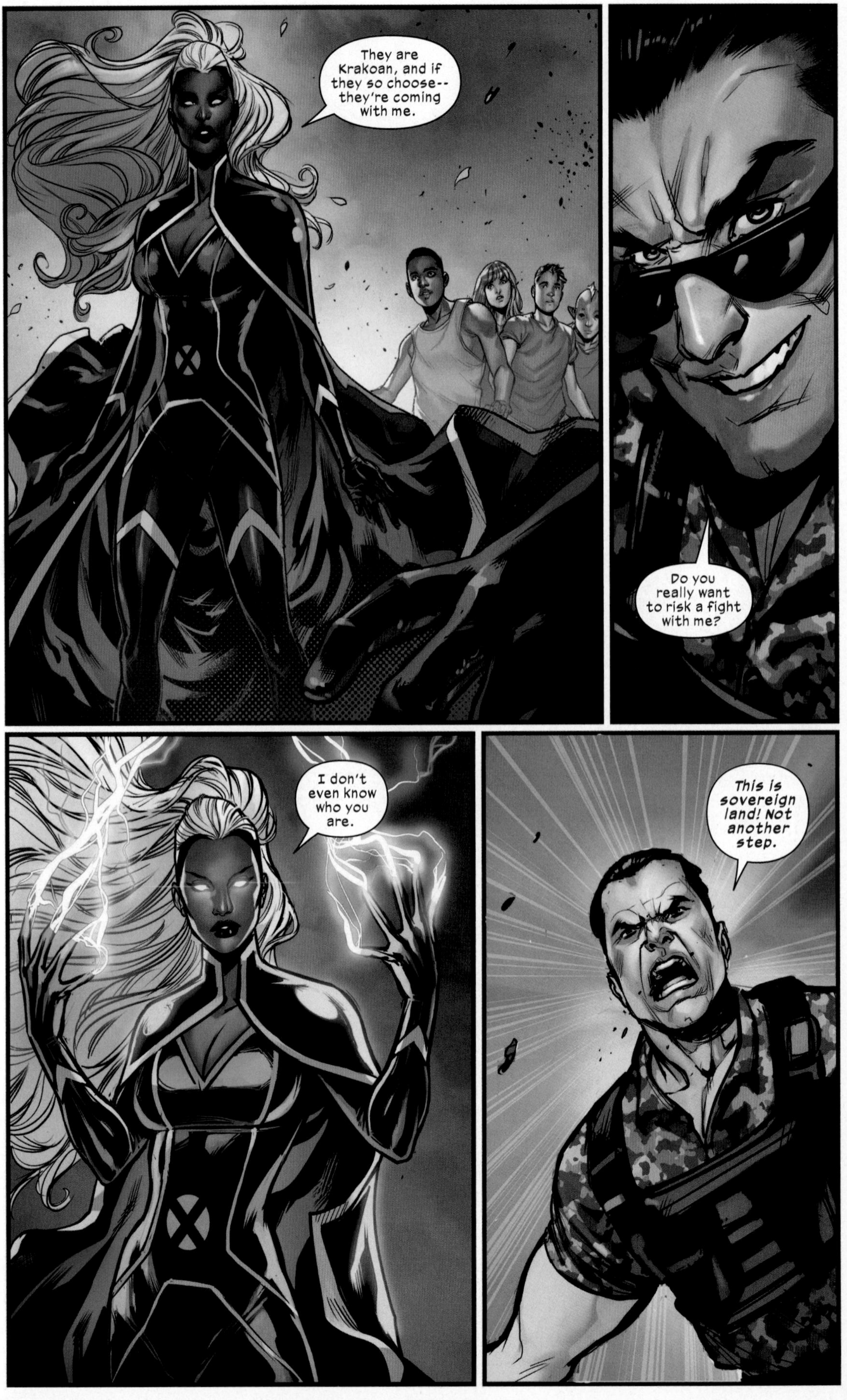
They are Krakoan, and if they so choose-- they're coming with me.
Do you really want to risk a fight with me?
I don't even know who you are.
This is sovereign land! Not another step.

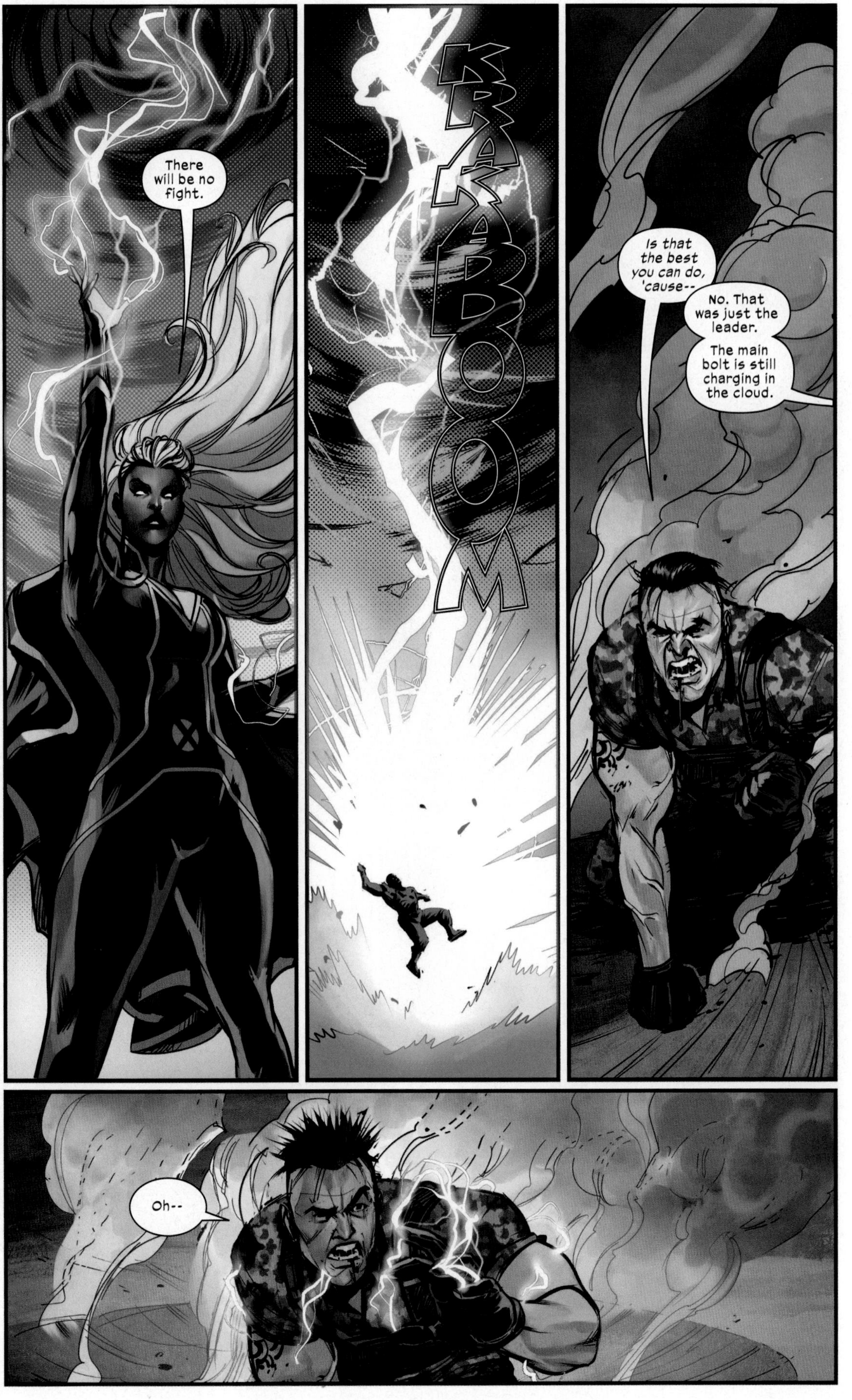
There will be no fight.
KRAKADOOM
Is that the best you can do, 'cause--
No. That was just the leader.
The main bolt is still charging in the cloud.
Oh--

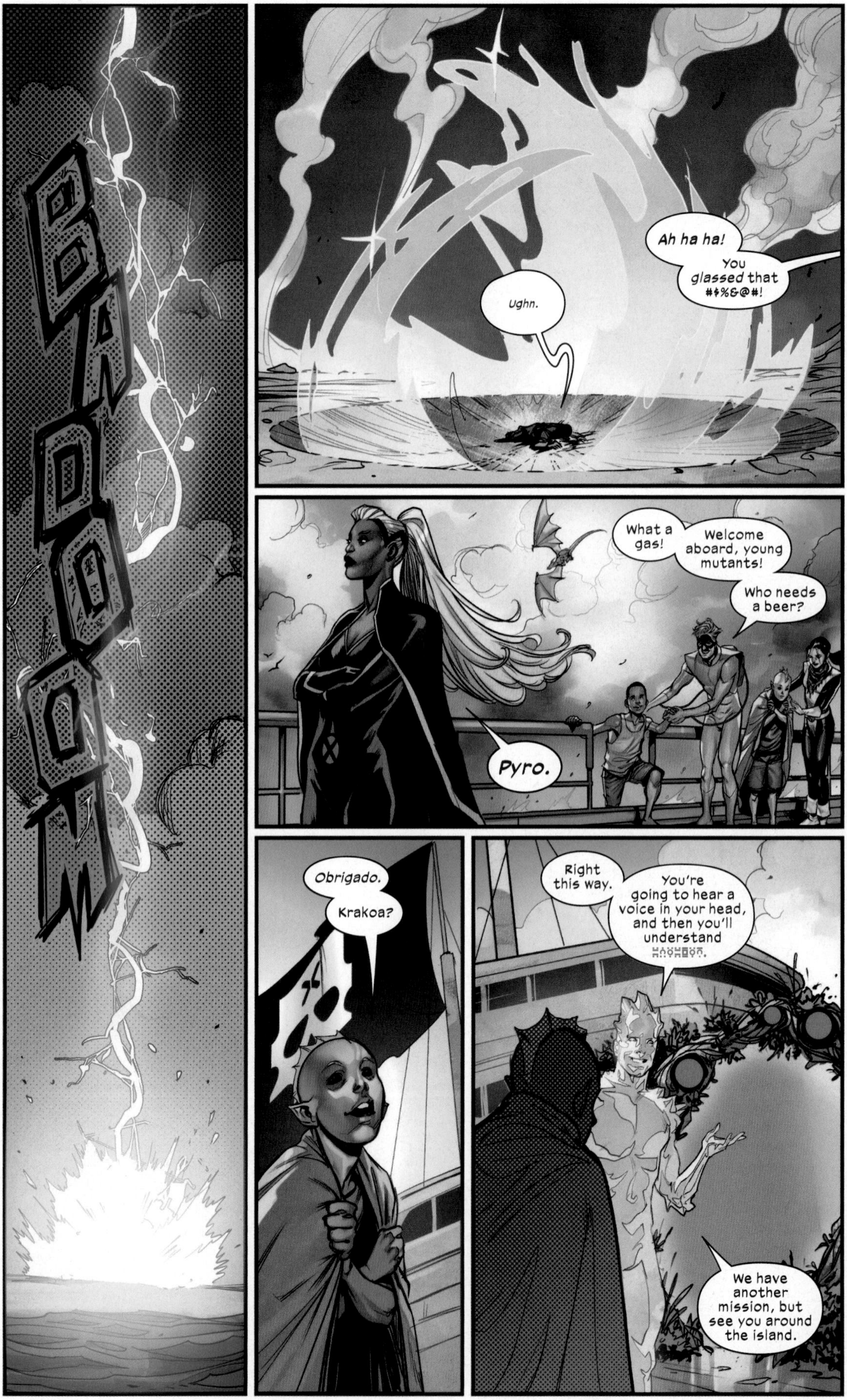
BADOOOM
Ah ha ha!
You glassed that #$%&@#!
Ughn.
What a gas!
Welcome aboard, young mutants!
Who needs a beer?
Pyro.
Obrigado.
Krakoa?
Right this way.
You're going to hear a voice in your head, and then you'll understand
We have another mission, but see you around the island.

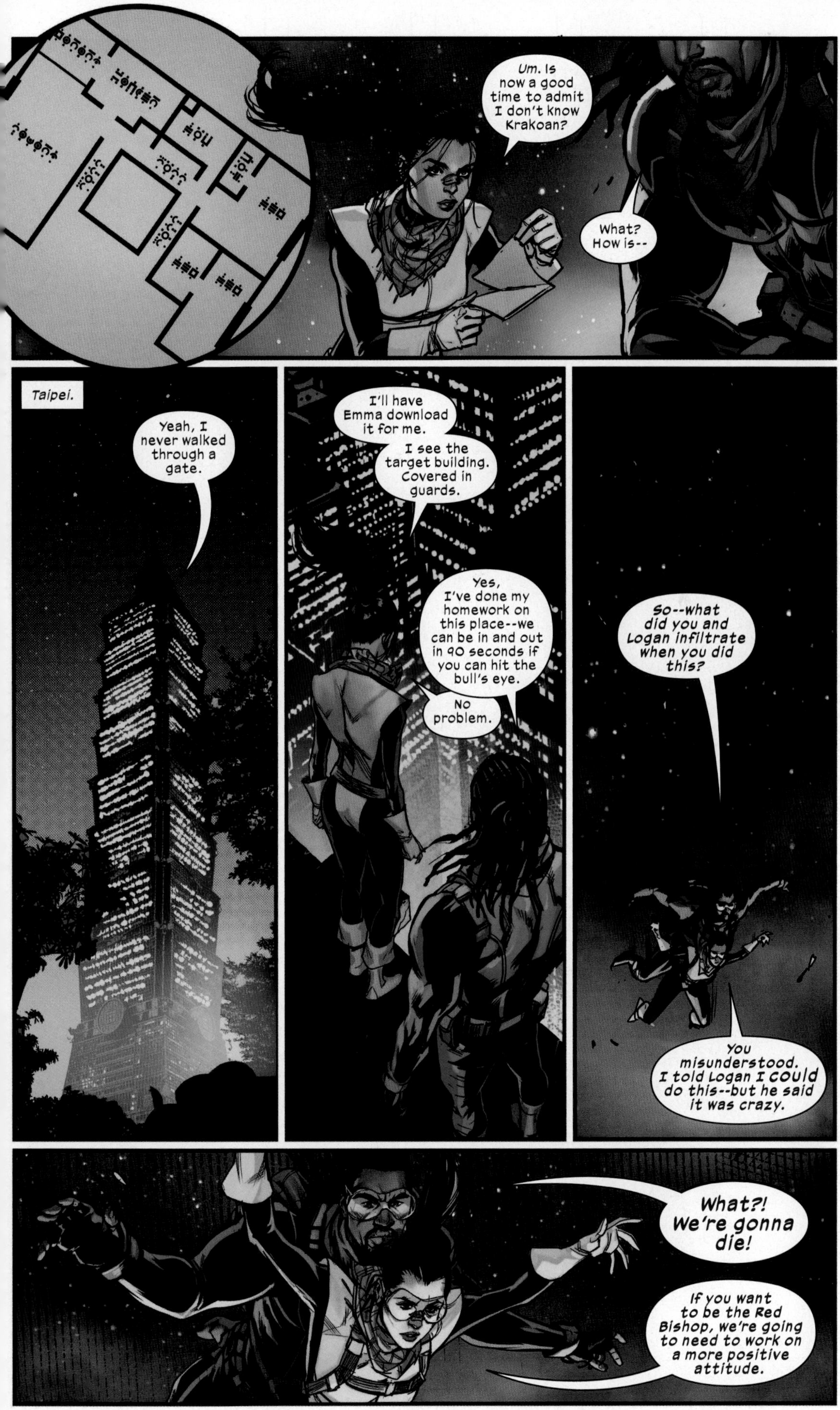
Um. Is now a good time to admit I don't know Krakoan?
What? How is--
Taipei.
Yeah, I never walked through a gate.
I'll have Emma download it for me.
I see the target building. Covered in guards.
Yes, I've done my homework on this place--we can be in and out in 90 seconds if you can hit the bull's eye.
No problem.
So--what did you and Logan infiltrate when you did this?
You misunderstood. I told Logan I COULD do this--but he said it was crazy.
What?! We're gonna die!
If you want to be the Red Bishop, we're going to need to work on a more positive attitude.

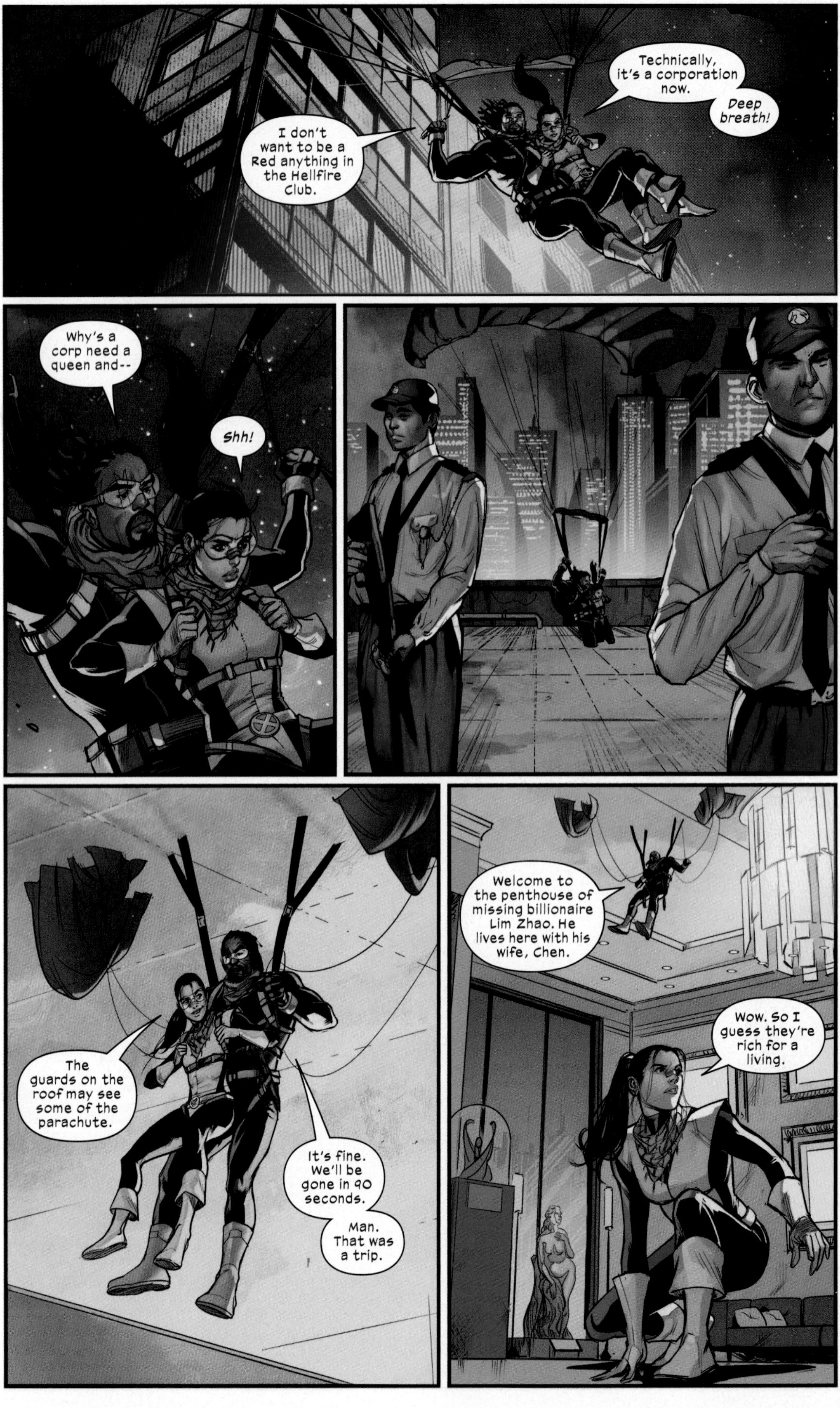

I don't want to be a Red anything in the Hellfire Club.
Technically, it's a corporation now.
Deep breath!
Why's a corp need a queen and--
Shh!
The guards on the roof may see some of the parachute.
It's fine. We'll be gone in 90 seconds.
Man. That was a trip.
Welcome to the penthouse of missing billionaire Lim Zhao. He lives here with his wife, Chen.
Wow. So I guess they're rich for a living.

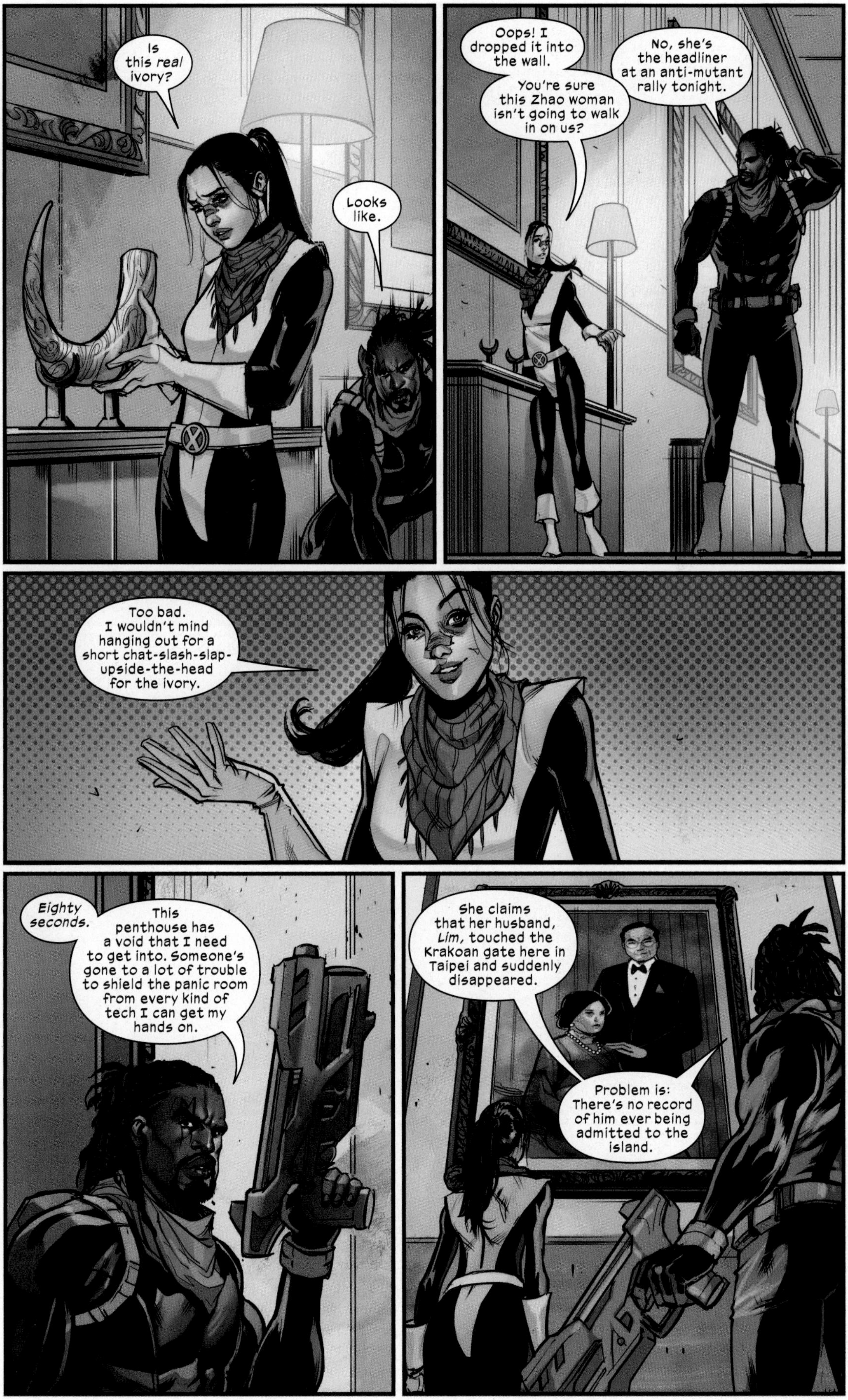
Is this *real* ivory?
Looks like.
Oops! I dropped it into the wall.
You're sure this Zhao woman isn't going to walk in on us?
No, she's the headliner at an anti-mutant rally tonight.
Too bad. I wouldn't mind hanging out for a short chat-slash-slap-upside-the-head for the ivory.
Eighty seconds.
This penthouse has a void that I need to get into. Someone's gone to a lot of trouble to shield the panic room from every kind of tech I can get my hands on.
She claims that her husband, *Lim,* touched the Krakoan gate here in Taipei and suddenly disappeared.
Problem is: There's no record of him ever being admitted to the island.

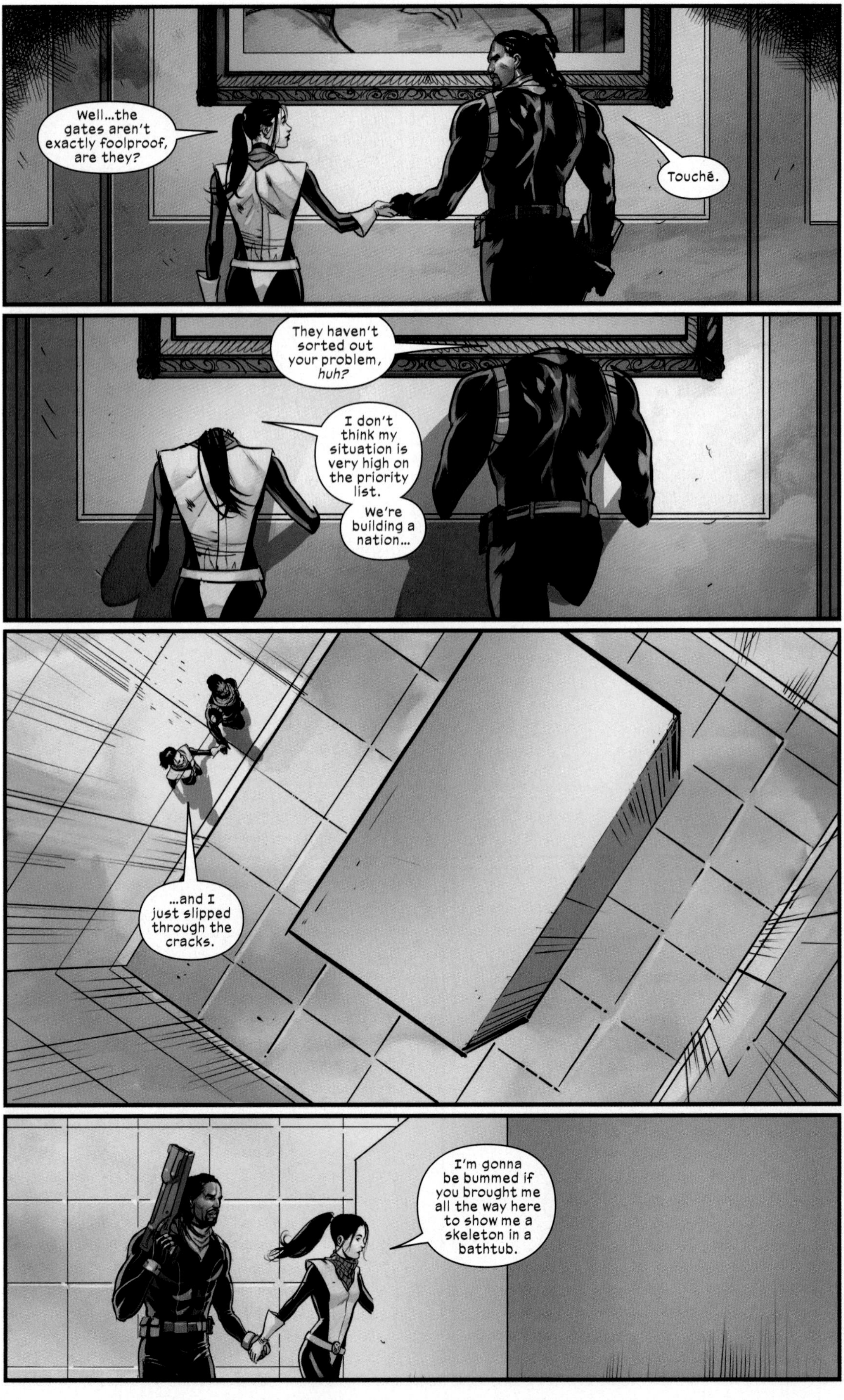
Well...the gates aren't exactly foolproof, are they?
Touché.
They haven't sorted out your problem, *huh?*
I don't think my situation is very high on the priority list.
We're building a nation...
...and I just slipped through the cracks.
I'm gonna be bummed if you brought me all the way here to show me a skeleton in a bathtub.

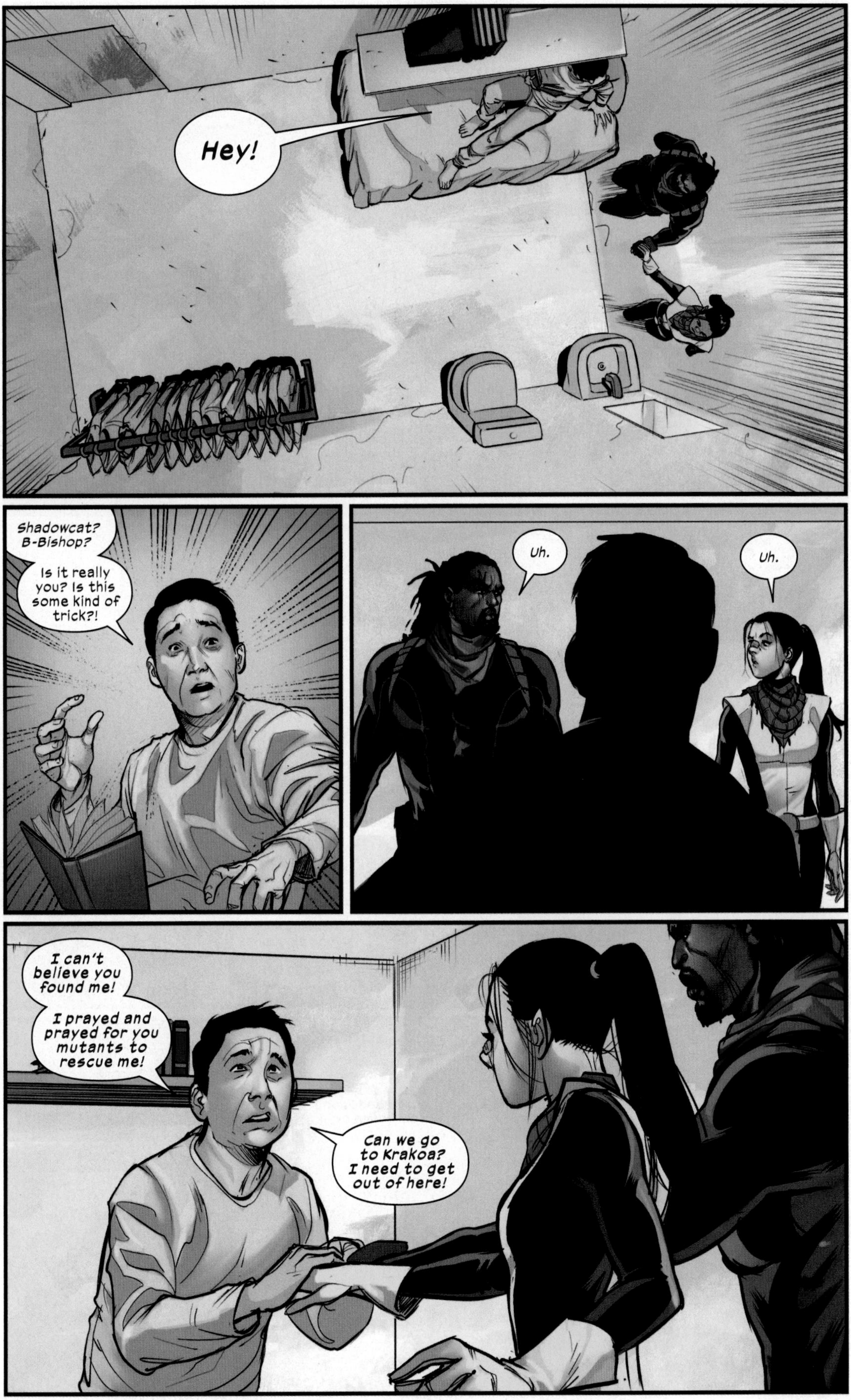
Hey!
Shadowcat? B-Bishop?
Is it really you? Is this some kind of trick?!
Uh.
Uh.
I can't believe you found me!
I prayed and prayed for you mutants to rescue me!
Can we go to Krakoa? I need to get out of here!

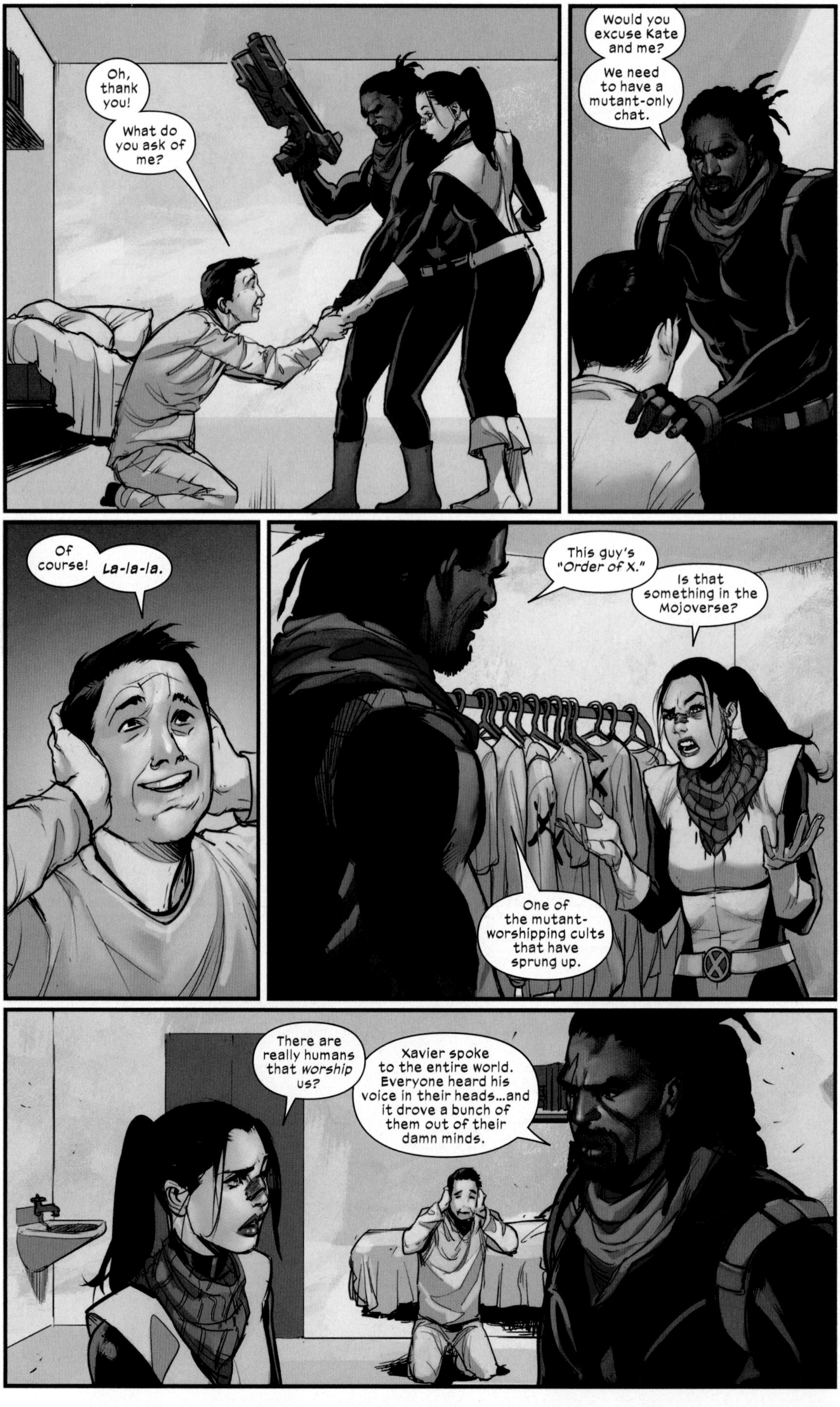

Oh, thank you!
What do you ask of me?
Would you excuse Kate and me?
We need to have a mutant-only chat.
Of course!
La-la-la.
This guy's "*Order of X.*"
Is that something in the Mojoverse?
One of the mutant-worshipping cults that have sprung up.
There are really humans that *worship* us?
Xavier spoke to the entire world. Everyone heard his voice in their heads...and it drove a bunch of them out of their damn minds.

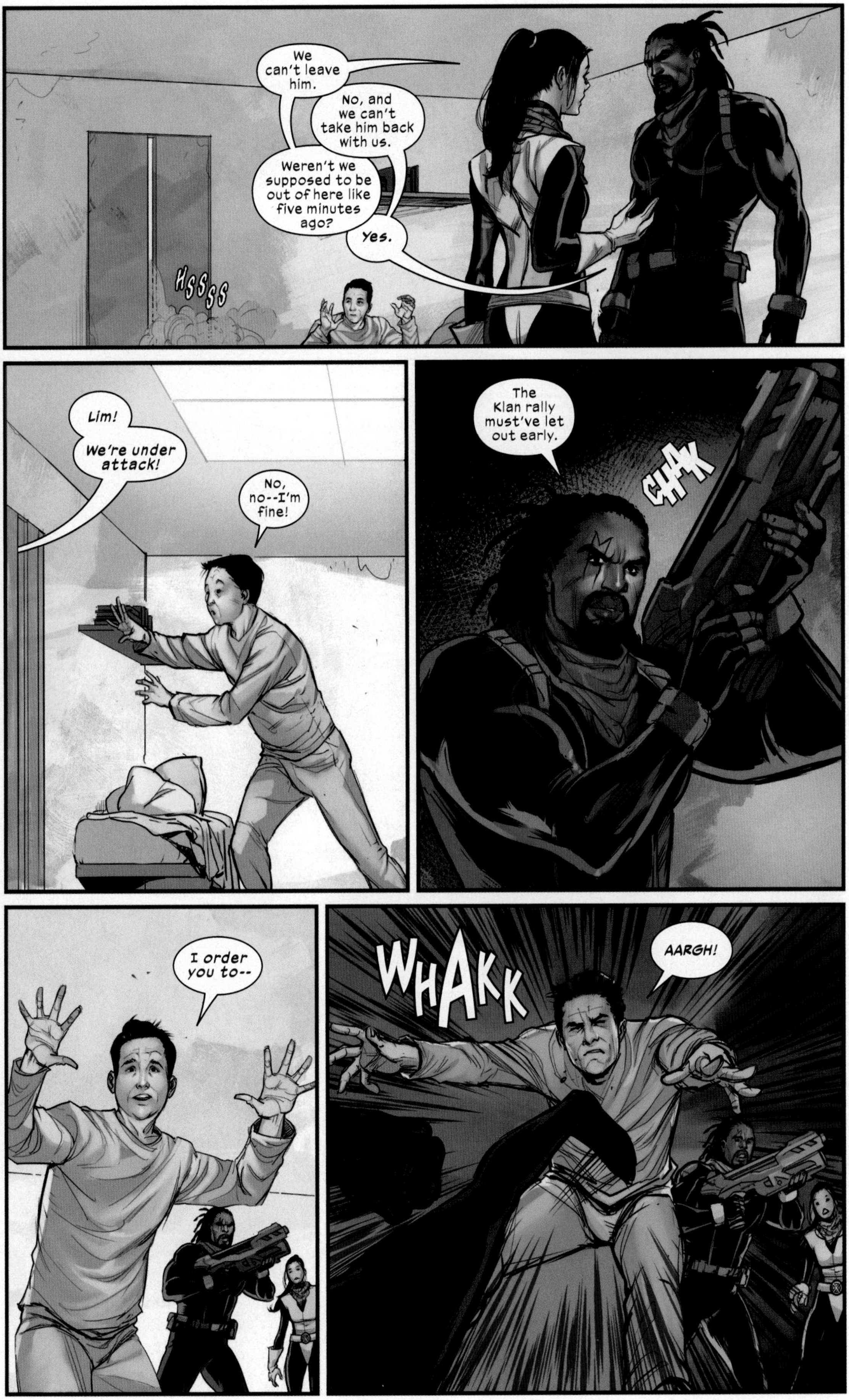
We can't leave him.
No, and we can't take him back with us.
Weren't we supposed to be out of here like five minutes ago?
Yes.
HSSSS
Lim!
We're under attack!
No, no--I'm fine!
The Klan rally must've let out early.
CHAK
I order you to--
WHAKK
AARGH!

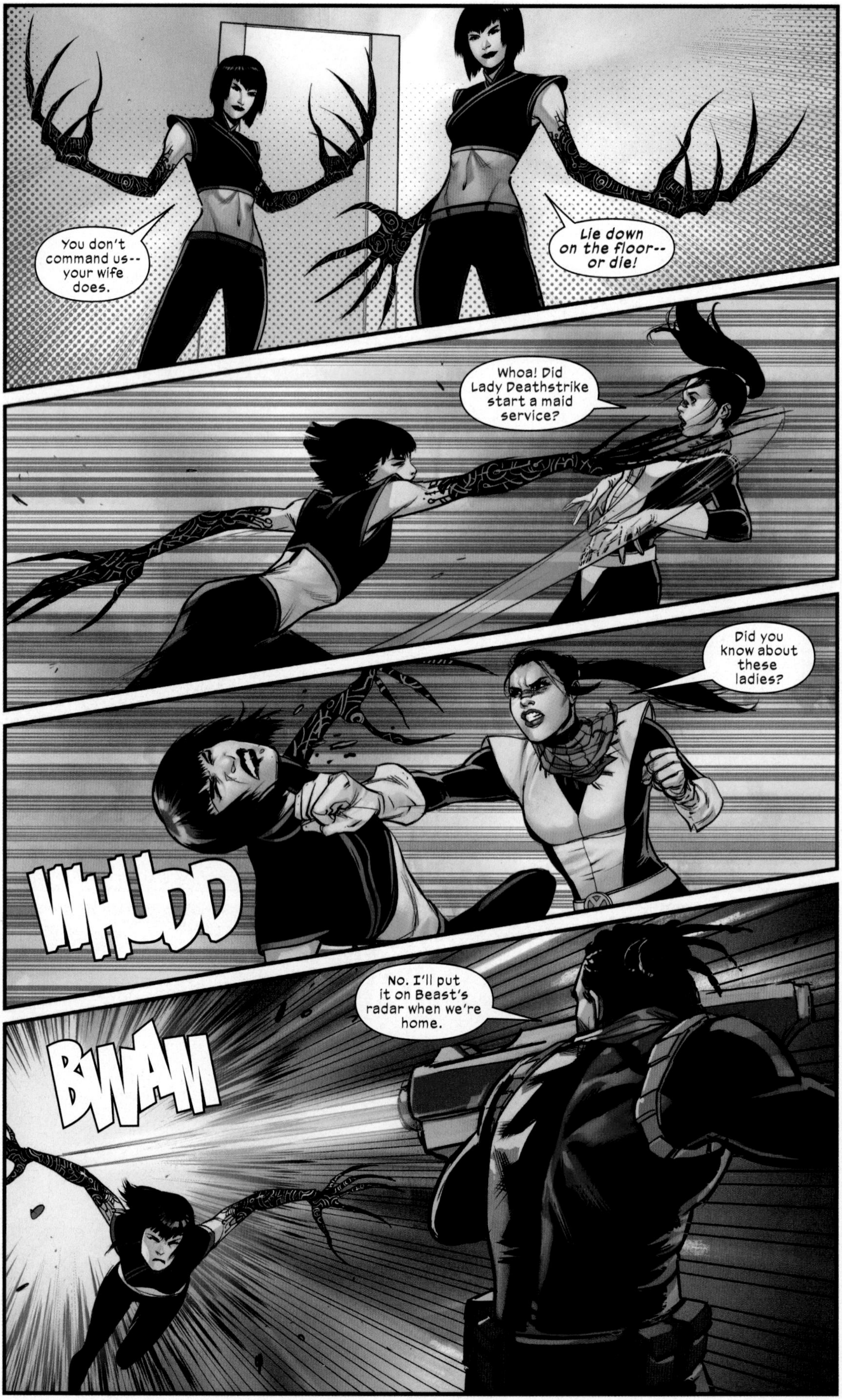

You don't command us--your wife does.
Lie down on the floor--or die!
Whoa! Did Lady Deathstrike start a maid service?
Did you know about these ladies?
WHUDD
No. I'll put it on Beast's radar when we're home.
BWAM

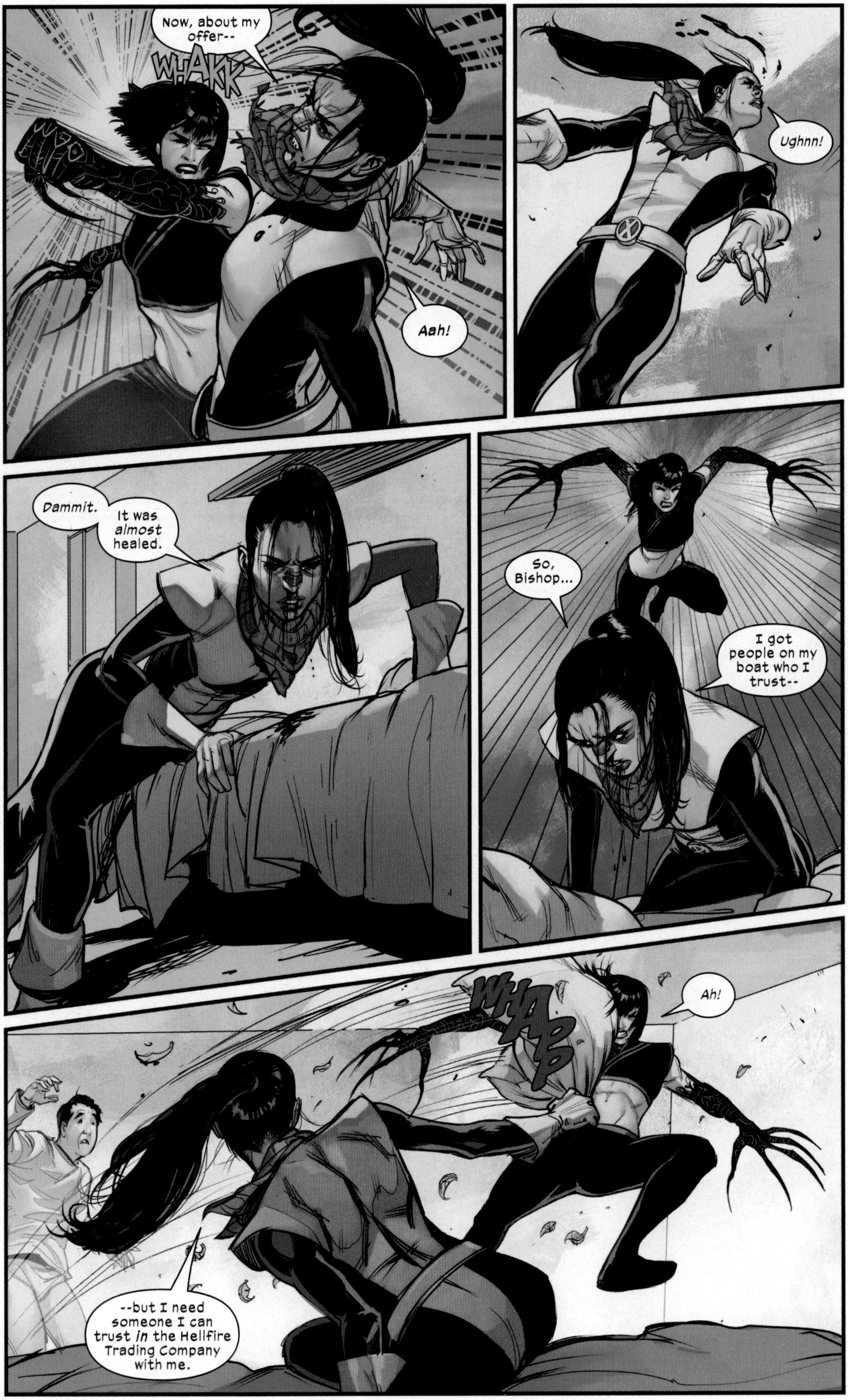

Now, about my offer--
WHAKK
Aah!
Ughnn!
Dammit.
It was *almost* healed.
So, Bishop...
I got people on my boat who I trust--
WHAP
Ah!
--but I need someone I can trust *in* the Hellfire Trading Company with me.

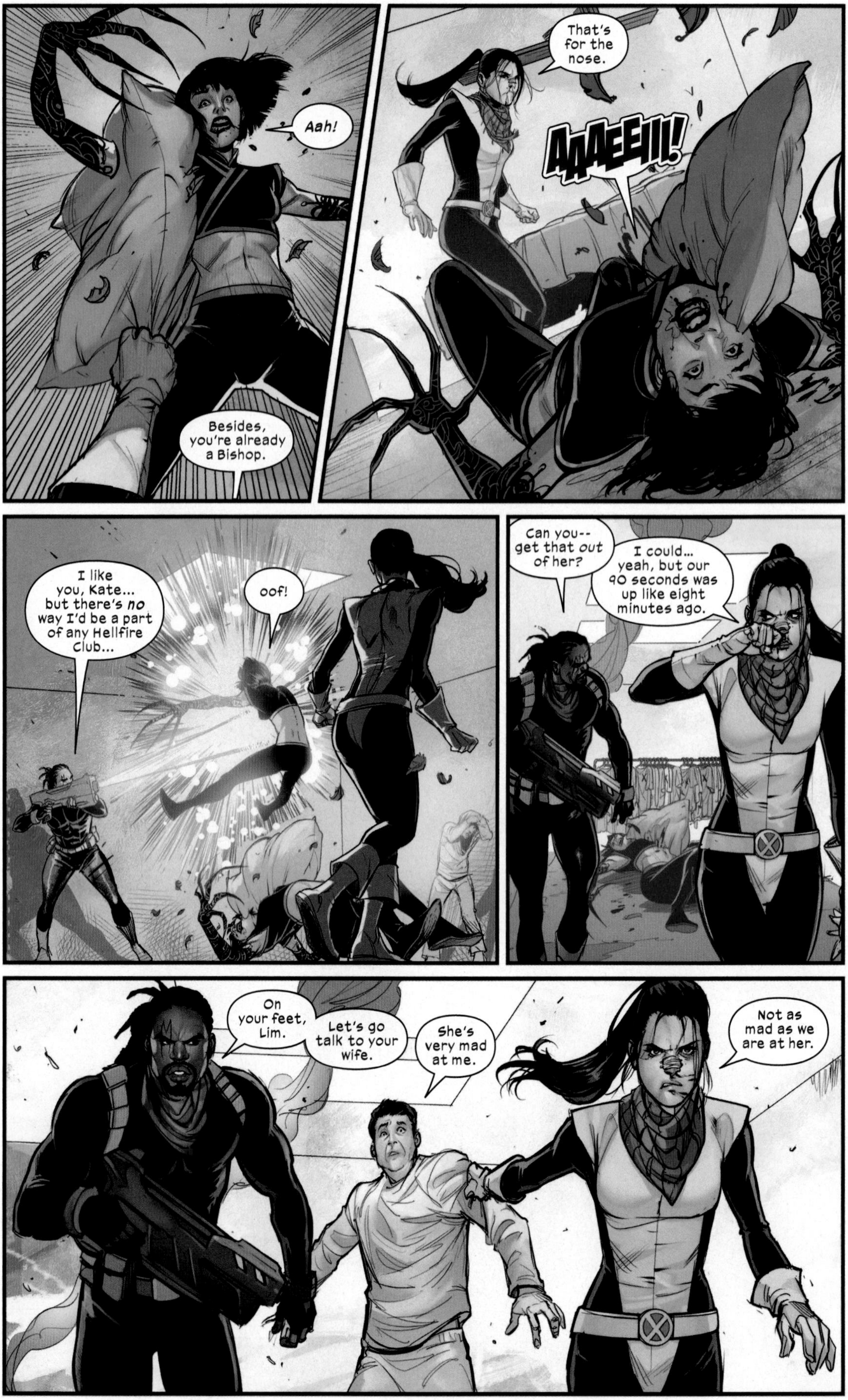
Aah!
Besides, you're already a Bishop.
That's for the nose.
AAAEEIIII!
I like you, Kate... but there's no way I'd be a part of any Hellfire Club...
oof!
Can you--get that out of her?
I could... yeah, but our 90 seconds was up like eight minutes ago.
On your feet, Lim.
Let's go talk to your wife.
She's very mad at me.
Not as mad as we are at her.

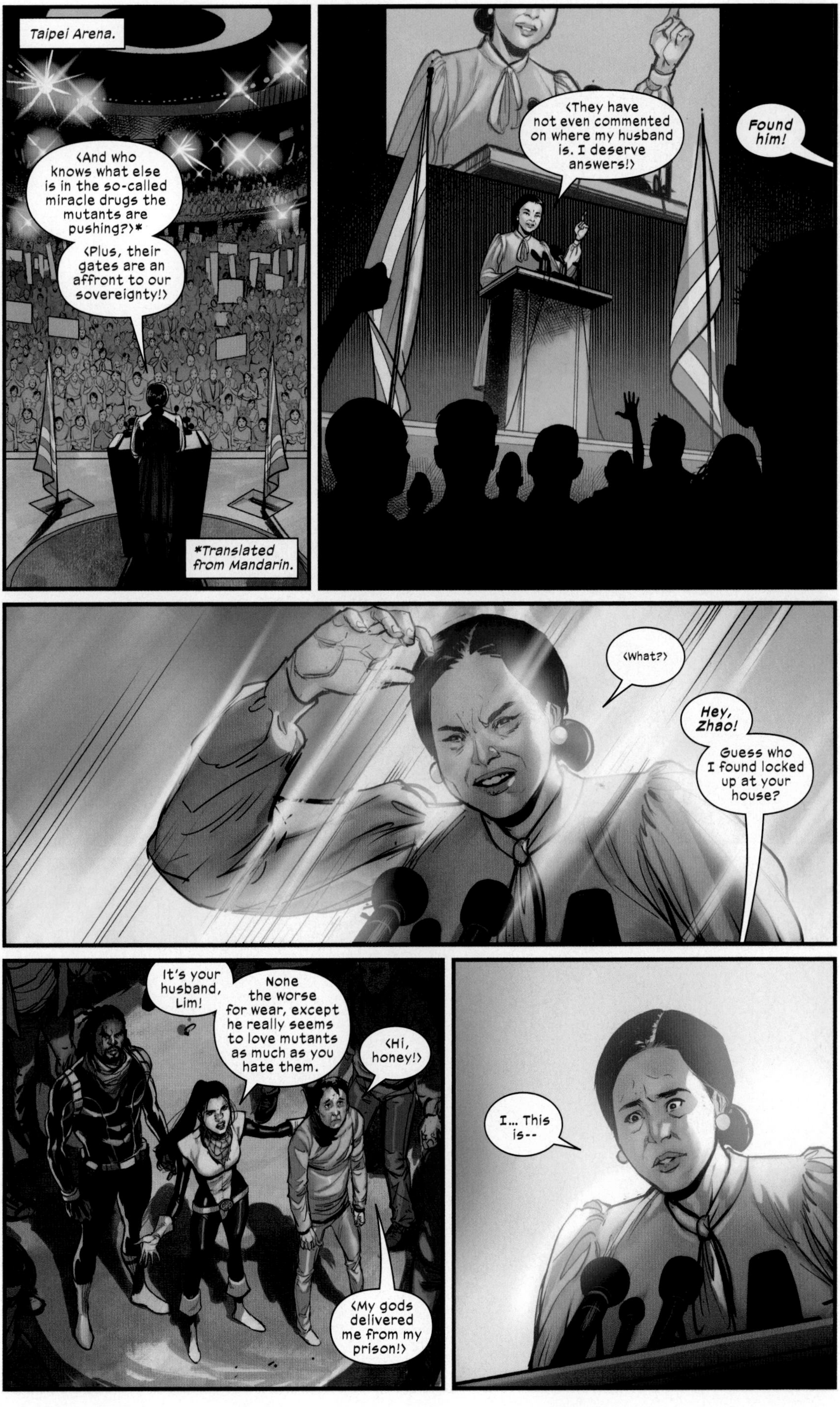

Taipei Arena.
‹And who knows what else is in the so-called miracle drugs the mutants are pushing?›*
‹Plus, their gates are an affront to our sovereignty!›
*Translated from Mandarin.
‹They have not even commented on where my husband is. I deserve answers!›
Found him!
‹What?›
Hey, Zhao!
Guess who I found locked up at your house?
It's your husband, Lim!
None the worse for wear, except he really seems to love mutants as much as you hate them.
‹Hi, honey!›
‹My gods delivered me from my prison!›
I... This is--

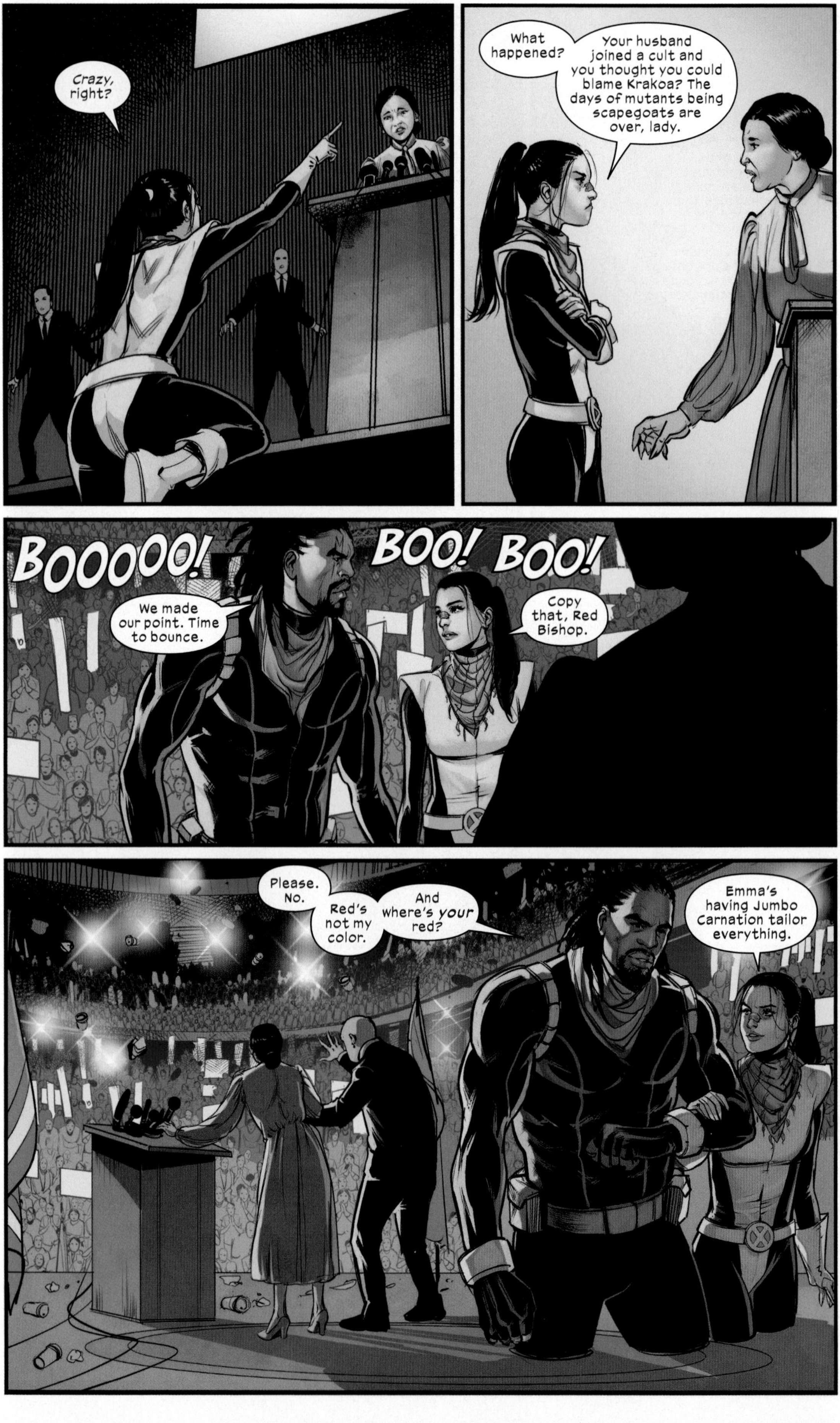
Crazy, right?
What happened?
Your husband joined a cult and you thought you could blame Krakoa? The days of mutants being scapegoats are over, lady.
BOOOOO!
BOO! BOO!
We made our point. Time to bounce.
Copy that, Red Bishop.
Please. No.
Red's not my color.
And where's *your* red?
Emma's having Jumbo Carnation tailor everything.

PRIVATE COMMUNICATION

 Hank,

You said to keep your head on a swivel for this kind of thing. I closed the Zhao case earlier today with Pryde. Spoiler: it was the spouse, like most domestics. Kitty seems fine, by the way. I know you were worried about her. The reason I'm writing is to let you know we were confronted by two post-humans with some nails by Lady Deathstrike. I don't know if the razors were Adamantium or not — I didn't let them get that close. The women had the equipment, not the training, but it could have been a real crapshoot if they'd had both. Seems like something we may want to keep tabs on. I guess that's your job. Speaking of jobs, Kitty wants me to join the Hellfire Club. I told her that making me a Bishop was a little on the nose.

-Bishop

Lucas,

Thank you. I'll add Deathstrike augmentations to the board. Re: Kitty's offer...you might consider it. You'd be another layer of protection for her and her mission, and you would be splitting your time between a world hostile to Krakoa...and the inside of the Hellfire organization...which has always been...less than transparent? I hope you consider the opportunity. It seems like it could yield a treasure trove of intel from abroad and the homeland.

Regards,
Hank

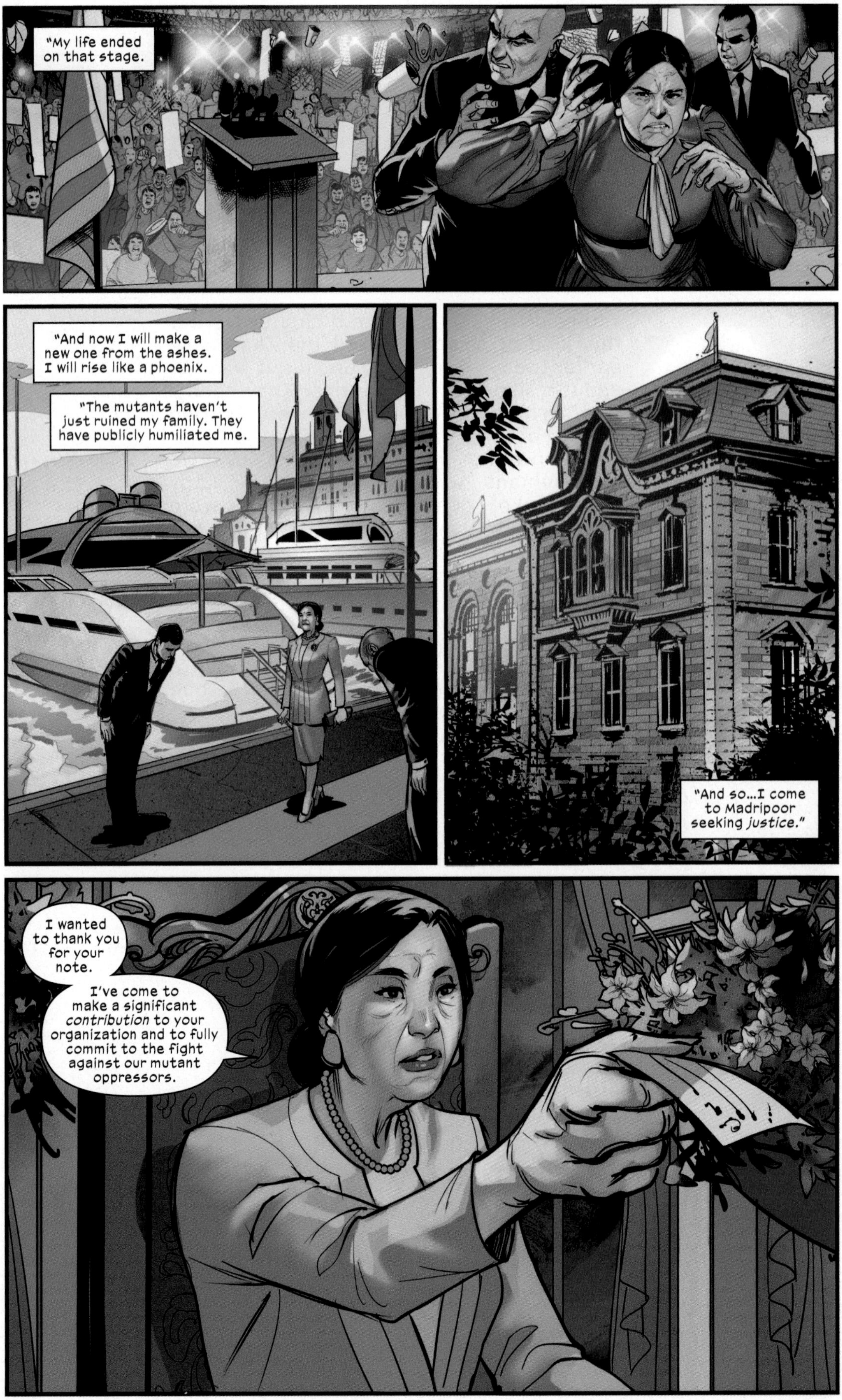
"My life ended on that stage.
"And now I will make a new one from the ashes. I will rise like a phoenix.
"The mutants haven't just ruined my family. They have publicly humiliated me.
"And so...I come to Madripoor seeking *justice*."
I wanted to thank you for your note.
I've come to make a significant *contribution* to your organization and to fully commit to the fight against our mutant oppressors.

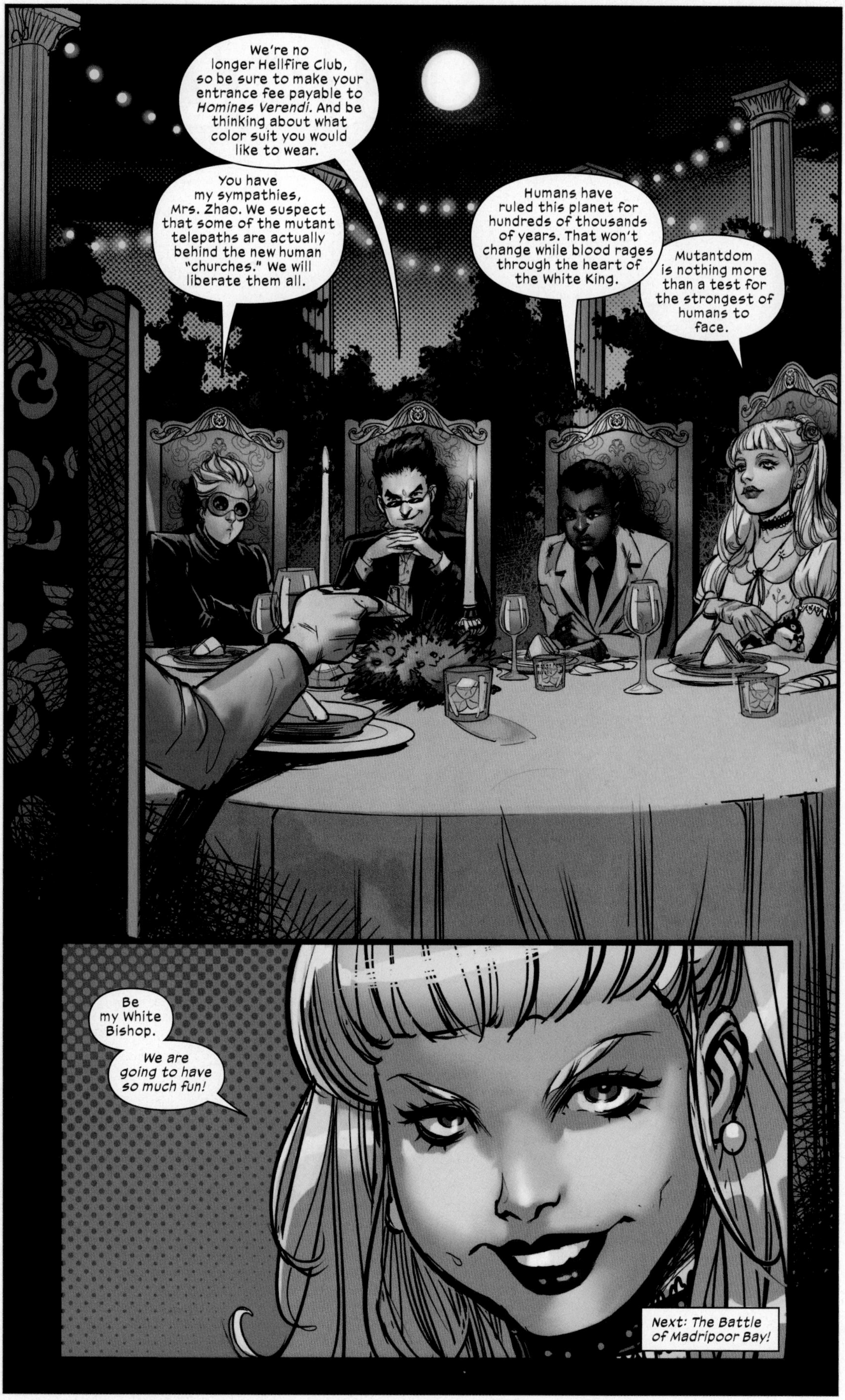
We're no longer Hellfire Club, so be sure to make your entrance fee payable to *Homines Verendi*. And be thinking about what color suit you would like to wear.
You have my sympathies, Mrs. Zhao. We suspect that some of the mutant telepaths are actually behind the new human "churches." We will liberate them all.
Humans have ruled this planet for hundreds of thousands of years. That won't change while blood rages through the heart of the White King.
Mutantdom is nothing more than a test for the strongest of humans to face.
Be my White Bishop.
We are going to have so much fun!
Next: The Battle of Madripoor Bay!

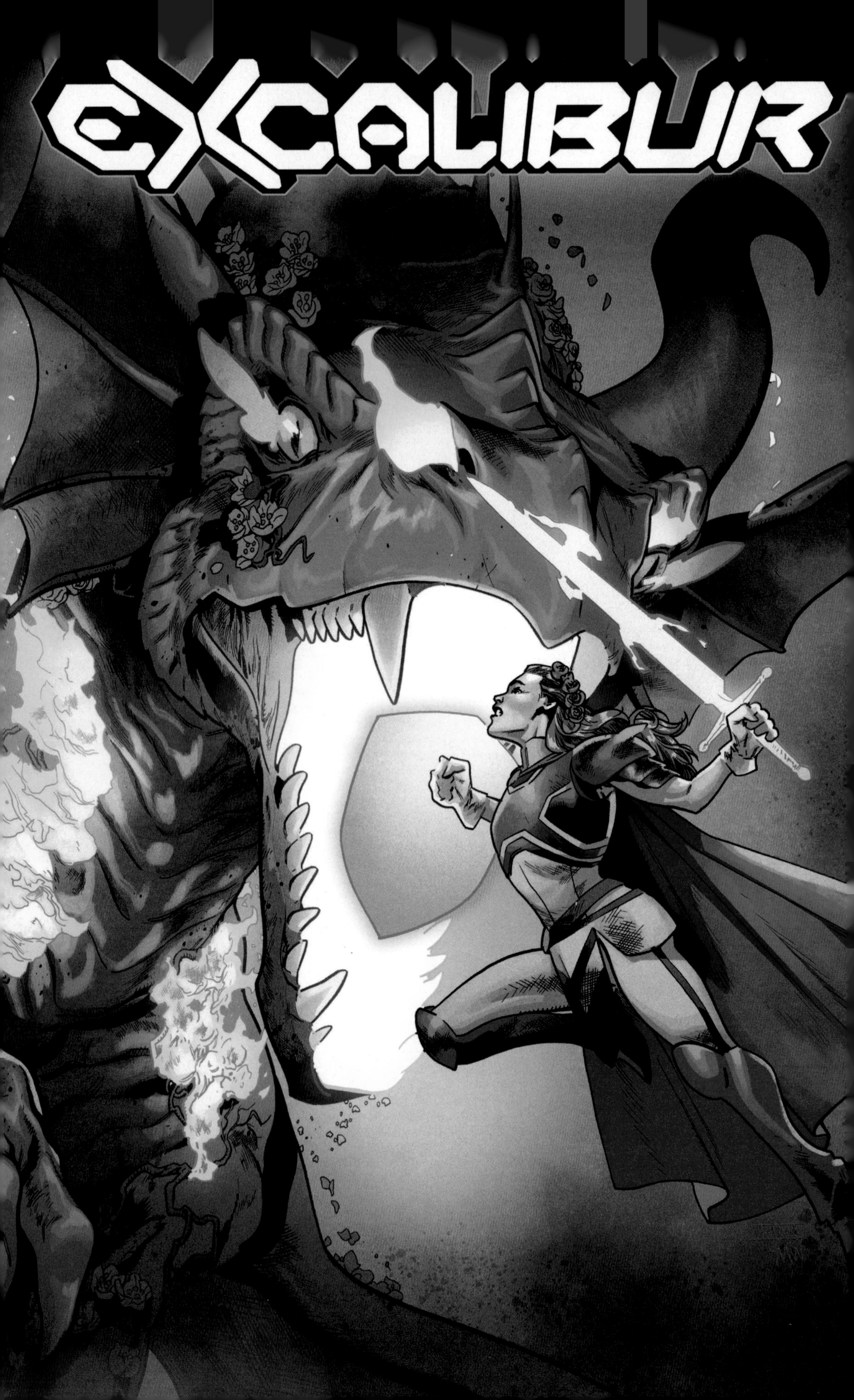
EXCALIBUR

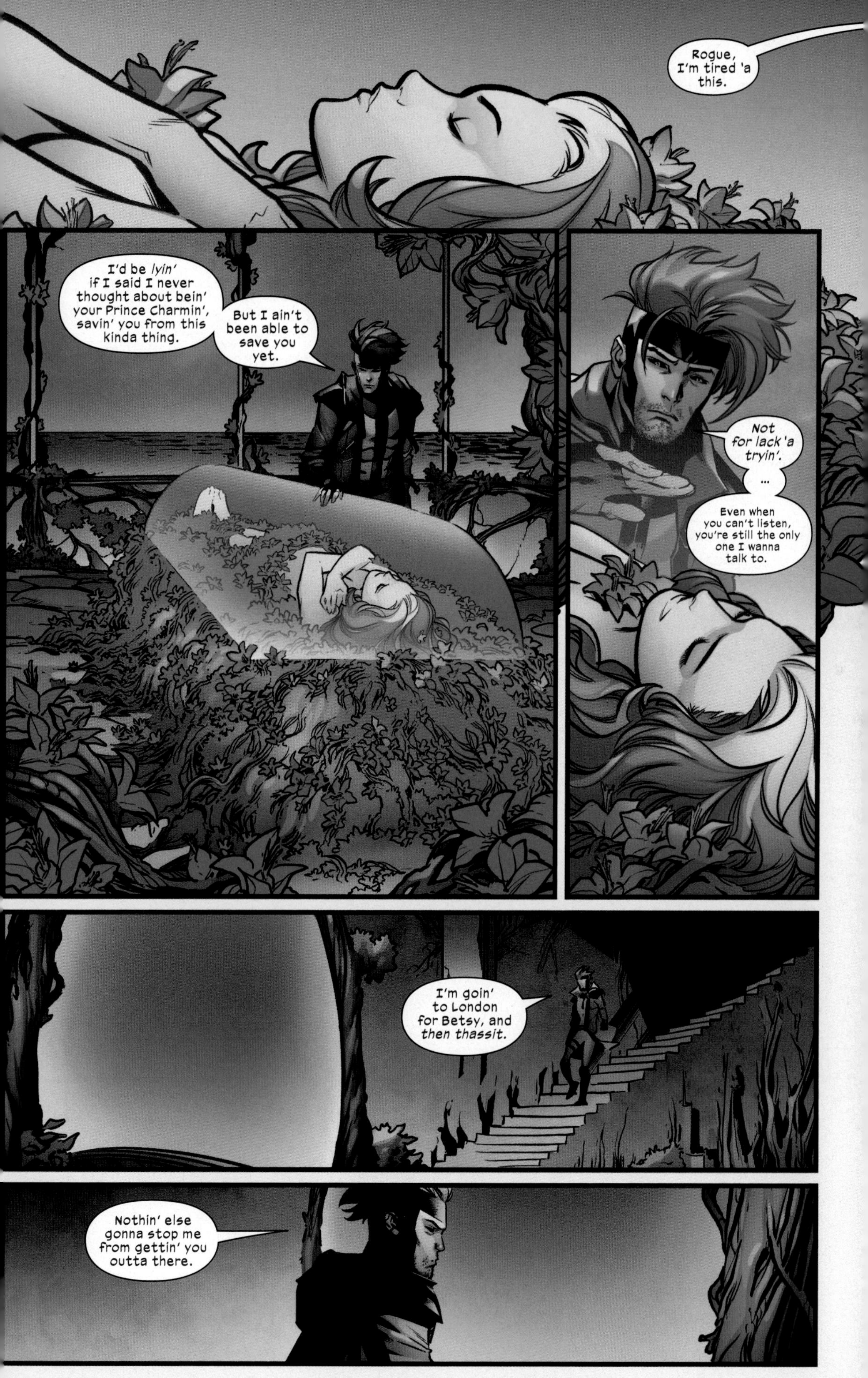

Rogue, I'm tired 'a this.
I'd be *lyin'* if I said I never thought about bein' your Prince Charmin', savin' you from this kinda thing.
But I ain't been able to save you yet.
Not for lack 'a tryin'.
...
Even when you can't listen, you're still the only one I wanna talk to.
I'm goin' to London for Betsy, and *then thassit.*
Nothin' else gonna stop me from gettin' you outta there.

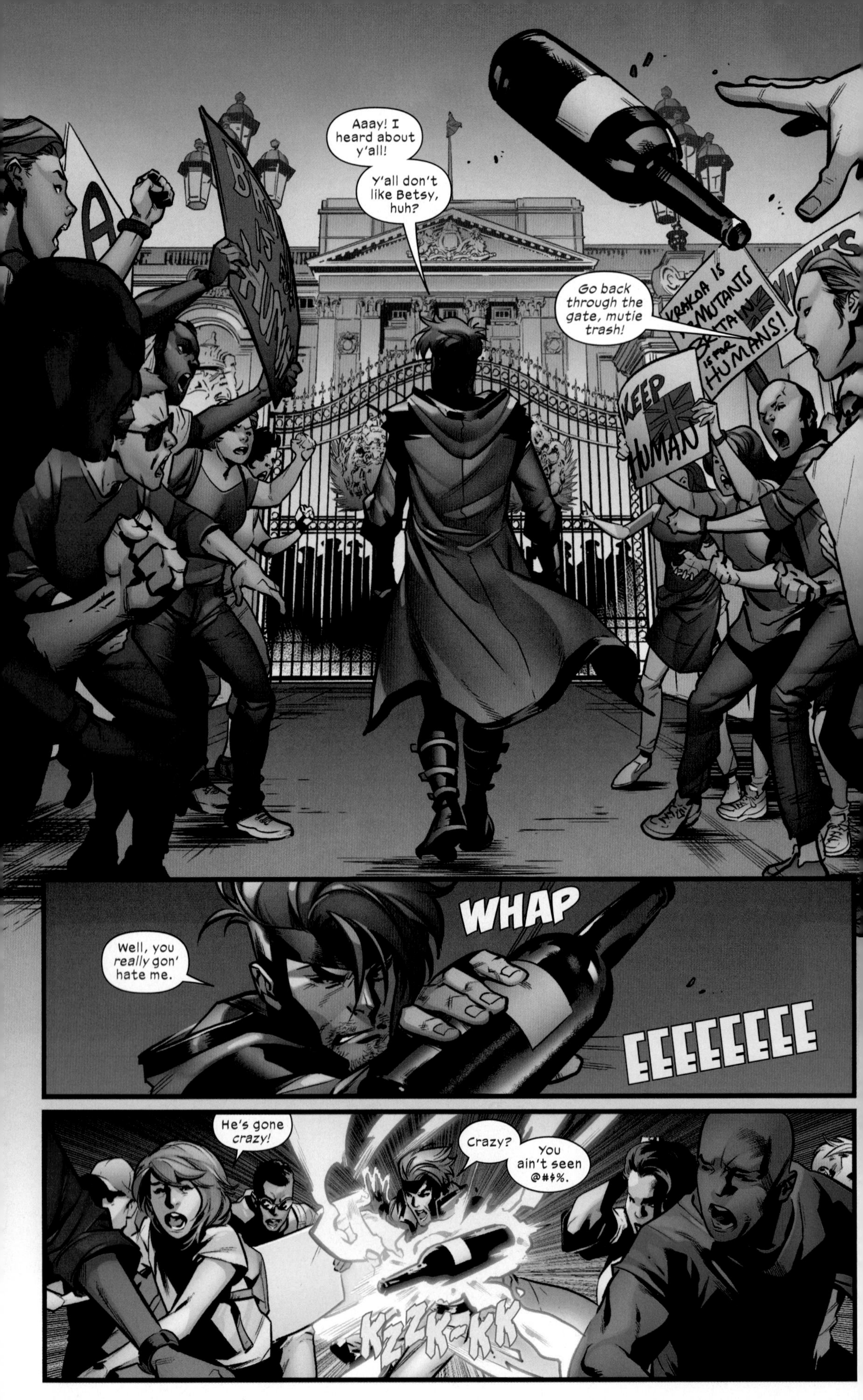

Aaay! I heard about y'all!
Y'all don't like Betsy, huh?
Go back through the gate, mutie trash!
KEEP HUMAN
WHAP
Well, you *really* gon' hate me.
EEEEEEEE
He's gone *crazy!*
Crazy?
You ain't seen @#$%.
KZZK-KK

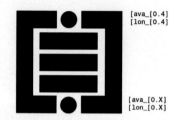

[ava_[0.4]
[lon_[0.4]

[ava_[0.X]
[lon_[0.X]

BLACK AIR, BLACK MAGIC

Mutants around the world are flocking to the island-nation of Krakoa for safety, for security and to be part of the first mutant society.

With her brother Brian possessed by an evil sorceress, Betsy Braddock has become Captain Britain -- and must bear the weight of all that name entails! Rogue has been trapped in a mysterious floral stasis, and while Apocalypse has been playing nice, Gambit sees evil lurking beneath the veneer of magic.

At least EXCALIBUR is back from Otherworld...and they know the rules of this world...right?

Gambit

Rogue

Rictor

Jubilee

Captain
Britain

Pete
Wisdom

Apocalypse

Meggan
Braddock

Jamie
Braddock

Marianna
Stern

[ava_[0.4]...]
[lon_[0.4]...]

[All....HAIL.]

[00_so_below_X]
[00_as_above_X]

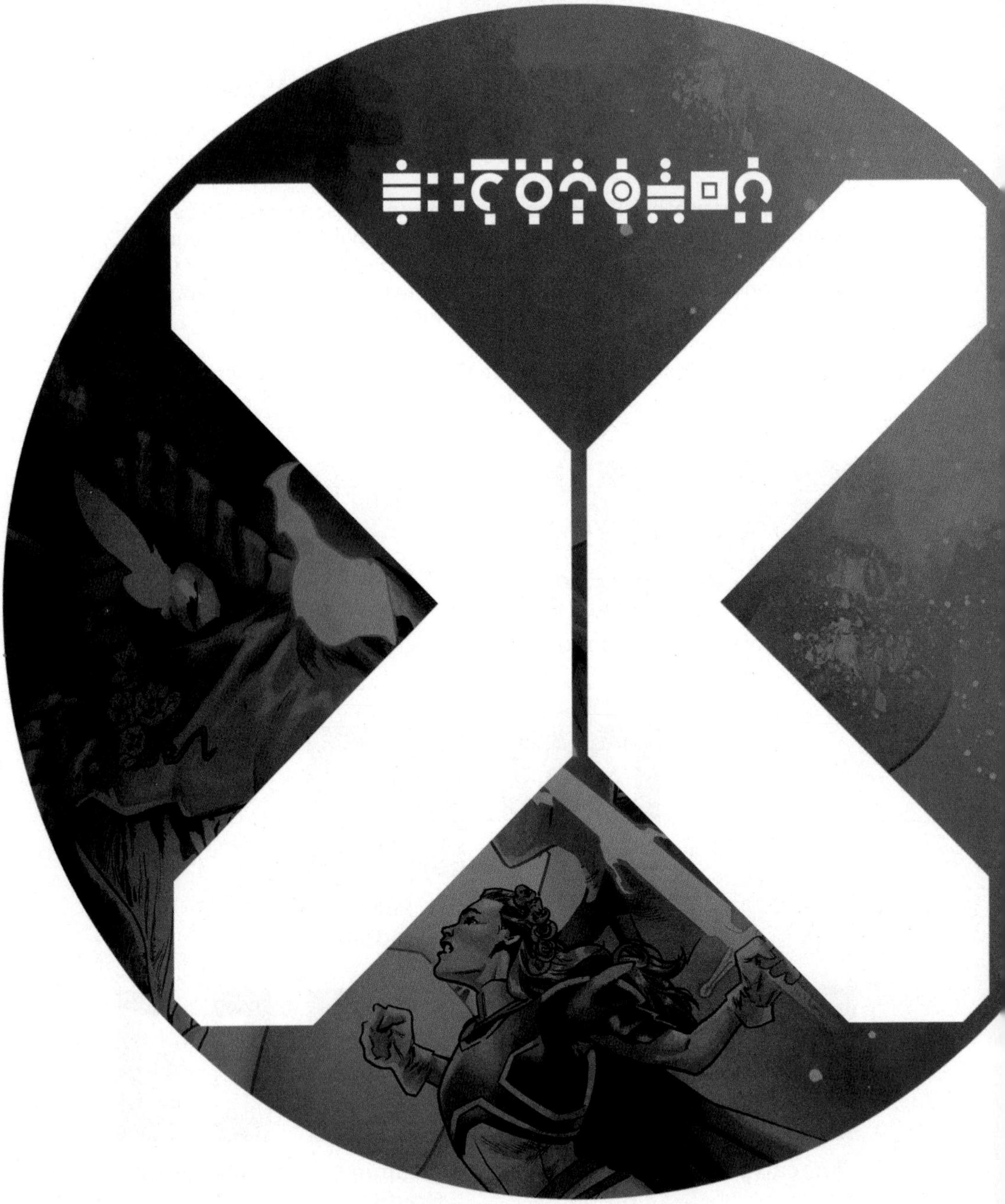

```
TINI HOWARD....................................[WRITER]
MARCUS TO......................................[ARTIST]
ERICK ARCINIEGA..........................[COLOR ARTIST]
VC's CORY PETIT..............................[LETTERER]
TOM MULLER.....................................[DESIGN]

MAHMUD ASRAR & MATTHEW WILSON...........[COVER ARTISTS]

KAEL NGU & DAVID CURIEL.........[VARIANT COVER ARTISTS]

NICK RUSSELL...............................[PRODUCTION]

JONATHAN HICKMAN...........................[HEAD OF X]
ANNALISE BISSA.....................[ASSISTANT EDITOR]
JORDAN D. WHITE...............................[EDITOR]
C.B. CEBULSKI.......................[EDITOR IN CHIEF]
JOE QUESADA..................[CHIEF CREATIVE OFFICER]
DAN BUCKLEY.................................[PRESIDENT]
ALAN FINE.........................[EXECUTIVE PRODUCER]
```

[04] EXCALIBUR

[ISSUE FOUR]....................VERSE IV:
..........Fall Back and Think of England!

[00_so_below_X]
[00_as_above_X]

[00_00.....0]
[00_00.....4]

[00_greater_]
[00_secrets_]

[00_____]

[00_exist___]

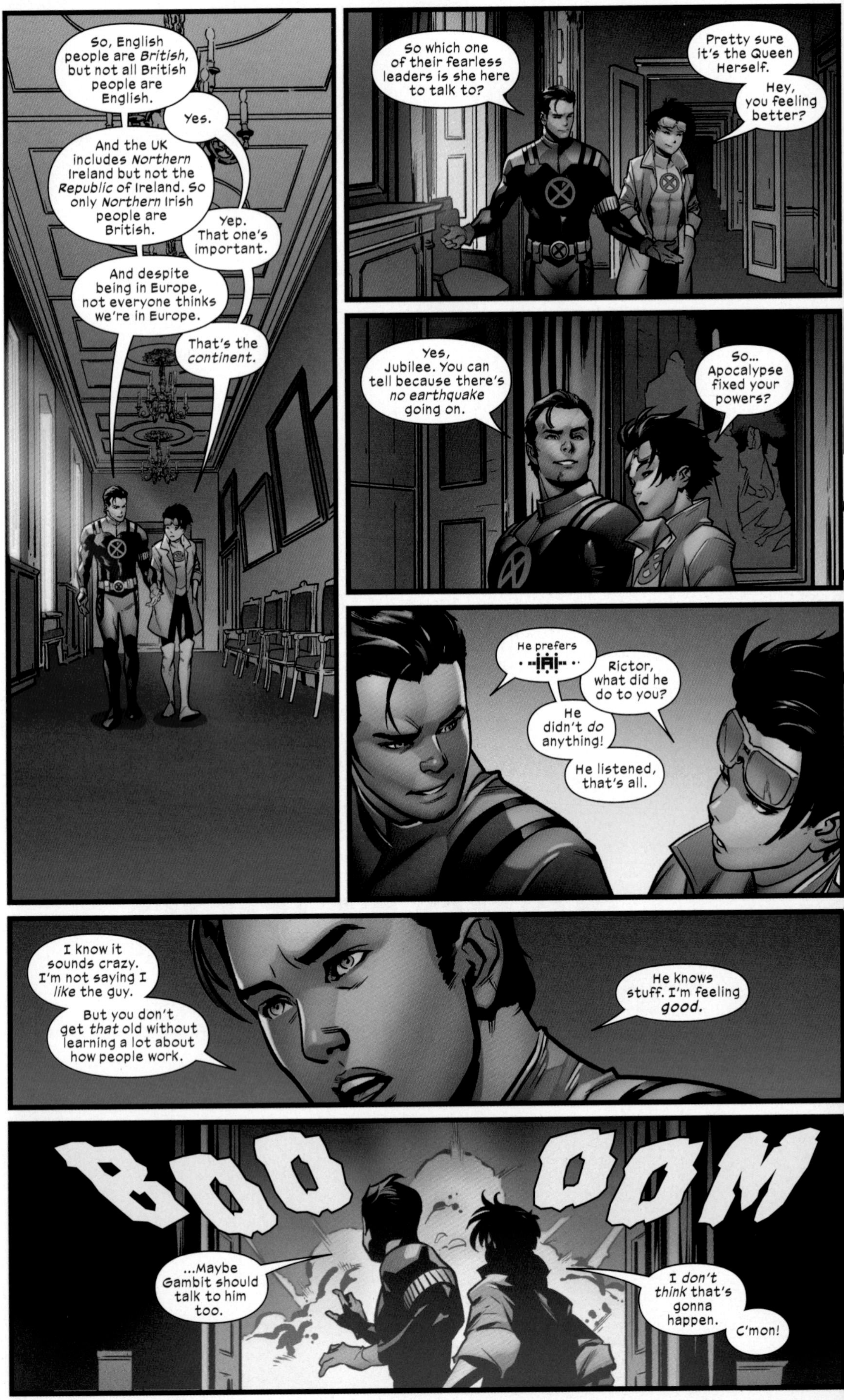

So, English people are *British*, but not all British people are English.
Yes.
And the UK includes *Northern* Ireland but not the *Republic* of Ireland. So only *Northern* Irish people are British.
Yep. That one's important.
And despite being in Europe, not everyone thinks we're in Europe.
That's the *continent*.
So which one of their fearless leaders is she here to talk to?
Pretty sure it's the Queen Herself.
Hey, you feeling better?
Yes, Jubilee. You can tell because there's *no earthquake* going on.
So... Apocalypse fixed your powers?
He prefers
Rictor, what did he do to you?
He didn't *do* anything!
He listened, that's all.
I know it sounds crazy. I'm not saying I *like* the guy.
But you don't get *that* old without learning a lot about how people work.
He knows stuff. I'm feeling *good*.
BOOOOM
...Maybe Gambit should talk to him too.
I *don't think* that's gonna happen.
C'mon!

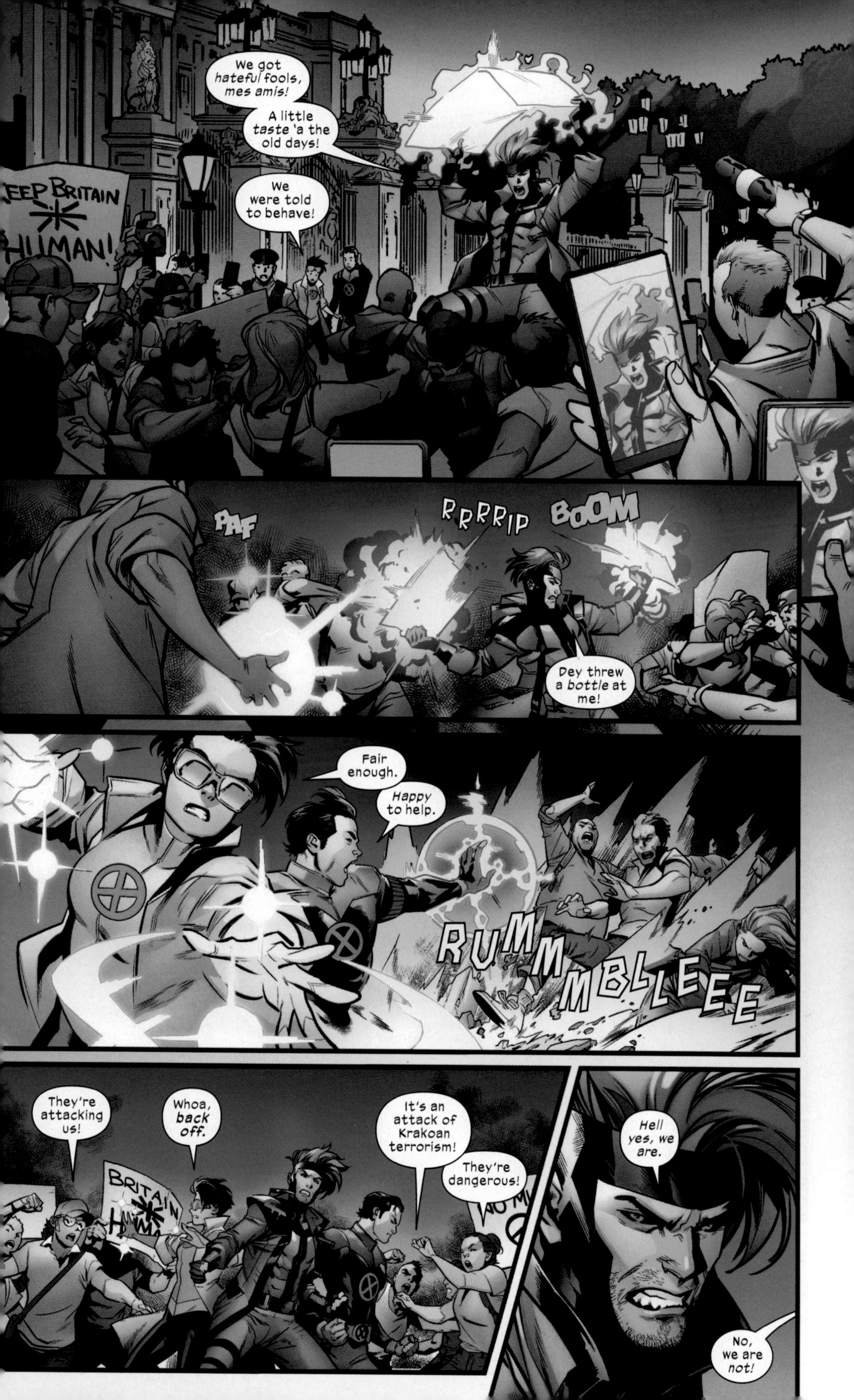
KEEP BRITAIN HUMAN!
We got hateful fools, mes amis!
A little taste 'a the old days!
We were told to behave!
PAF
RRRRIP
BOOM
Dey threw a bottle at me!
Fair enough.
Happy to help.
RUMMMBLLEEE
They're attacking us!
Whoa, back off.
It's an attack of Krakoan terrorism!
They're dangerous!
Hell yes, we are.
No, we are not!

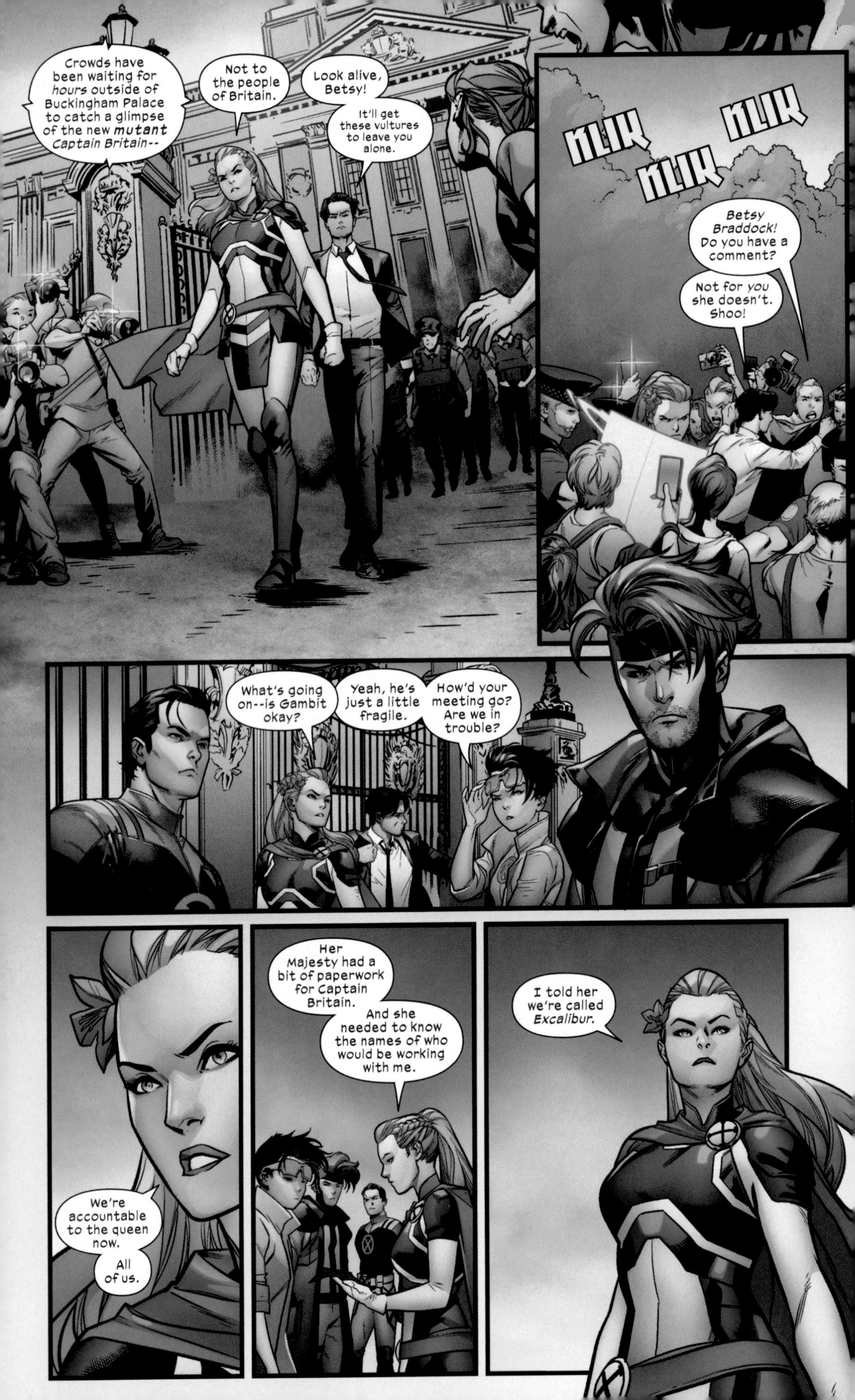

Crowds have been waiting for hours outside of Buckingham Palace to catch a glimpse of the new mutant Captain Britain--
Not to the people of Britain.
Look alive, Betsy!
It'll get these vultures to leave you alone.
KLIK
KLIK
KLIK
Betsy Braddock! Do you have a comment?
Not for you she doesn't. Shoo!
What's going on--is Gambit okay?
Yeah, he's just a little fragile.
How'd your meeting go? Are we in trouble?
We're accountable to the queen now.
All of us.
Her Majesty had a bit of paperwork for Captain Britain.
And she needed to know the names of who would be working with me.
I told her we're called Excalibur.

ACT

An ACT; Protecting and Dividing the United Kingdom and Otherworld

It is hereby ordered in protection and preservation of the realm that all occurrences regarding matters not being sourced from obvious Earthly or Celestial causes, with answers not found in the firmament or heavens, and deriving from lineage including but not limited to the Matter of Britain, shall be officially deemed *Otherworldly.*

The Crown recognizes the *Otherworld* as an extraplanar realm, separate from but alongside the United Kingdom of Great Britain and Northern Ireland, with separate governance, rights and laws distinct from our own.

Matters regarding the realm of Otherworld shall be under the representation and protection of heritor and titleholder Captain Britain. In these matters alone, Captain Britain is the Crown's highest authority.

In all other matters Earthly and Celestial, Captain Britain remains an honored servant to the Crown and shall be called on as a citizen to protect Crown and Country.

The Captain may be called upon to serve as the Crown's representative against Otherworld.

In such matters, their defense of the realm is expected to be as a shield before the throne.

—

Here's the official text of the act for your files. Hasn't been updated in a while.

Drinks on the island later?

—PW

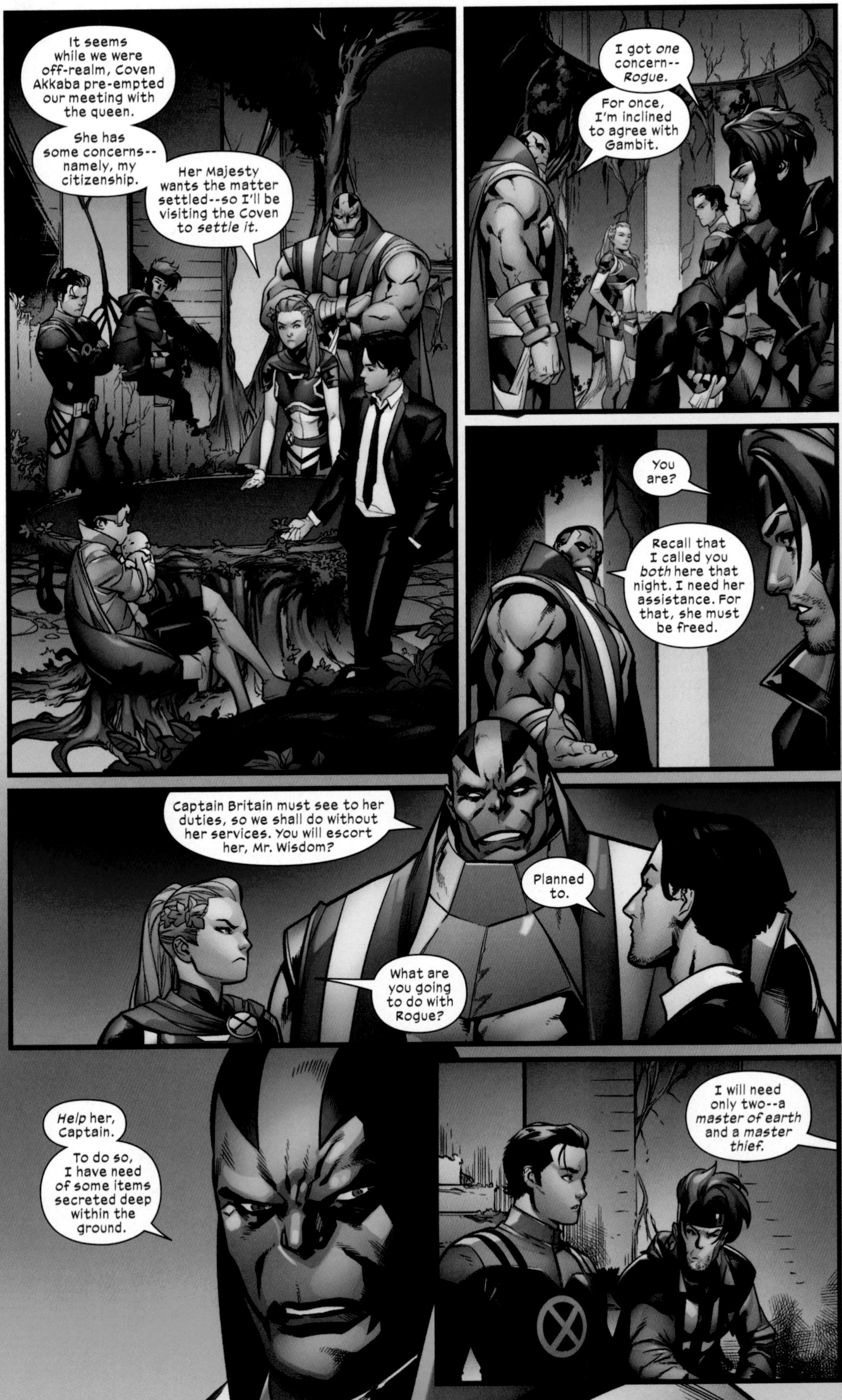
It seems while we were off-realm, Coven Akkaba pre-empted our meeting with the queen.
She has some concerns--namely, my citizenship.
Her Majesty wants the matter settled--so I'll be visiting the Coven to settle it.
I got one concern--Rogue.
For once, I'm inclined to agree with Gambit.
You are?
Recall that I called you both here that night. I need her assistance. For that, she must be freed.
Captain Britain must see to her duties, so we shall do without her services. You will escort her, Mr. Wisdom?
Planned to.
What are you going to do with Rogue?
Help her, Captain.
To do so, I have need of some items secreted deep within the ground.
I will need only two--a master of earth and a master thief.

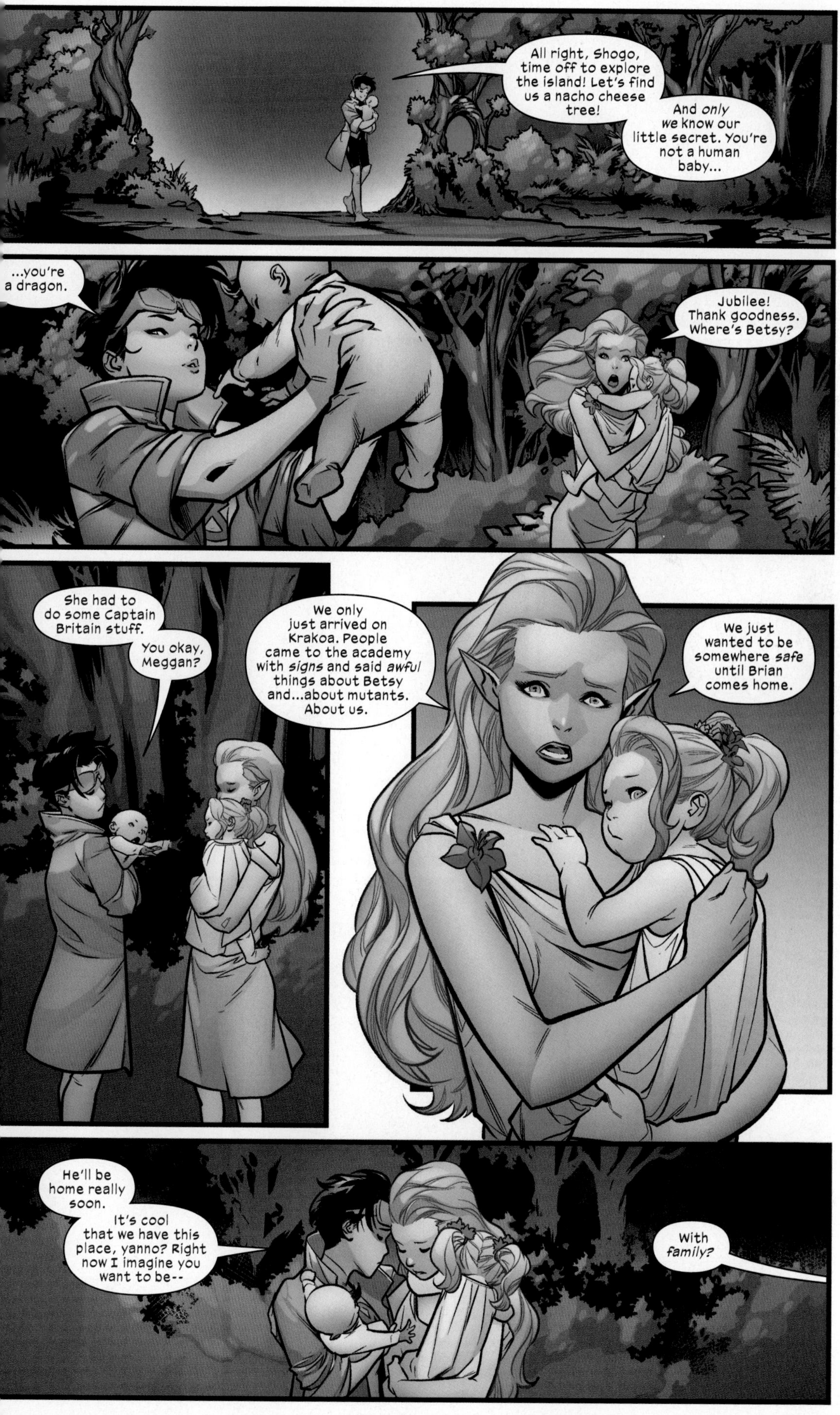
All right, Shogo, time off to explore the island! Let's find us a nacho cheese tree!
And *only* we know our little secret. You're not a human baby...
...you're a dragon.
Jubilee! Thank goodness. Where's Betsy?
She had to do some Captain Britain stuff.
You okay, Meggan?
We only just arrived on Krakoa. People came to the academy with *signs* and said *awful* things about Betsy and...about mutants. About us.
We just wanted to be somewhere *safe* until Brian comes home.
He'll be home really soon.
It's cool that we have this place, yanno? Right now I imagine you want to be--
With *family?*

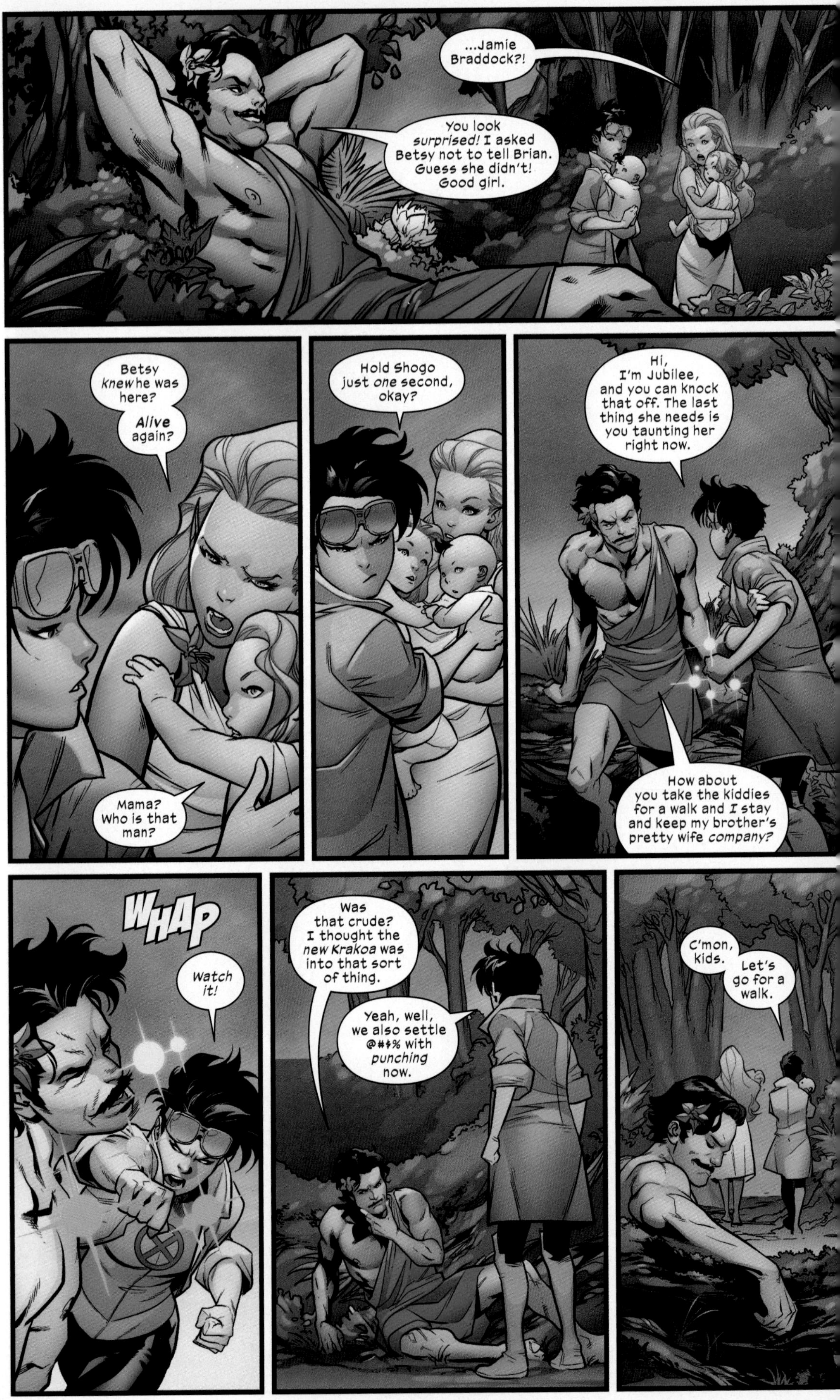
...Jamie Braddock?!
You look *surprised!* I asked Betsy not to tell Brian. Guess she didn't! Good girl.
Betsy *knew* he was here?
Alive again?
Mama? Who is that man?
Hold Shogo just *one* second, okay?
Hi, I'm Jubilee, and you can knock that off. The last thing she needs is you taunting her right now.
How about you take the kiddies for a walk and *I* stay and keep my brother's pretty wife *company?*
WHAP
Watch it!
Was that crude? I thought the *new Krakoa* was into that sort of thing.
Yeah, well, we also settle @#$% with *punching* now.
C'mon, kids.
Let's go for a walk.

THE FAMILY BRADDOCK

Their lineage a closely guarded secret, most known members of the Braddock family have ties to Otherworld.

"Not by Sword Alone"

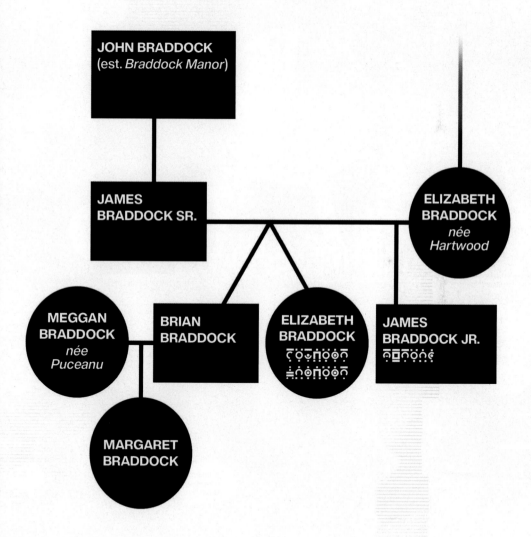

JOHN BRADDOCK
(est. *Braddock Manor*)

JAMES BRADDOCK SR.

ELIZABETH BRADDOCK
née Hartwood

MEGGAN BRADDOCK
née Puceanu

BRIAN BRADDOCK

ELIZABETH BRADDOCK

JAMES BRADDOCK JR.

MARGARET BRADDOCK

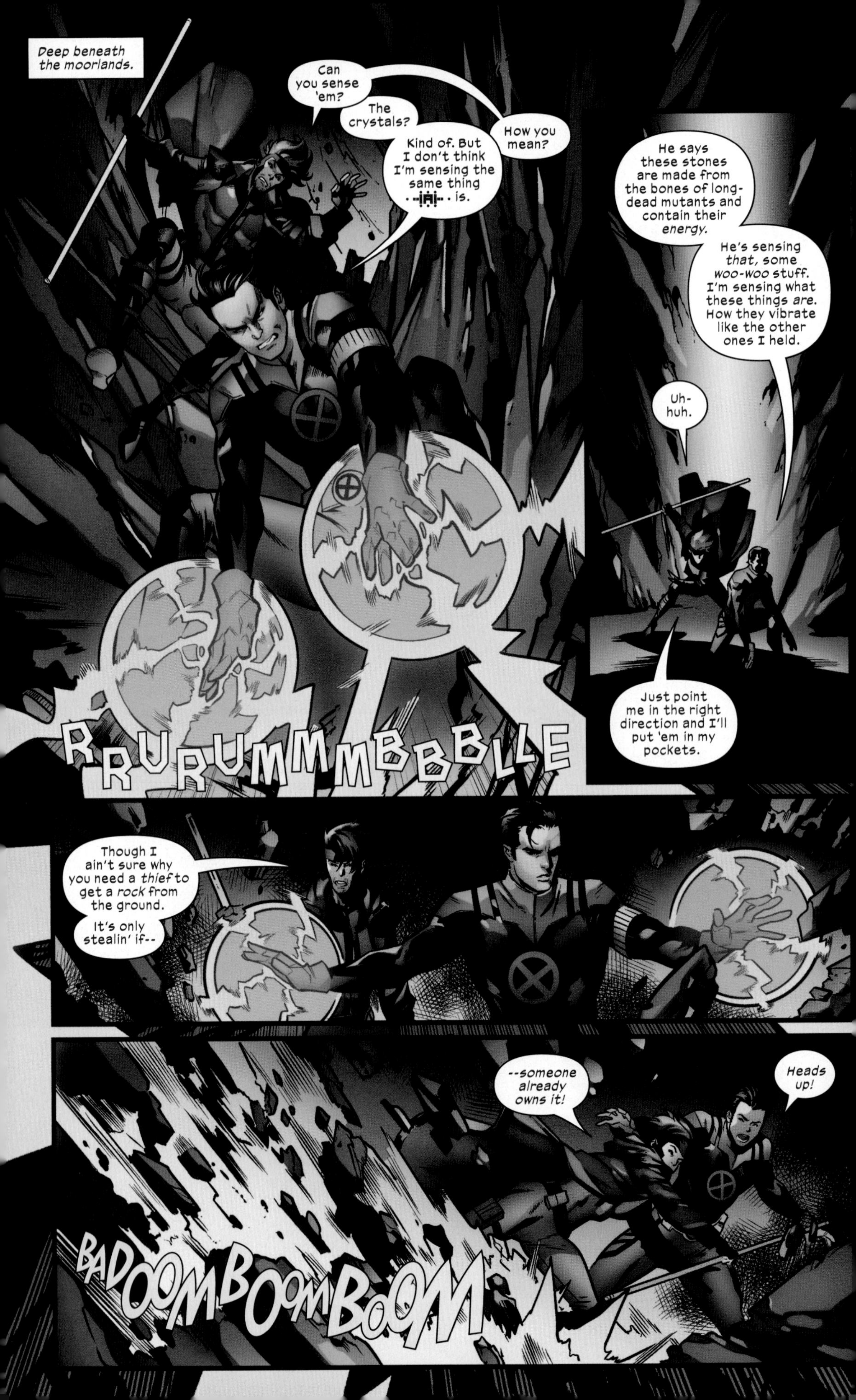

Deep beneath the moorlands.
Can you sense 'em?
The crystals?
How you mean?
Kind of. But I don't think I'm sensing the same thing is.
He says these stones are made from the bones of long-dead mutants and contain their *energy.*
He's sensing *that,* some *woo-woo* stuff. I'm sensing what these things *are.* How they vibrate like the other ones I held.
Uh-huh.
Just point me in the right direction and I'll put 'em in my pockets.
RRURUMMMMBBBLLE
Though I ain't sure why you need a *thief* to get a *rock* from the ground.
It's only stealin' if--
--someone already owns it!
Heads up!
BADOOMBOOMBOOM

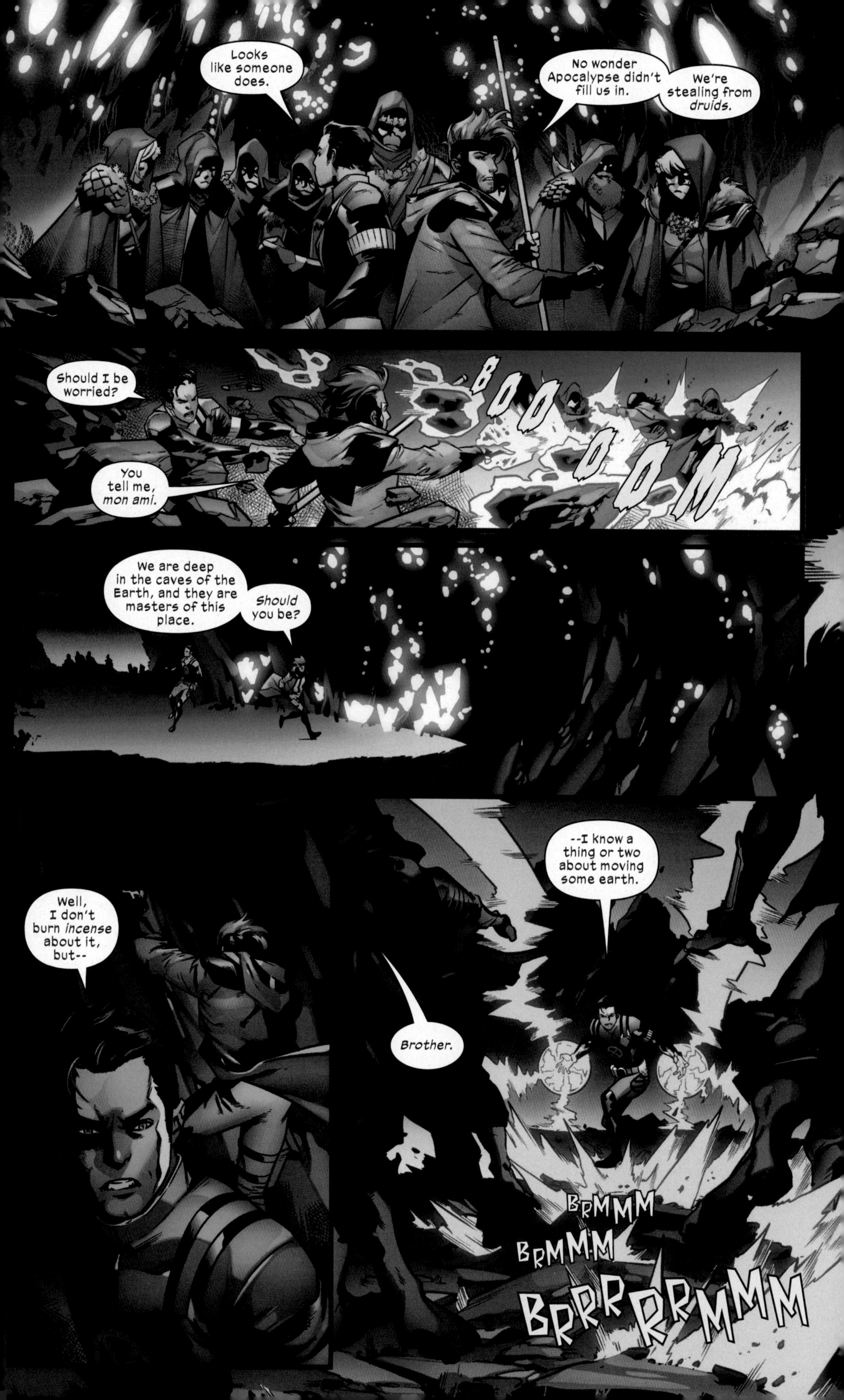

Looks like someone does.
No wonder Apocalypse didn't fill us in.
We're stealing from *druids*.
Should I be worried?
You tell me, *mon ami*.
BOOOOM
We are deep in the caves of the Earth, and they are masters of this place.
Should you be?
Well, I don't burn *incense* about it, but--
--I know a thing or two about moving some earth.
Brother.
BRMMM
BRMMM
BRRRRRMMM

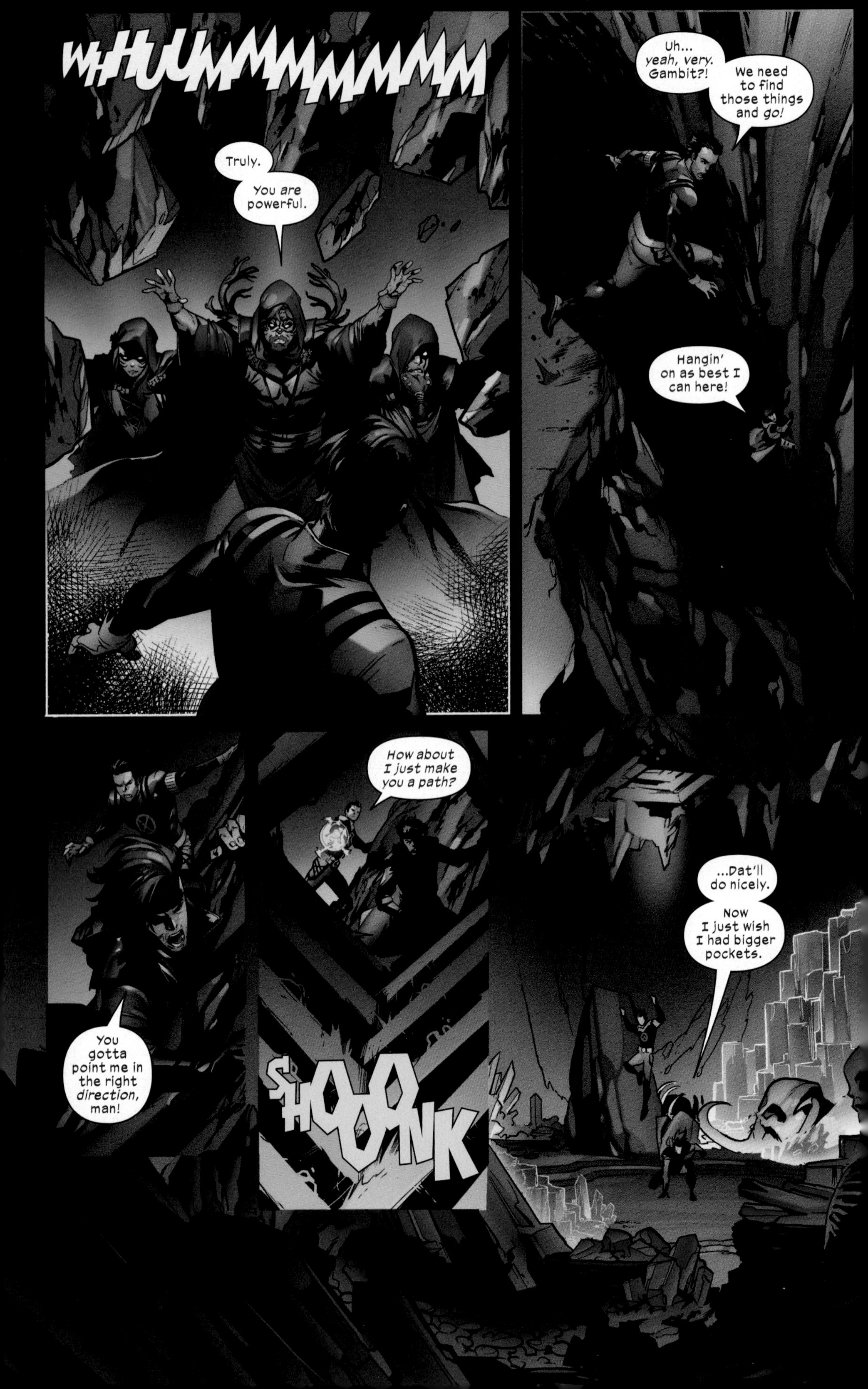
WHUMMMMMMMM
Truly.
You are powerful.
Uh... yeah, very. Gambit?!
We need to find those things and go!
Hangin' on as best I can here!
You gotta point me in the right direction, man!
How about I just make you a path?
SHOOONK
...Dat'll do nicely.
Now I just wish I had bigger pockets.

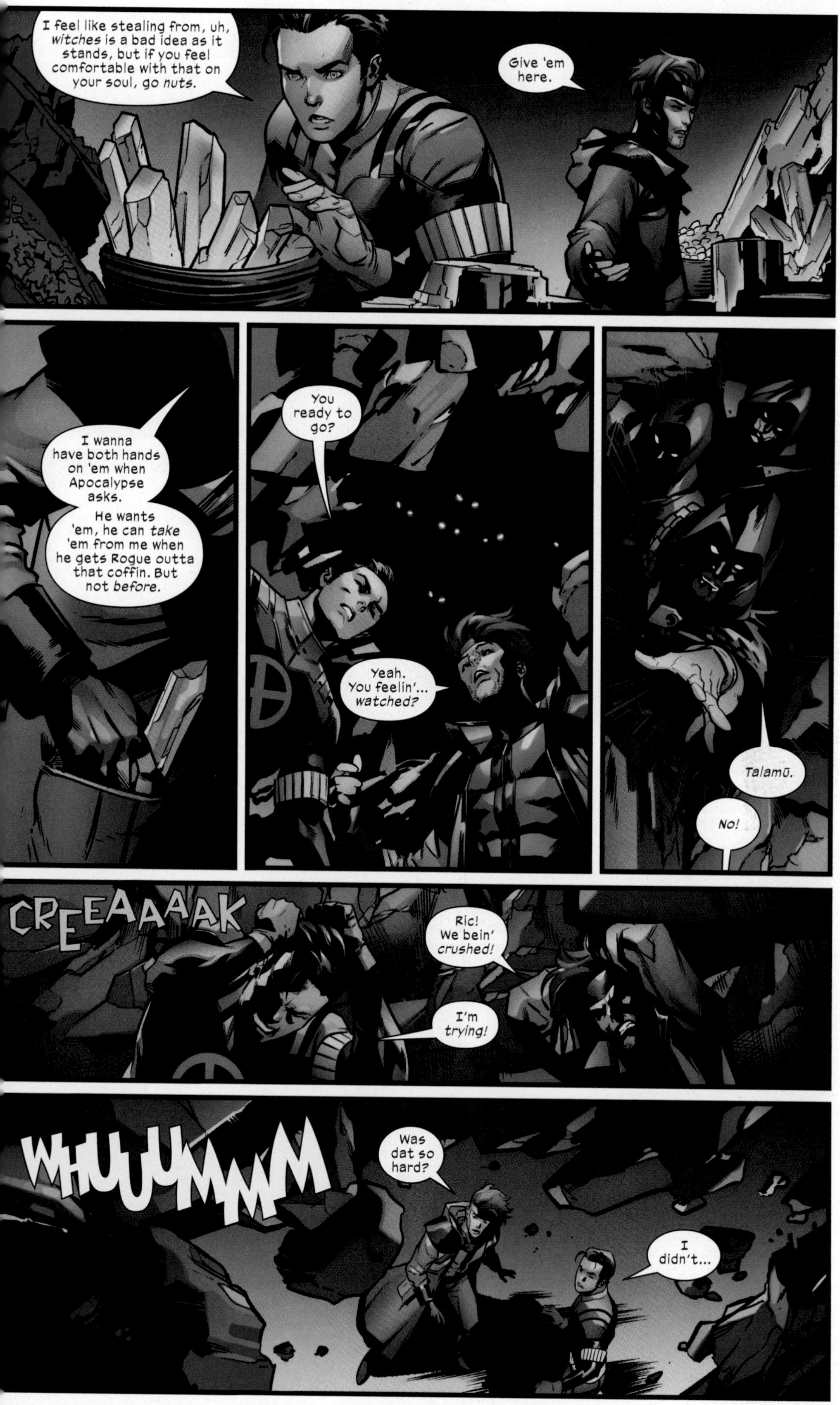
I feel like stealing from, uh, *witches* is a bad idea as it stands, but if you feel comfortable with that on your soul, go *nuts.*
Give 'em here.
I wanna have both hands on 'em when Apocalypse asks.
He wants 'em, he can *take* 'em from me when he gets Rogue outta that coffin. But not *before.*
You ready to go?
Yeah. You feelin'... *watched?*
Talamū.
No!
CREEAAAAK
Ric! We bein' *crushed!*
I'm *trying!*
WHUUMMMM
Was dat so hard?
I didn't...

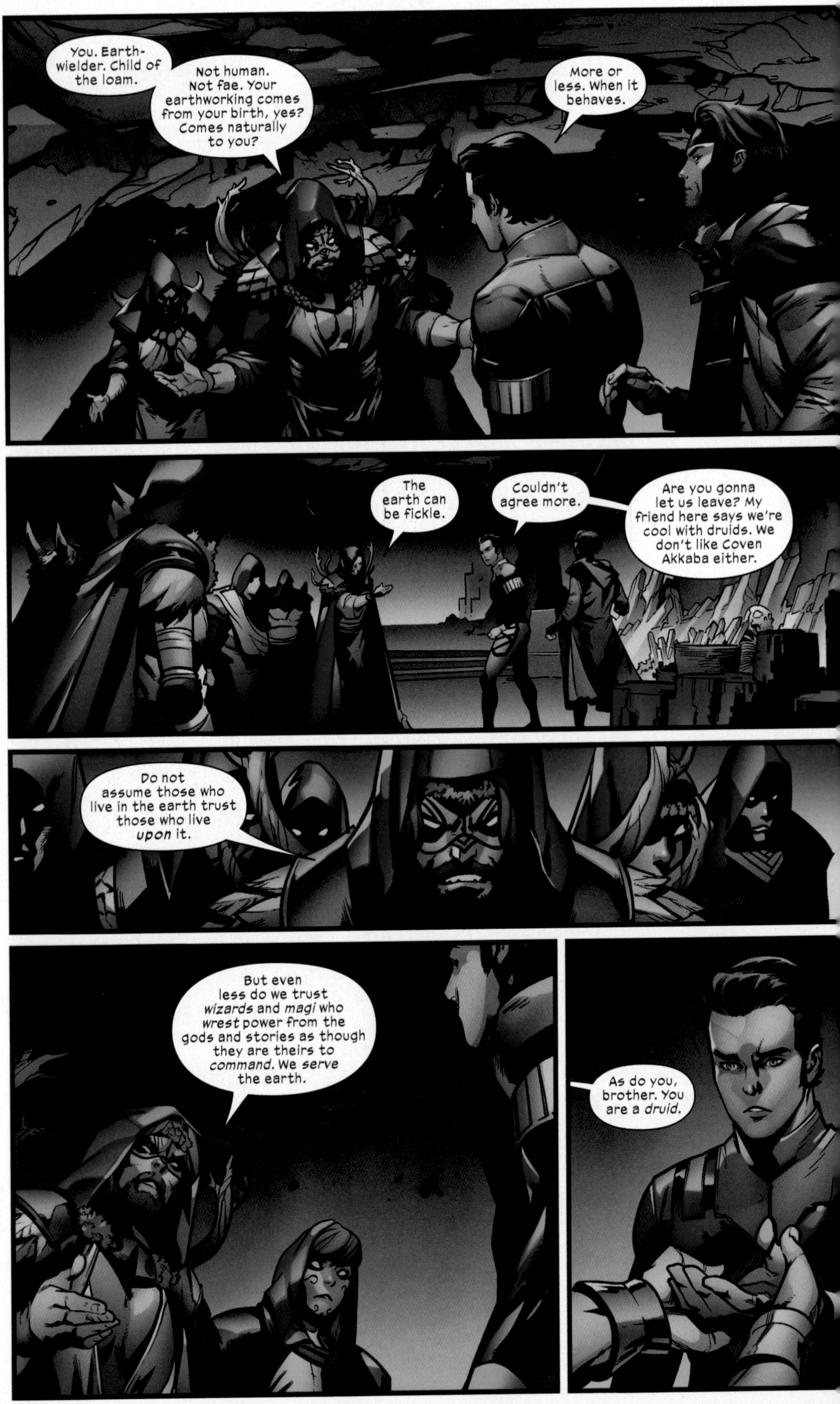

You. Earth-wielder. Child of the loam.
Not human. Not fae. Your earthworking comes from your birth, yes? Comes naturally to you?
More or less. When it behaves.
The earth can be fickle.
Couldn't agree more.
Are you gonna let us leave? My friend here says we're cool with druids. We don't like Coven Akkaba either.
Do not assume those who live in the earth trust those who live *upon* it.
But even less do we trust *wizards* and *magi* who *wrest* power from the gods and stories as though they are theirs to *command*. We *serve* the earth.
As do you, brother. You are a *druid*.

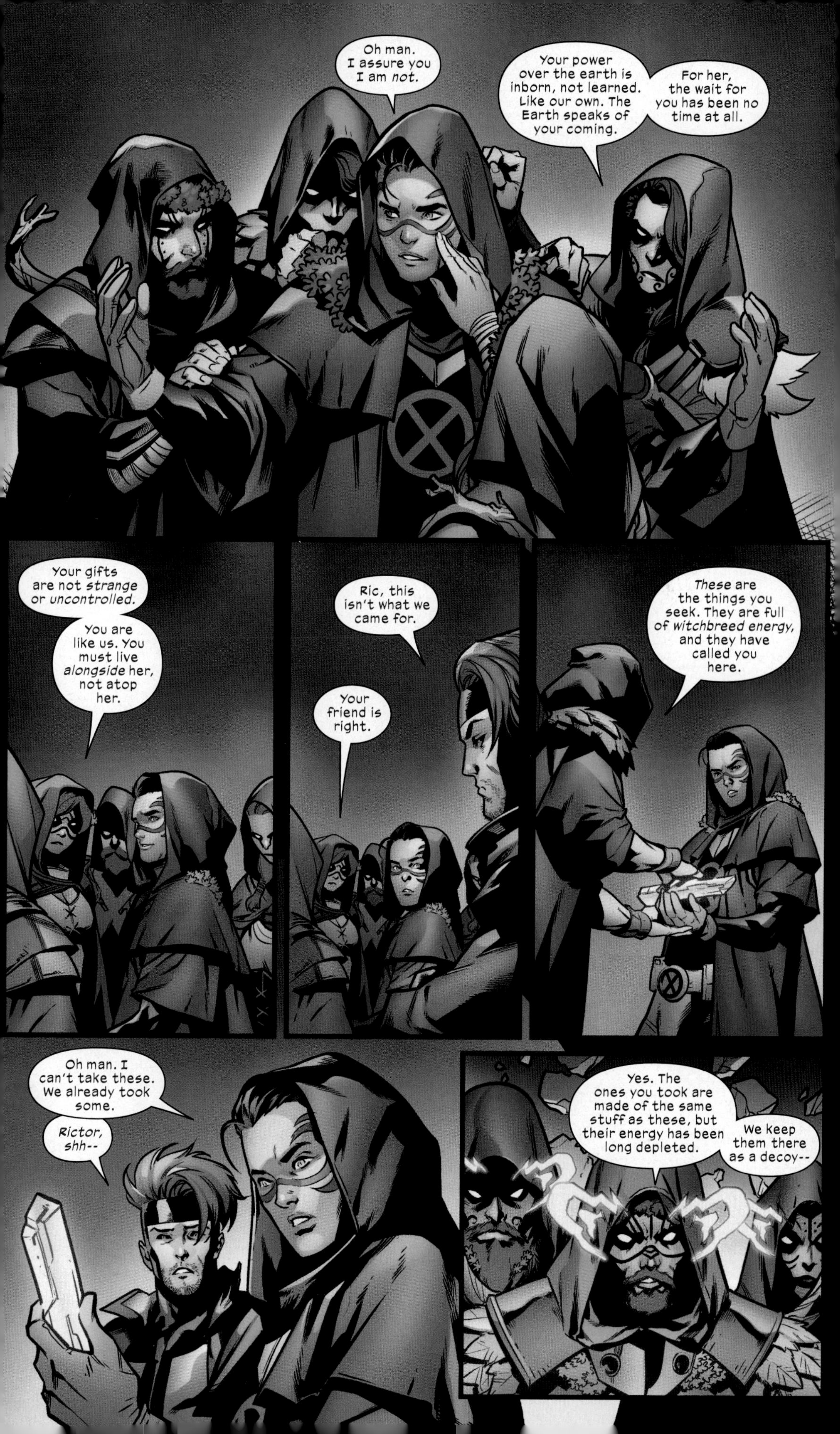

Oh man. I assure you I am *not*.
Your power over the earth is inborn, not learned. Like our own. The Earth speaks of your coming.
For her, the wait for you has been no time at all.
Your gifts are not *strange* or *uncontrolled*.
You are like us. You must live *alongside* her, not atop her.
Ric, this isn't what we came for.
Your friend is right.
These are the things you seek. They are full of *witchbreed energy*, and they have called you here.
Oh man. I can't take these. We already took some.
Rictor, shh--
Yes. The ones you took are made of the same stuff as these, but their energy has been long depleted.
We keep them there as a decoy--

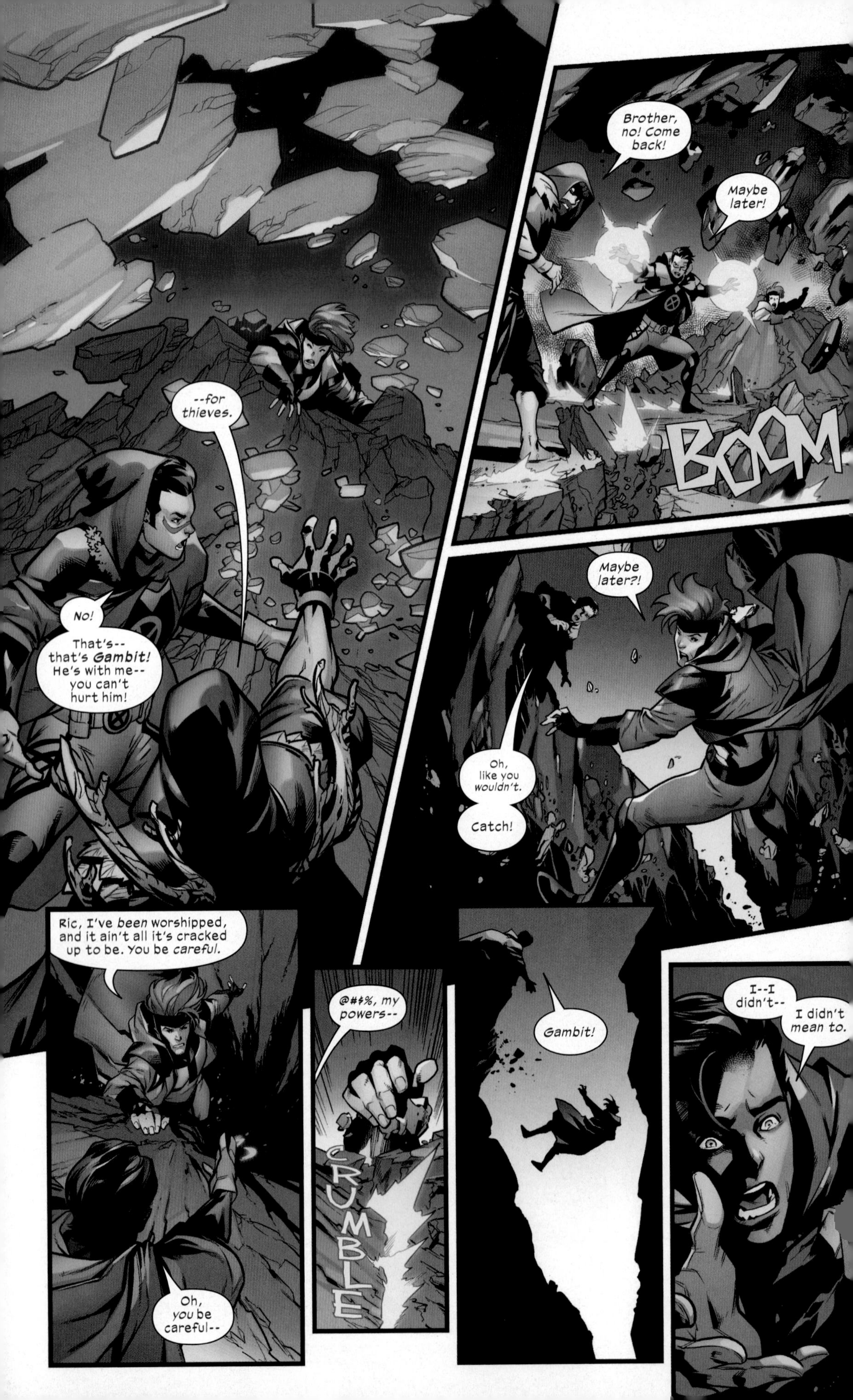
--for thieves.
No!
That's-- that's Gambit! He's with me-- you can't hurt him!
Brother, no! Come back!
Maybe later!
BOOM
Maybe later?!
Oh, like you wouldn't.
Catch!
Ric, I've been worshipped, and it ain't all it's cracked up to be. You be careful.
Oh, you be careful--
@#$%, my powers--
CRUMBLE
Gambit!
I--I didn't--
I didn't mean to.

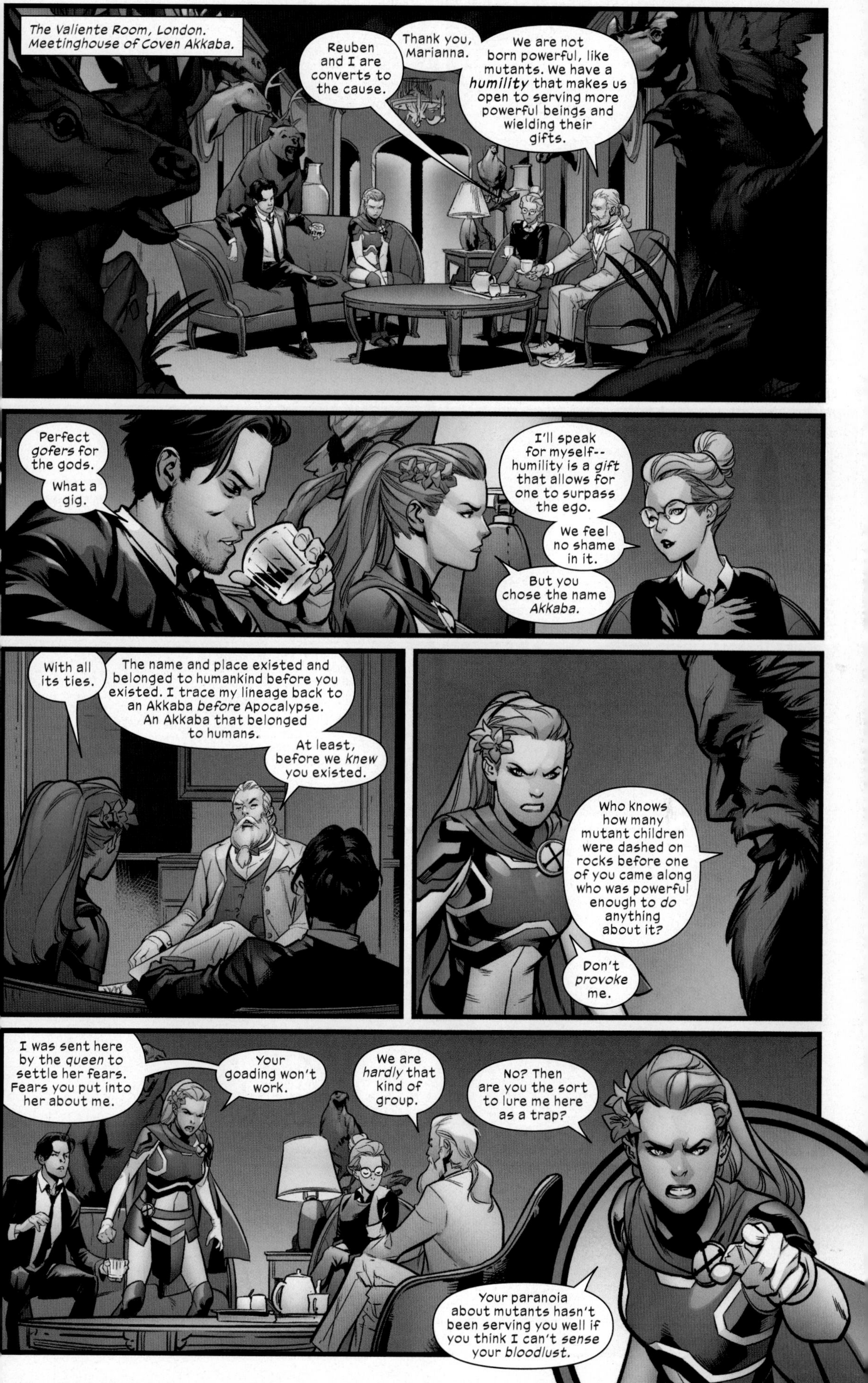
The Valiente Room, London. Meetinghouse of Coven Akkaba.
Reuben and I are converts to the cause.
Thank you, Marianna.
We are not born powerful, like mutants. We have a *humility* that makes us open to serving more powerful beings and wielding their gifts.
Perfect *gofers* for the gods.
What a gig.
I'll speak for myself-- humility is a *gift* that allows for one to surpass the ego.
We feel no shame in it.
But you chose the name *Akkaba.*
With all its ties.
The name and place existed and belonged to humankind before you existed. I trace my lineage back to an Akkaba *before* Apocalypse. An Akkaba that belonged to humans.
At least, before we *knew* you existed.
Who knows how many mutant children were dashed on rocks before one of you came along who was powerful enough to *do* anything about it?
Don't *provoke* me.
I was sent here by the *queen* to settle her fears. Fears you put into her about me.
Your goading won't work.
We are *hardly* that kind of group.
No? Then are you the sort to lure me here as a trap?
Your paranoia about mutants hasn't been serving you well if you think I can't *sense* your *bloodlust.*

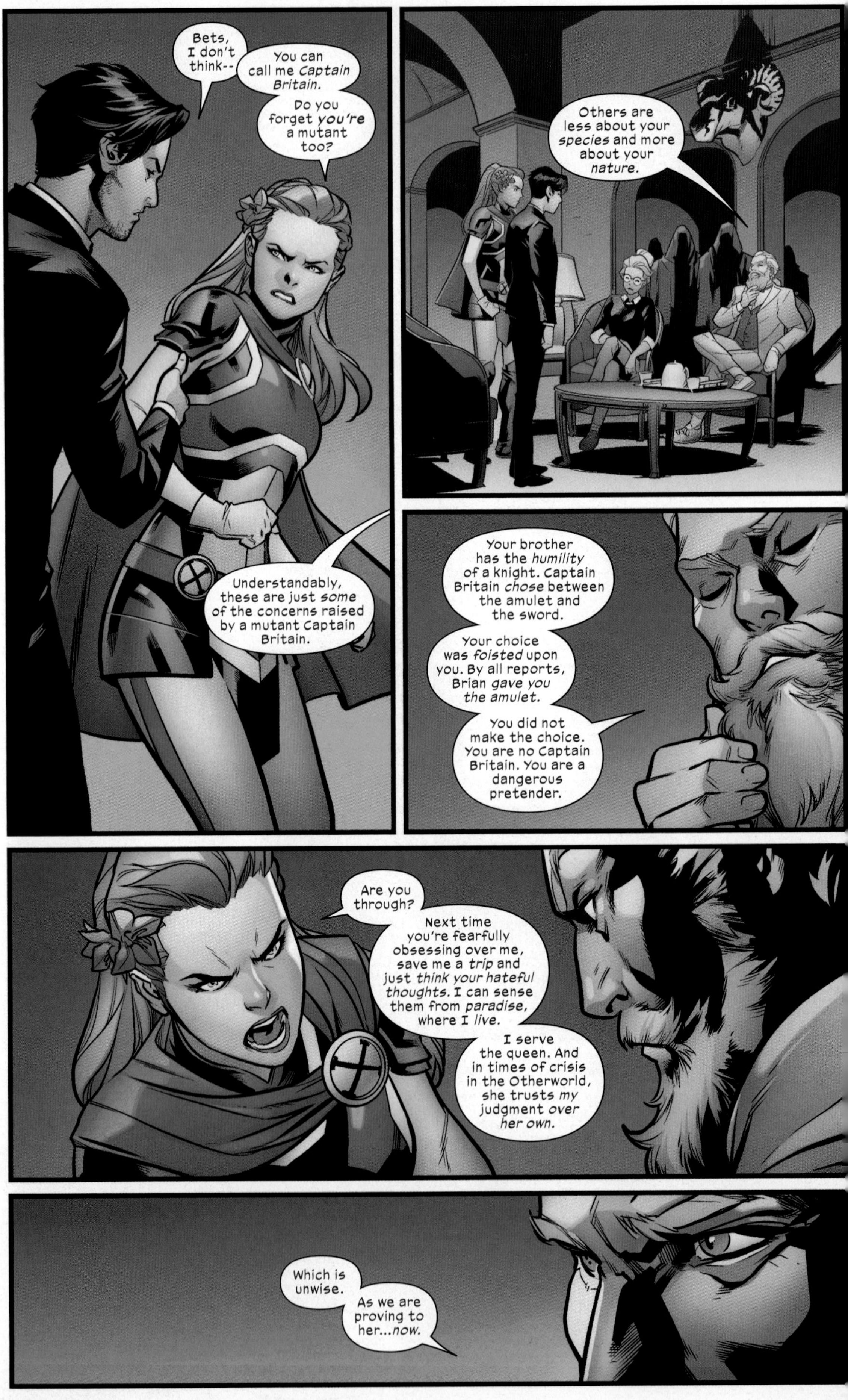
Bets, I don't think--
You can call me *Captain Britain.*
Do you forget *you're* a mutant too?
Others are less about your *species* and more about your *nature.*
Understandably, these are just *some* of the concerns raised by a mutant Captain Britain.
Your brother has the *humility* of a knight. Captain Britain *chose* between the amulet and the sword.
Your choice was *foisted* upon you. By all reports, Brian *gave you the amulet.*
You did not make the choice. You are no Captain Britain. You are a dangerous pretender.
Are you through?
Next time you're fearfully obsessing over me, save me a *trip* and just *think your hateful thoughts.* I can sense them from *paradise,* where I *live.*
I serve the queen. And in times of crisis in the Otherworld, she trusts *my* judgment *over her own.*
Which is unwise.
As we are proving to her...*now.*

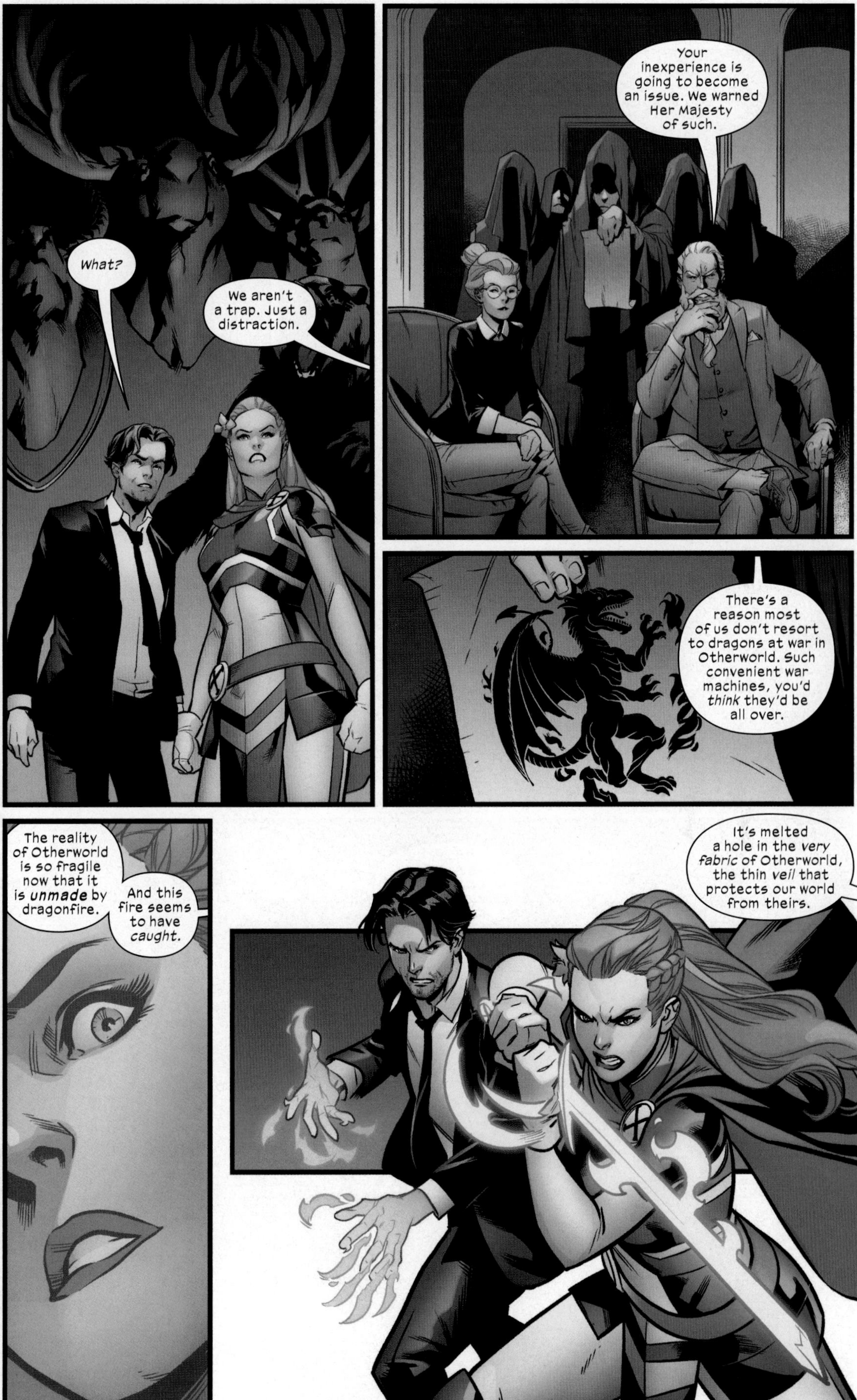
What?
We aren't a trap. Just a distraction.
Your inexperience is going to become an issue. We warned Her Majesty of such.
There's a reason most of us don't resort to dragons at war in Otherworld. Such convenient war machines, you'd *think* they'd be all over.
The reality of Otherworld is so fragile now that it is *unmade* by dragonfire.
And this fire seems to have *caught*.
It's melted a hole in the *very fabric* of Otherworld, the thin *veil* that protects our world from theirs.

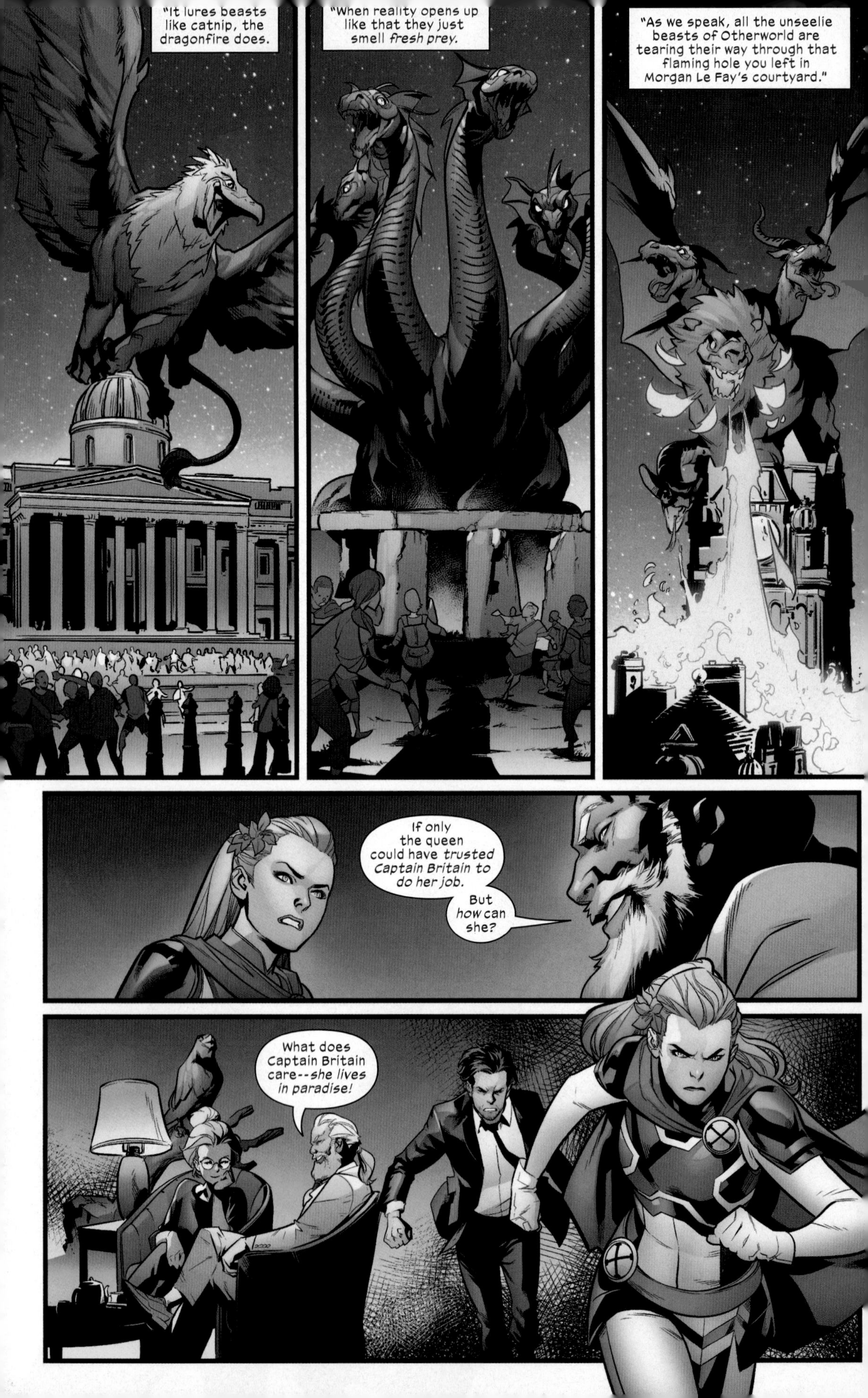
"It lures beasts like catnip, the dragonfire does.
"When reality opens up like that they just smell *fresh prey*.
"As we speak, all the unseelie beasts of Otherworld are tearing their way through that flaming hole you left in Morgan Le Fay's courtyard."
If only the queen could have *trusted* Captain Britain to do her job.
But *how* can she?
What does Captain Britain care--*she lives in paradise!*

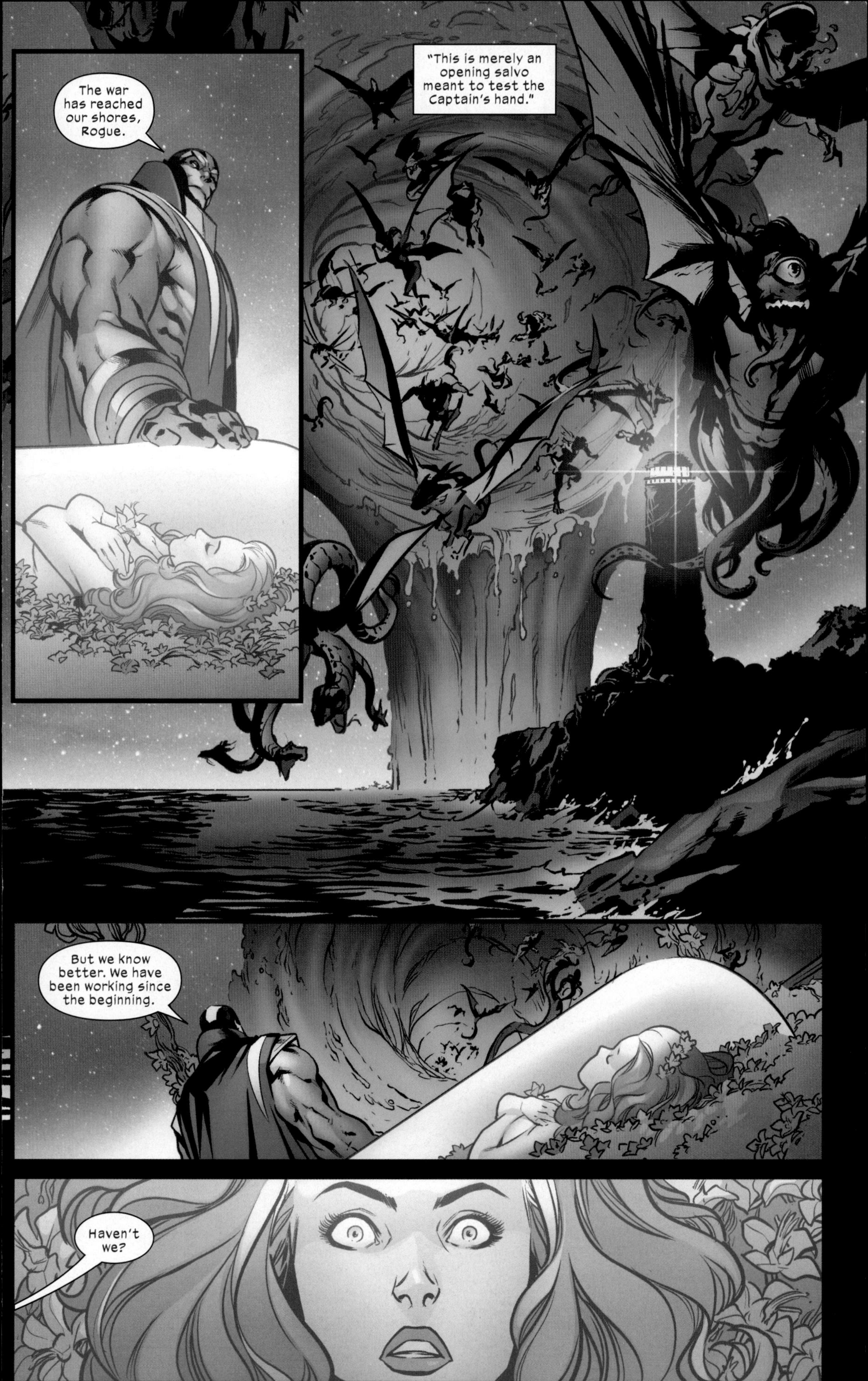
The war has reached our shores, Rogue.
"This is merely an opening salvo meant to test the Captain's hand."
But we know better. We have been working since the beginning.
Haven't we?

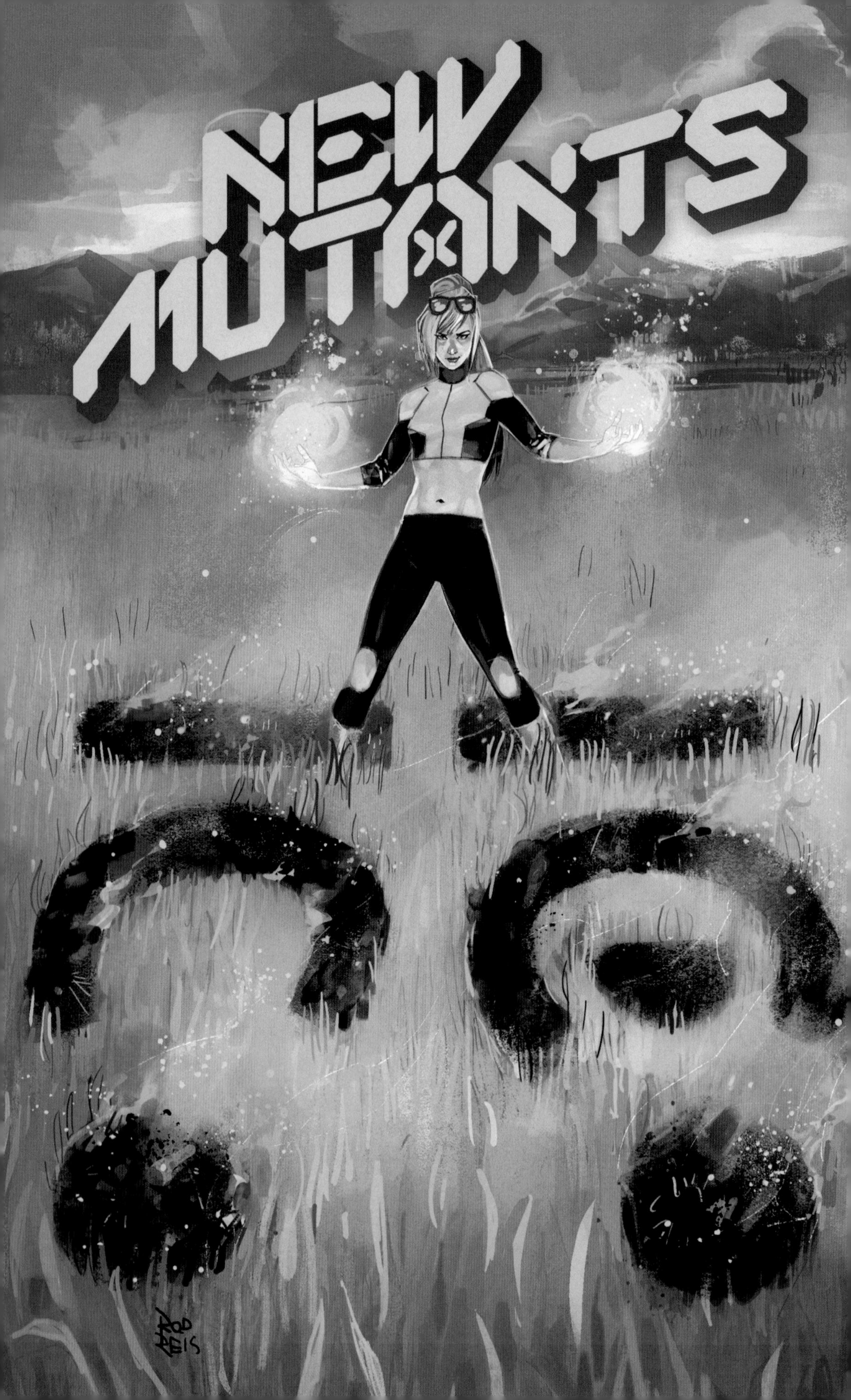
NEW MUTANTS
ROD REIS

[kra_[0.4]
[koa_[0.4]

[kra_[0.X]
[koa_[0.X]

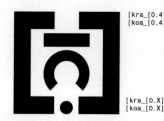

NIGHTMARE IN NEBRASKA

Discovering that old friends Beak and Angel were missing from the mutant nation of Krakoa due to Beak's ailing father, Armor, Glob, Maxime and Manon traveled to Nebraska, bringing with them Krakoan medicine. The reunion was joyful -- the medication worked miraculously -- and all was well...until armed gunmen arrived in the front yard.

Armor

Glob

Sage

Boom-Boom

Maxime

Manon

Beak

Angel

[kra_[0.4]...]
[koa_[0.4]...]

[search..find]

[00_search____X]
[00_find______X]

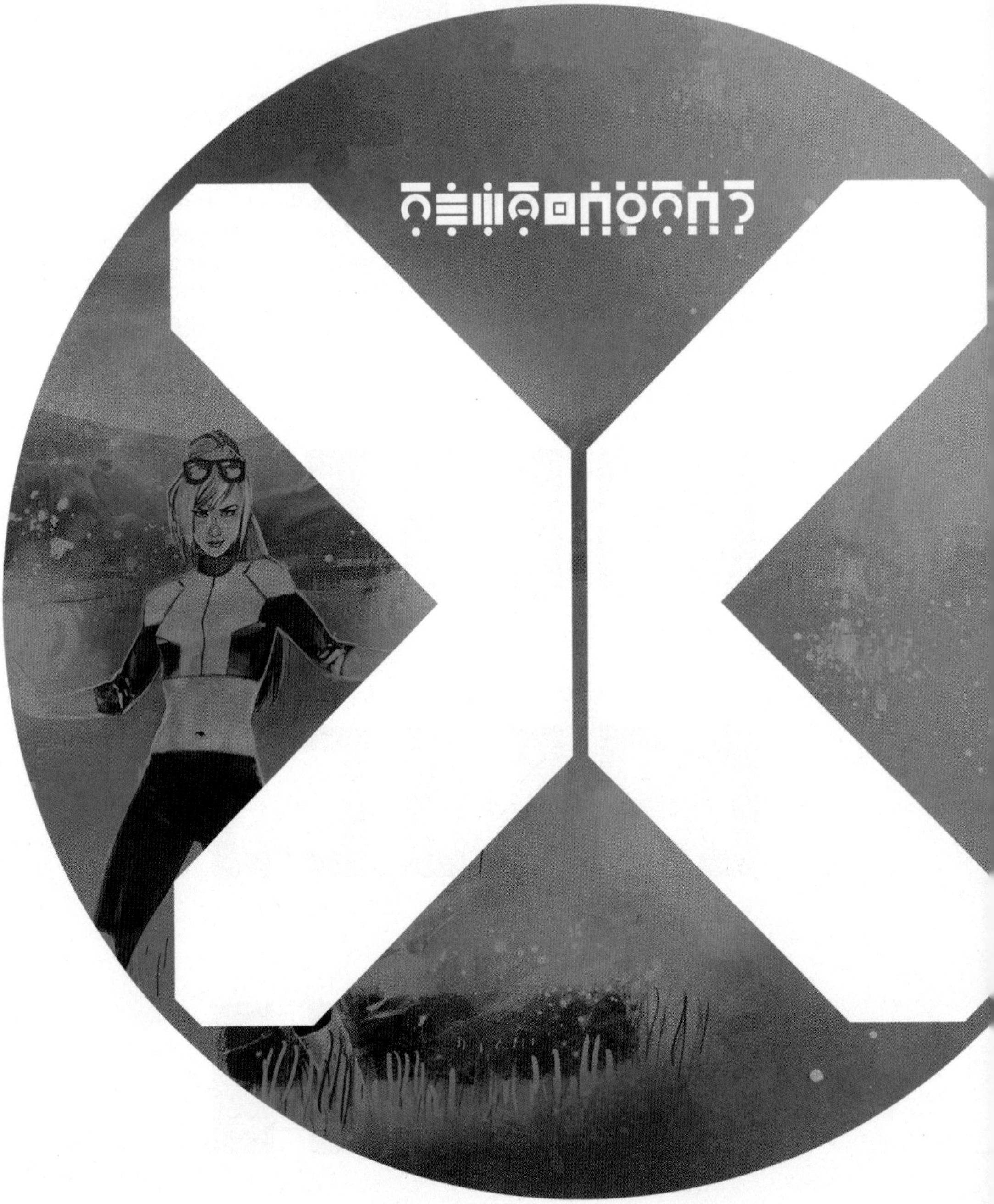

ED BRISSON.....................................[WRITER]
MARCO FAILLA...................................[ARTIST]
CARLOS LOPEZ.............................[COLOR ARTIST]
VC's TRAVIS LANHAM..........................[LETTERER]
TOM MULLER....................................[DESIGN]

ROD REIS.................................[COVER ARTIST]

NICK RUSSELL..............................[PRODUCTION]

JONATHAN HICKMAN..........................[HEAD OF X]
ANNALISE BISSA................................[EDITOR]
JORDAN D. WHITE........................[SENIOR EDITOR]
C.B. CEBULSKI........................[EDITOR IN CHIEF]
JOE QUESADA...................[CHIEF CREATIVE OFFICER]
DAN BUCKLEY................................[PRESIDENT]
ALAN FINE........................[EXECUTIVE PRODUCER]

[04] NEW MUTANTS

[ISSUE FOUR]...........FAST AND FURIOUS

[00_search__X]
[00_find____X]

[00_00.....0]
[00_00.....4]

[00___krakoa]
[00_is_____]

[00_calling_]

[00_answer?_]

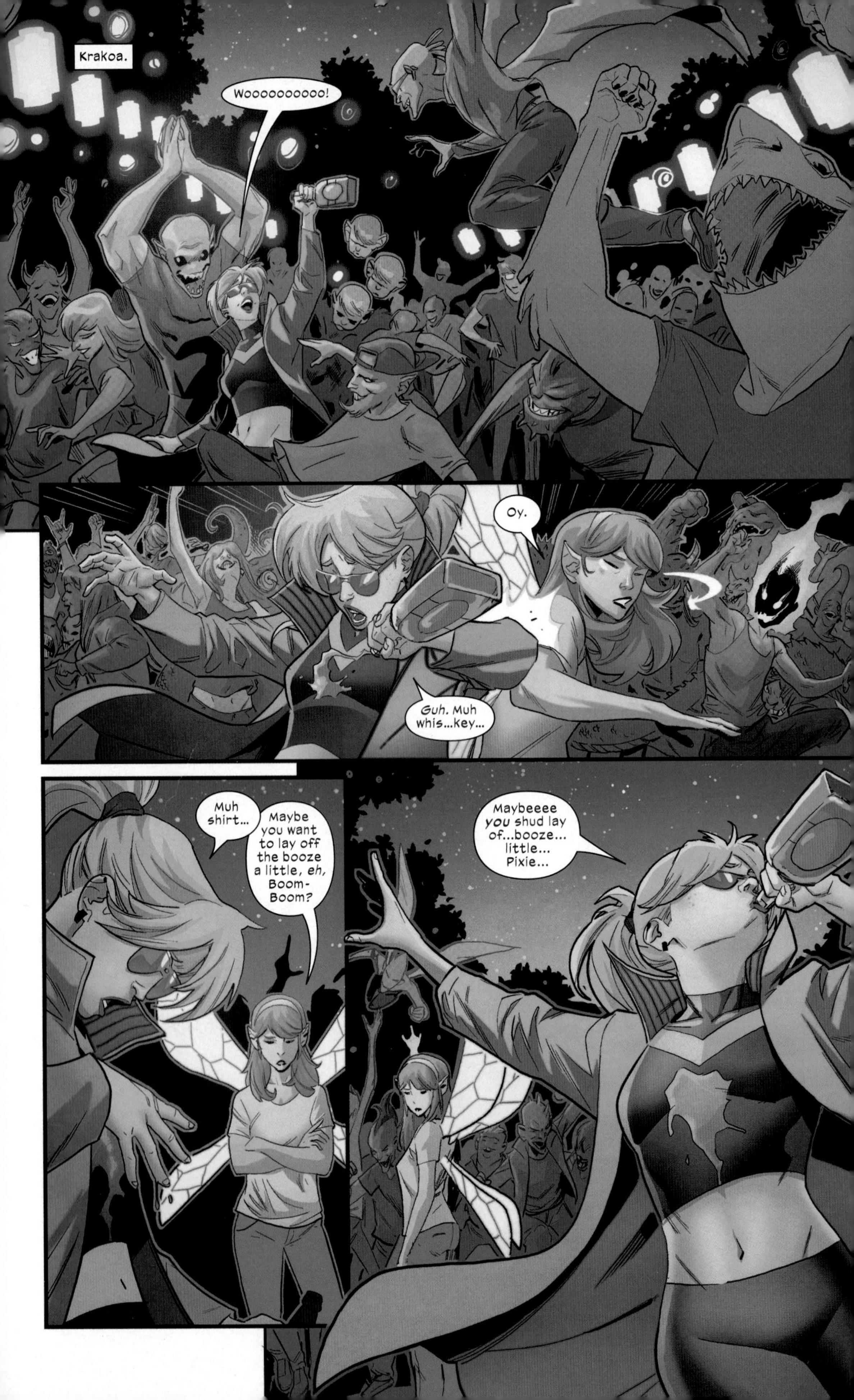
Krakoa.
Woooooooooo!
Oy.
Guh. Muh whis...key...
Muh shirt...
Maybe you want to lay off the booze a little, eh, Boom-Boom?
Maybeeee you shud lay of...booze... little... Pixie...

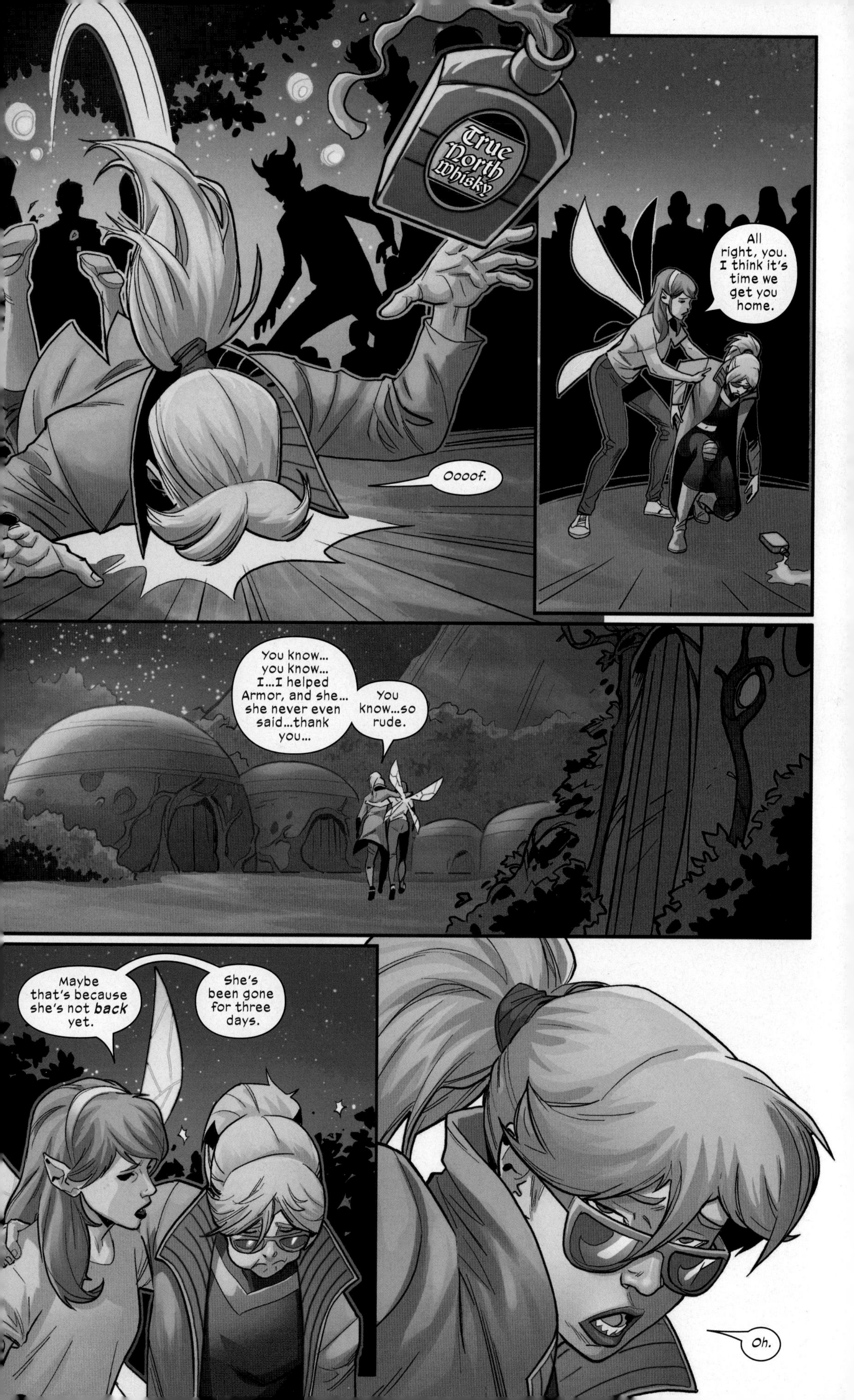
True North Whisky
Oooof.
All right, you. I think it's time we get you home.
You know... you know... I...I helped Armor, and she... she never even said...thank you...
You know...so rude.
Maybe that's because she's not *back* yet.
She's been gone for three days.
Oh.

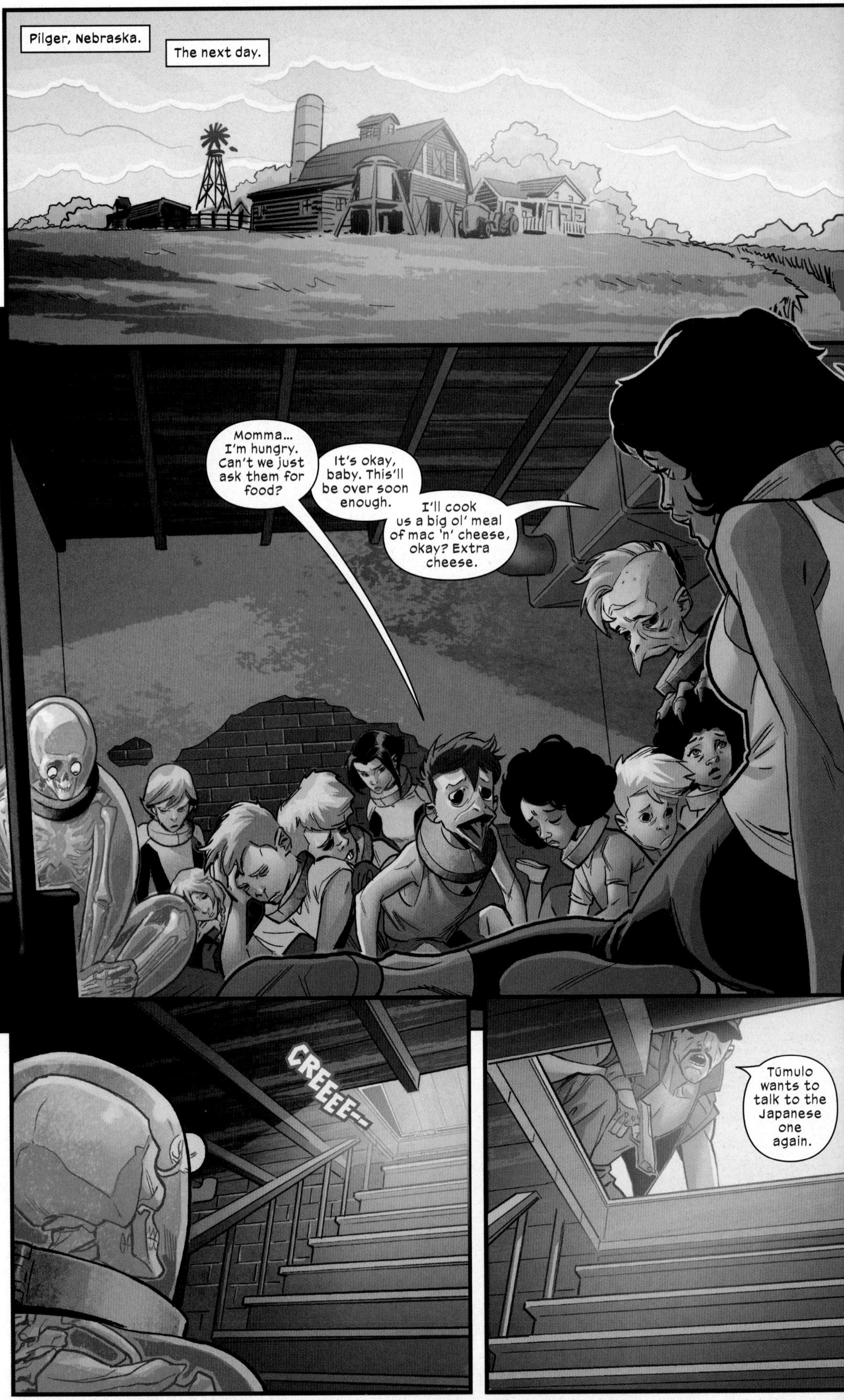
Pilger, Nebraska.
The next day.
Momma... I'm hungry. Can't we just ask them for food?
It's okay, baby. This'll be over soon enough.
I'll cook us a big ol' meal of mac 'n' cheese, okay? Extra cheese.
CREEEE--
Tūmulo wants to talk to the Japanese one again.

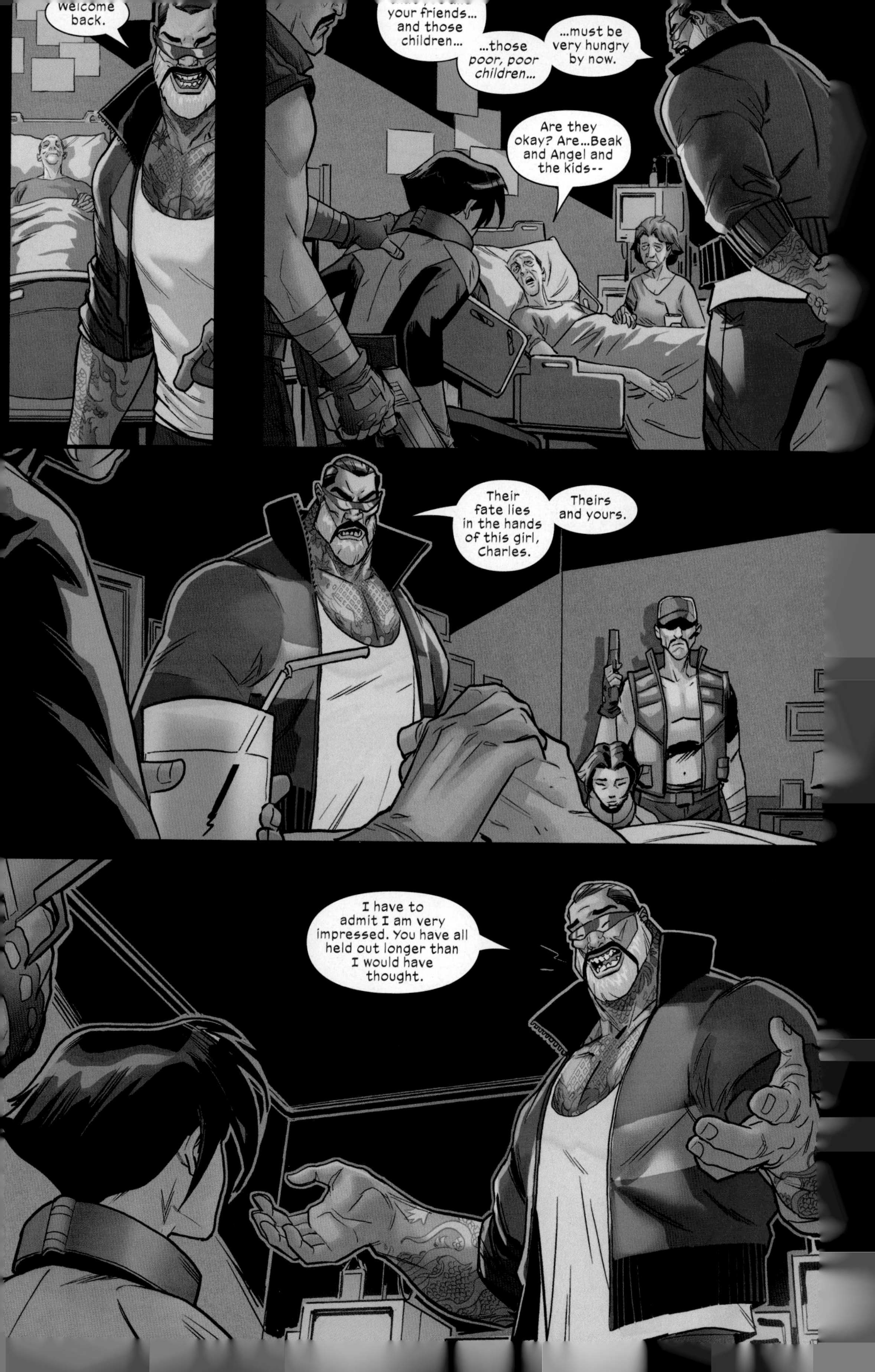
welcome back.
your friends... and those children...
...those *poor, poor* children...
...must be very hungry by now.
Are they okay? Are...Beak and Angel and the kids--
Their fate lies in the hands of this girl, Charles.
Theirs and yours.
I have to admit I am very impressed. You have all held out longer than I would have thought.

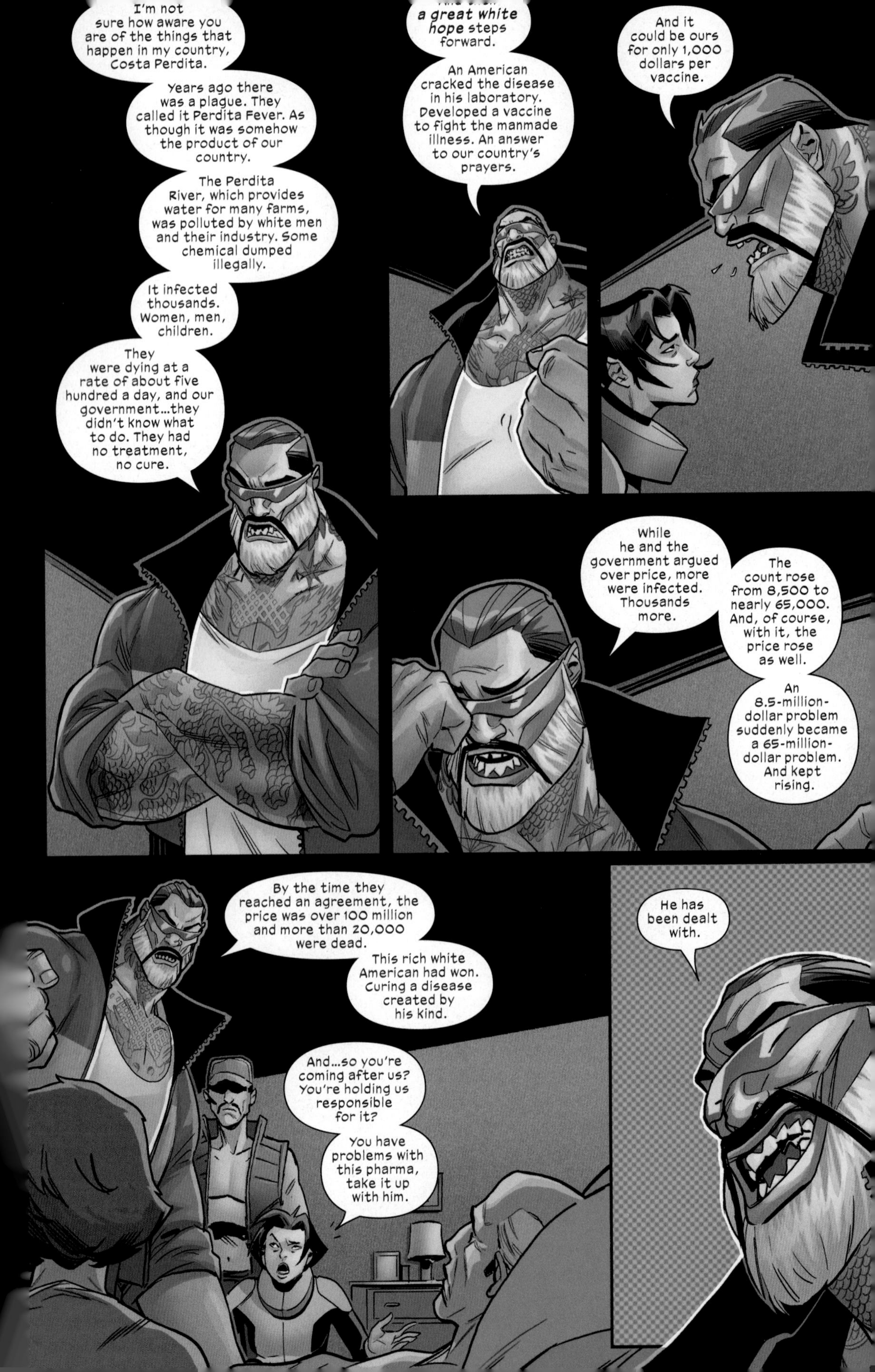
I'm not sure how aware you are of the things that happen in my country, Costa Perdita.
Years ago there was a plague. They called it Perdita Fever. As though it was somehow the product of our country.
The Perdita River, which provides water for many farms, was polluted by white men and their industry. Some chemical dumped illegally.
It infected thousands. Women, men, children.
They were dying at a rate of about five hundred a day, and our government...they didn't know what to do. They had no treatment, no cure.
a great white hope steps forward.
An American cracked the disease in his laboratory. Developed a vaccine to fight the manmade illness. An answer to our country's prayers.
And it could be ours for only 1,000 dollars per vaccine.
While he and the government argued over price, more were infected. Thousands more.
The count rose from 8,500 to nearly 65,000. And, of course, with it, the price rose as well.
An 8.5-million-dollar problem suddenly became a 65-million-dollar problem. And kept rising.
By the time they reached an agreement, the price was over 100 million and more than 20,000 were dead.
This rich white American had won. Curing a disease created by his kind.
And...so you're coming after us? You're holding us responsible for it?
You have problems with this pharma, take it up with him.
He has been dealt with.

EXCERPT FROM NEWSPAPER

CONTROVERSIAL PHARMA C.E.O. FOUND DEAD AT 35

The NYPD Homicide Unit is investigating the death of a man identified as MAK Pharmaceutical C.E.O. Kevin MacKinnon. MacKinnon was found dead in his Manhattan apartment early Tuesday morning after officers were called to the luxury apartment complex shortly after 3:00 a.m. in response to multiple 9-1-1 reports of gunshots from MacKinnon's unit. The NYPD says that MacKinnon suffered a gunshot wound, but would not say how many wounds or whether the wounds were self-inflicted.

Kevin MacKinnon had become a controversial figure in the pharmaceutical world, having acquired several smaller pharmaceutical companies and increased the cost of life-saving medications by upward of 5,300%. He was also the subject of a recently launched investigation by the FTC and FBI for securities fraud.

Recently, MAK Pharmaceutical was criticized for raising the price of Talimrelic, a vaccine for "Perdita Fever," by more than 1,000% in an intense series of negotiations with the government of Costa Perdita. During the negotiations, MAK Pharmaceutical held back its supply of the life-saving drug, resulting in more than 20,000 casualties in Costa Perdita.

The NYPD is asking any witnesses to come forward. Officers are currently canvassing door-to-door in the area looking for potential witnesses.

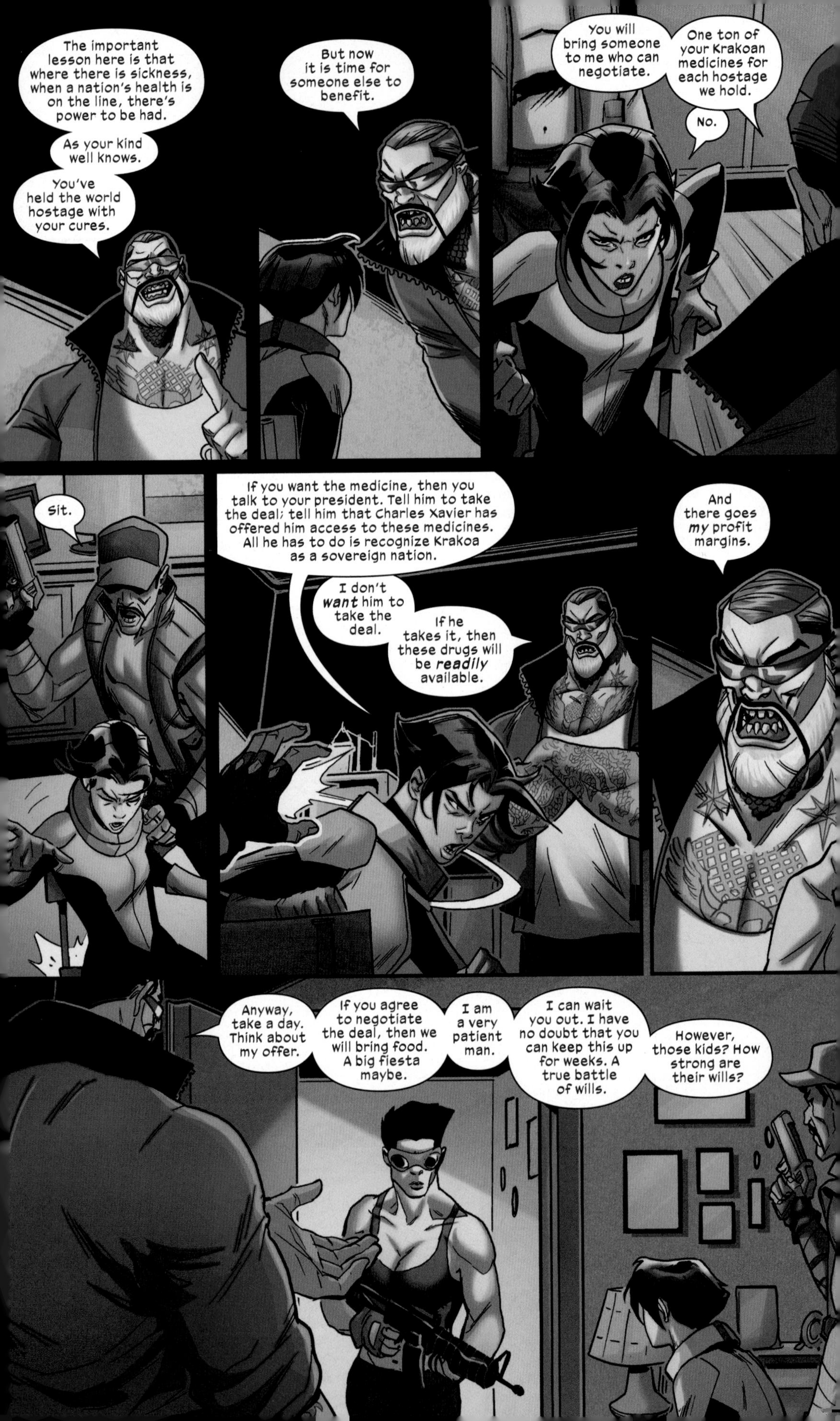
The important lesson here is that where there is sickness, when a nation's health is on the line, there's power to be had.
As your kind well knows.
You've held the world hostage with your cures.
But now it is time for someone else to benefit.
You will bring someone to me who can negotiate.
One ton of your Krakoan medicines for each hostage we hold.
No.
Sit.
If you want the medicine, then you talk to your president. Tell him to take the deal; tell him that Charles Xavier has offered him access to these medicines. All he has to do is recognize Krakoa as a sovereign nation.
I don't *want* him to take the deal.
If he takes it, then these drugs will be *readily* available.
And there goes *my* profit margins.
Anyway, take a day. Think about my offer.
If you agree to negotiate the deal, then we will bring food. A big fiesta maybe.
I am a very patient man.
I can wait you out. I have no doubt that you can keep this up for weeks. A true battle of wills.
However, those kids? How strong are their wills?

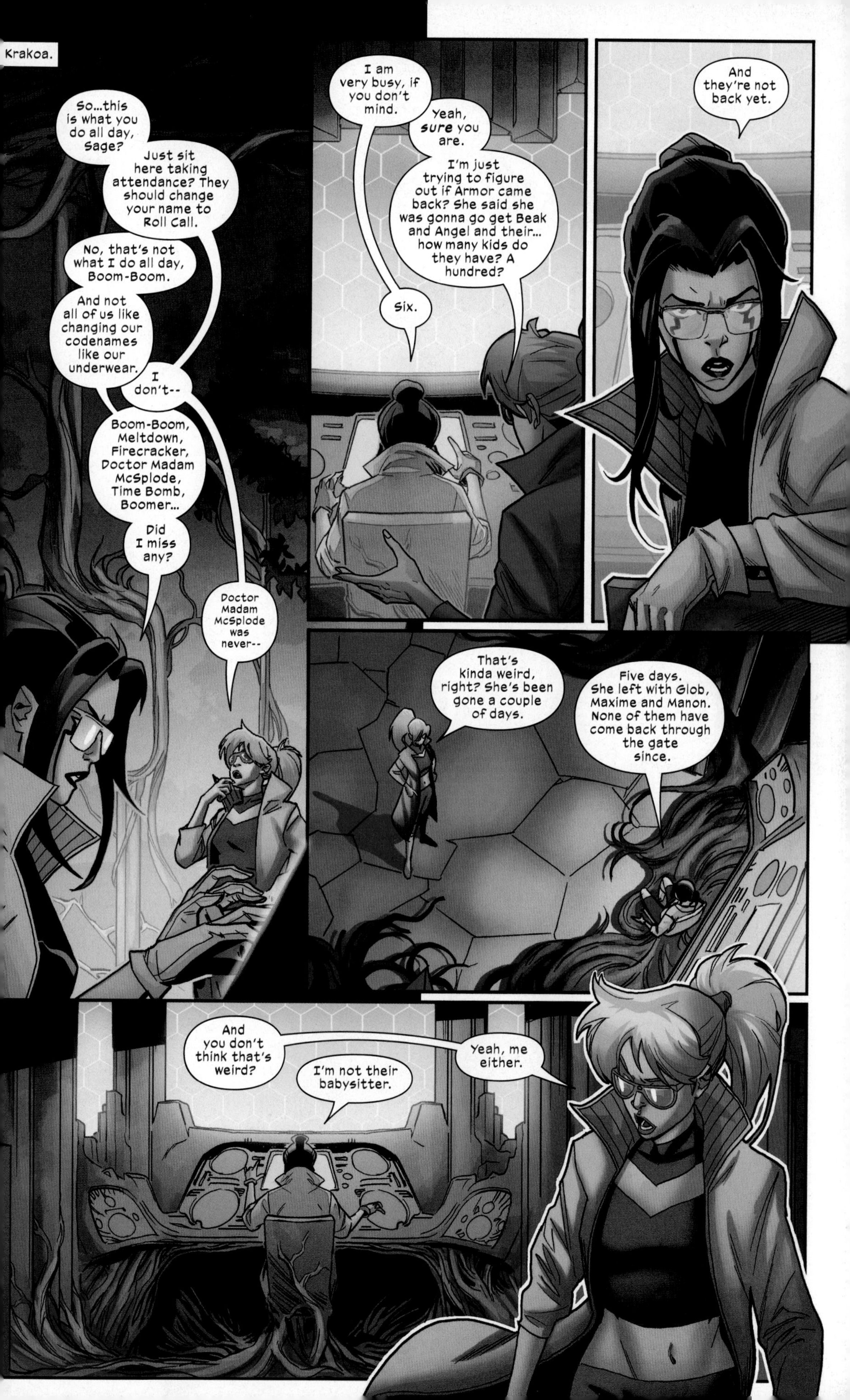

Krakoa.
So...this is what you do all day, Sage?
Just sit here taking attendance? They should change your name to Roll Call.
No, that's not what I do all day, Boom-Boom.
And not all of us like changing our codenames like our underwear.
I don't--
Boom-Boom, Meltdown, Firecracker, Doctor Madam McSplode, Time Bomb, Boomer...
Did I miss any?
Doctor Madam McSplode was never--
I am very busy, if you don't mind.
Yeah, sure you are.
I'm just trying to figure out if Armor came back? She said she was gonna go get Beak and Angel and their... how many kids do they have? A hundred?
Six.
And they're not back yet.
That's kinda weird, right? She's been gone a couple of days.
Five days. She left with Glob, Maxime and Manon. None of them have come back through the gate since.
And you don't think that's weird?
I'm not their babysitter.
Yeah, me either.

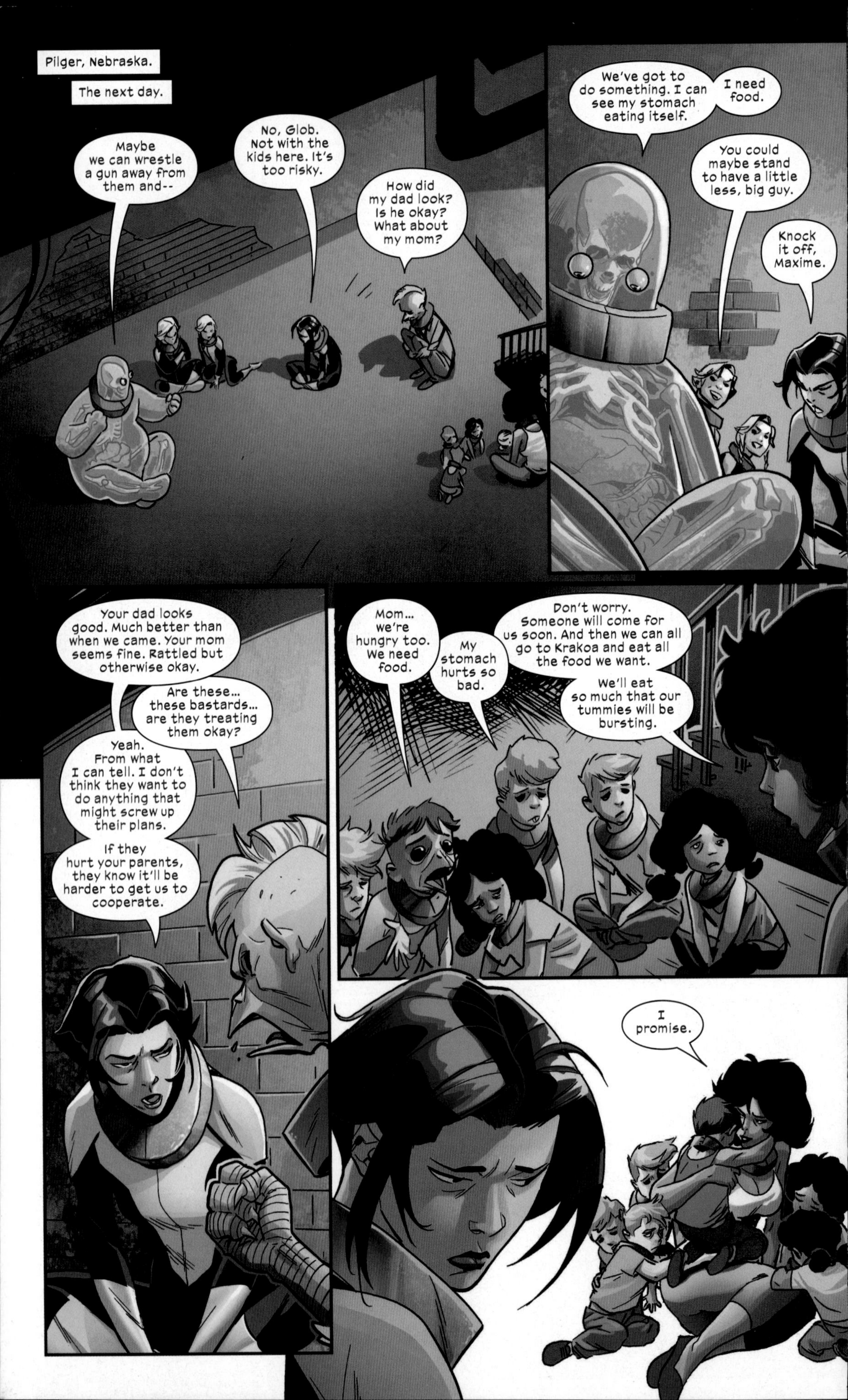
Pilger, Nebraska.
The next day.
Maybe we can wrestle a gun away from them and--
No, Glob. Not with the kids here. It's too risky.
How did my dad look? Is he okay? What about my mom?
We've got to do something. I can see my stomach eating itself.
I need food.
You could maybe stand to have a little less, big guy.
Knock it off, Maxime.
Your dad looks good. Much better than when we came. Your mom seems fine. Rattled but otherwise okay.
Are these... these bastards... are they treating them okay?
Yeah. From what I can tell. I don't think they want to do anything that might screw up their plans.
If they hurt your parents, they know it'll be harder to get us to cooperate.
Mom... we're hungry too. We need food.
My stomach hurts so bad.
Don't worry. Someone will come for us soon. And then we can all go to Krakoa and eat all the food we want.
We'll eat so much that our tummies will be bursting.
I promise.

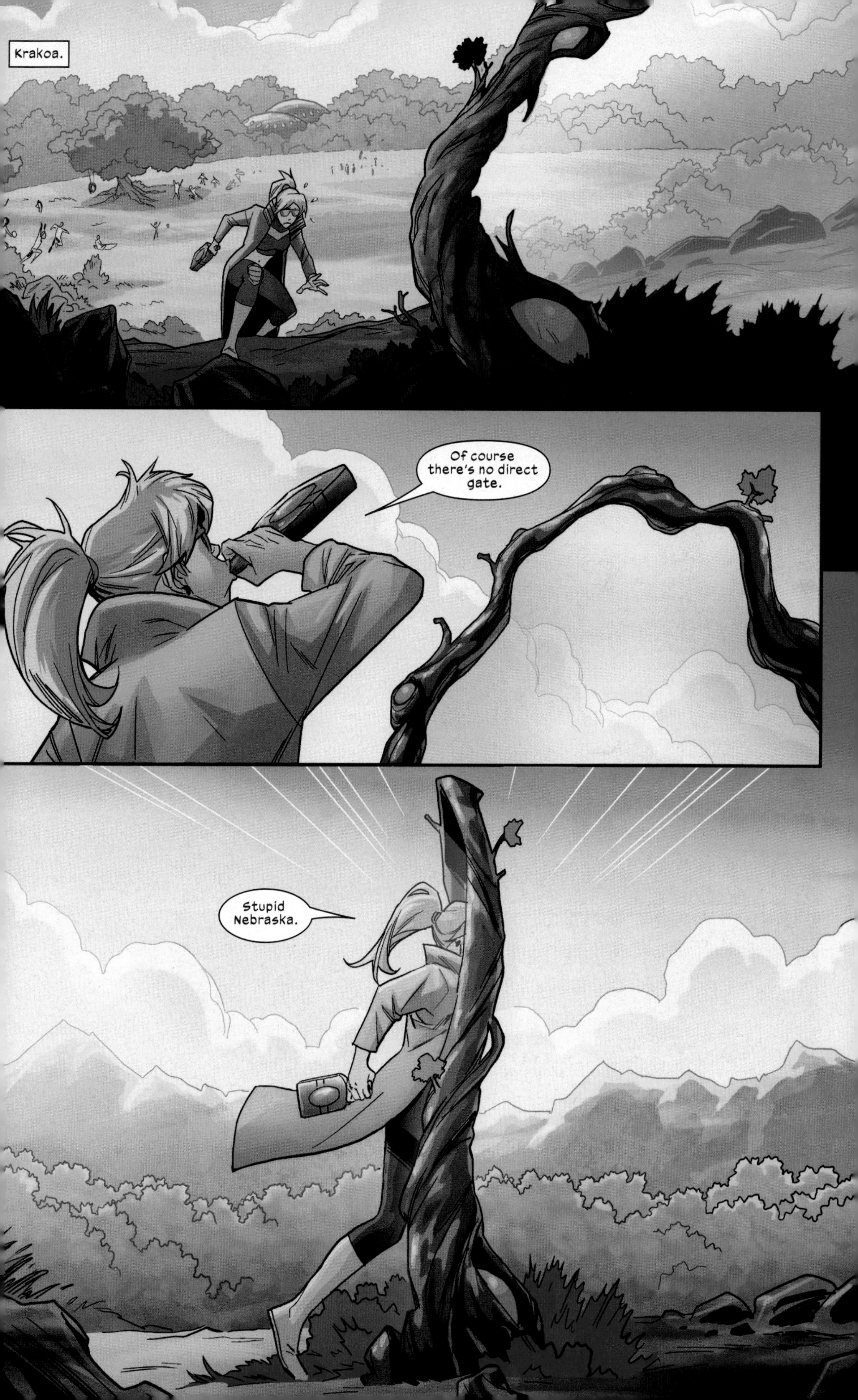
Krakoa.
Of course there's no direct gate.
Stupid Nebraska.

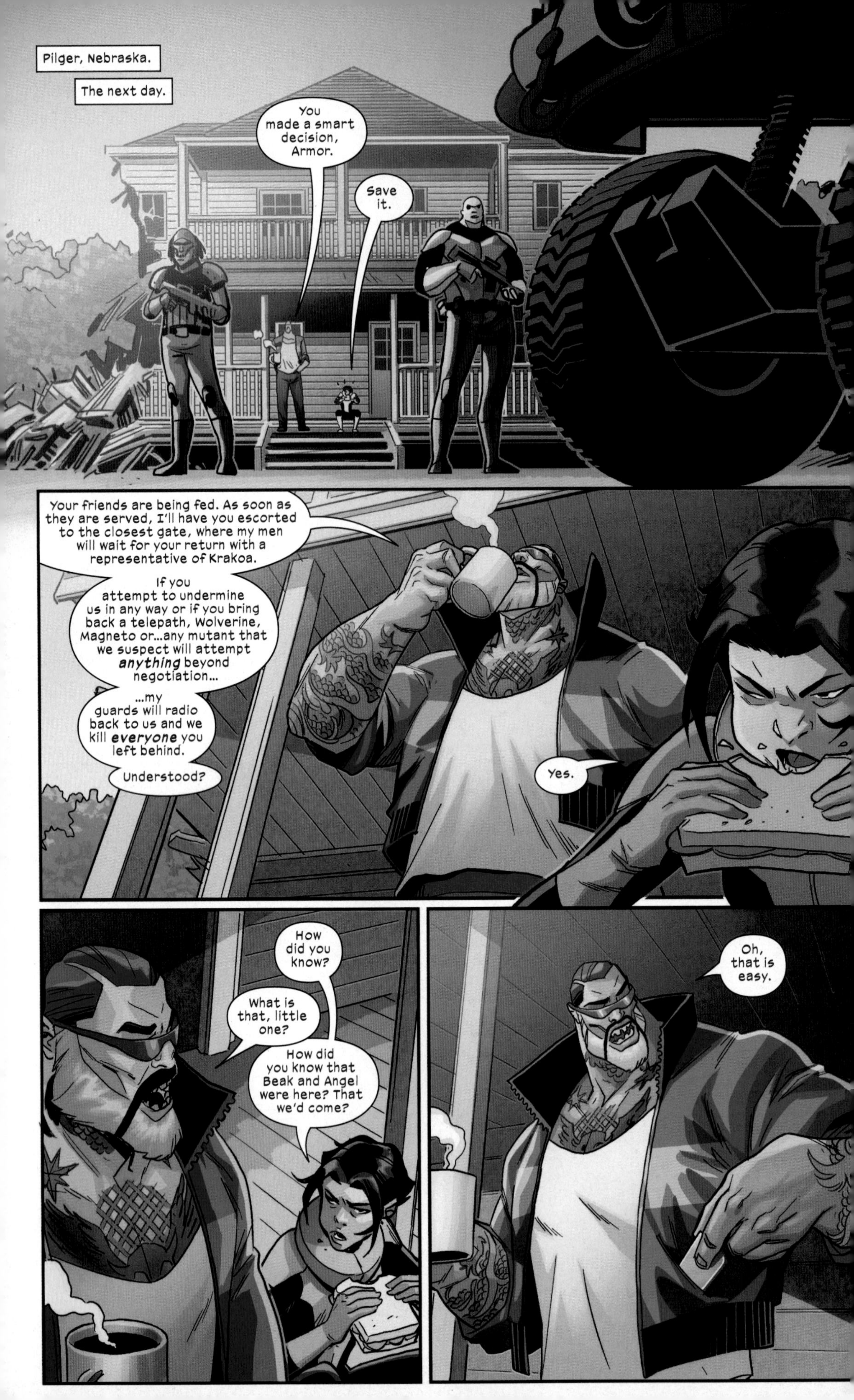
Pilger, Nebraska.
The next day.
You made a smart decision, Armor.
Save it.
Your friends are being fed. As soon as they are served, I'll have you escorted to the closest gate, where my men will wait for your return with a representative of Krakoa.
If you attempt to undermine us in any way or if you bring back a telepath, Wolverine, Magneto or...any mutant that we suspect will attempt *anything* beyond negotiation...
...my guards will radio back to us and we kill *everyone* you left behind.
Understood?
Yes.
How did you know?
What is that, little one?
How did you know that Beak and Angel were here? That we'd come?
Oh, that is easy.

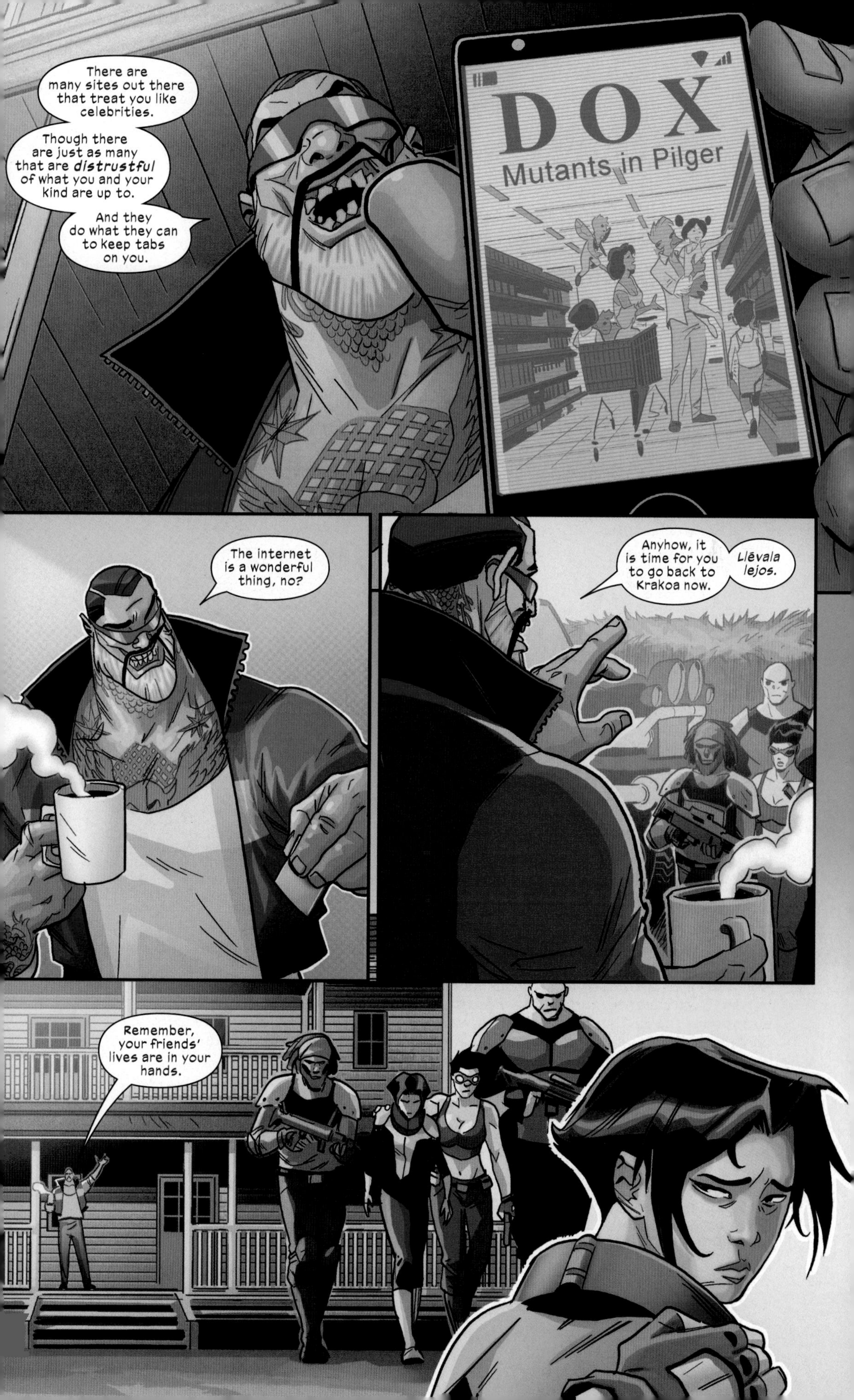
There are many sites out there that treat you like celebrities.
Though there are just as many that are *distrustful* of what you and your kind are up to.
And they do what they can to keep tabs on you.
DOX
Mutants in Pilger
The internet is a wonderful thing, no?
Anyhow, it is time for you to go back to Krakoa now.
Llévala lejos.
Remember, your friends' lives are in your hands.

COSTA PERDITA

GULF
OF MEXICO
MEXICO
TROPIC OF CANCER
PACIFIC
OCEAN
BELIZE
COSTA DIALBLO
TERRA VERDE
COSTA VERDE
COSTA PERDITA
GUATEMALA
RIO DE MUERTE

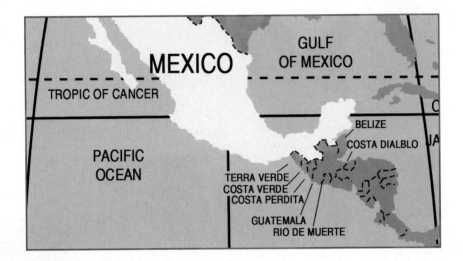

OFFICIAL NAME: Republic of Costa Perdita *(República de Costa Perdita)*

POPULATION: 1,200,000

AREA: 140,000 square kilometers

CAPITAL CITY: Bohem

GOVERNMENT: Republic

MAJOR LANGUAGES: Spanish, Portuguese

MAJOR RESOURCES: Fishing, timber

Formerly a Spanish colony, Costa Perdita gained independence from Spain in 1823 after a brief civil war involving the allied nations of Terra Verde, Costa Verde and Costa Perdita. The three countries had the support of the British Empire, which was looking to further disrupt the control of Spain within major trade routes. After less than a year, the war ended with the signing of the The Treaty of Verdita.

A small country, Costa Perdita has little in the way of homegrown industry beyond natural resources. In recent years, large biochemical corporations have moved their manufacturing and testing facilities into the country, taking advantage of oft-criticized relaxed health and safety and human rights regulations.

It has been estimated that more than 50,000 citizens have died in the last two decades due to contamination of both the air and water from biochemical waste and spill-off.

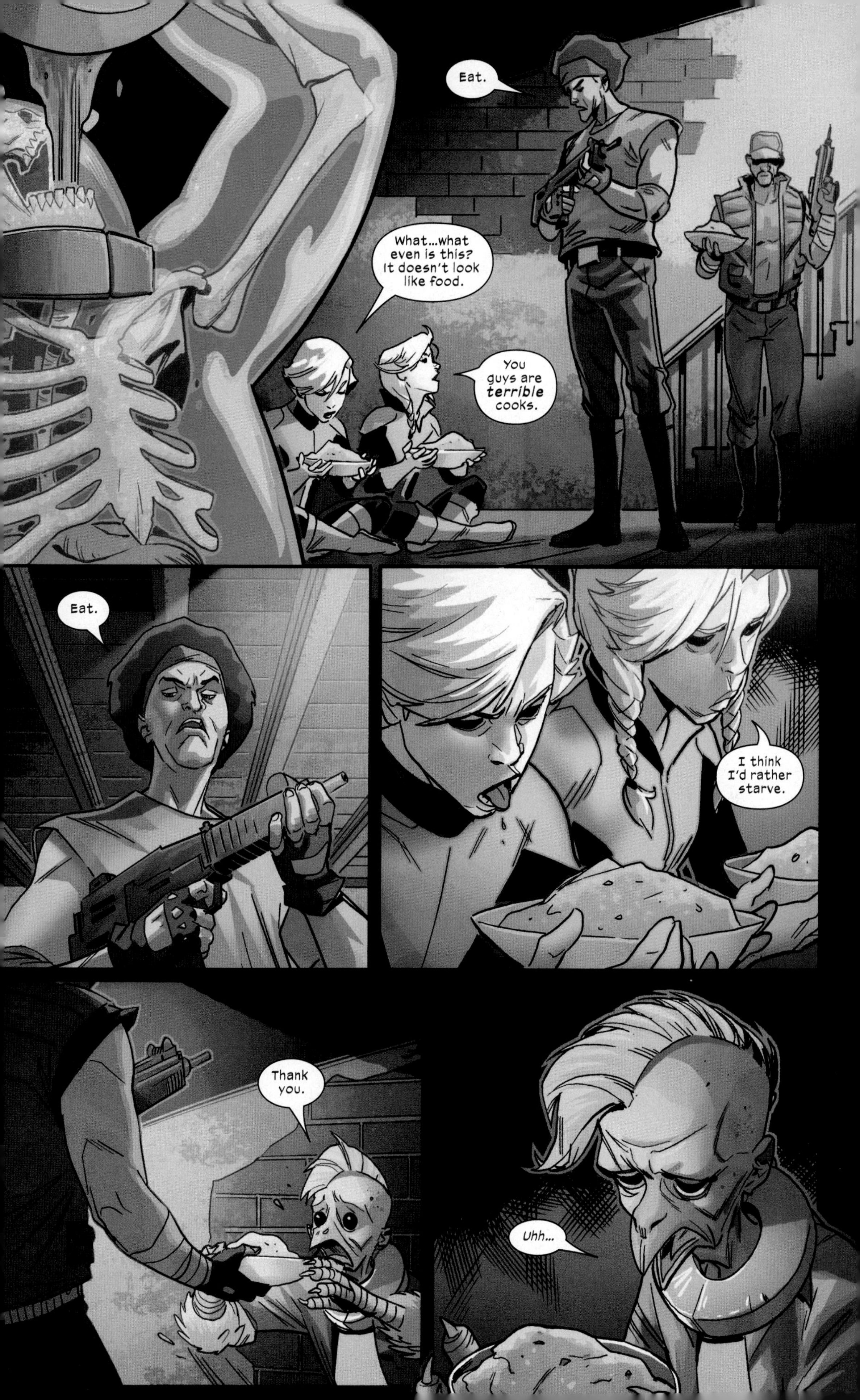
Eat.
What...what even is this? It doesn't look like food.
You guys are *terrible* cooks.
Eat.
I think I'd rather starve.
Thank you.
Uhh...

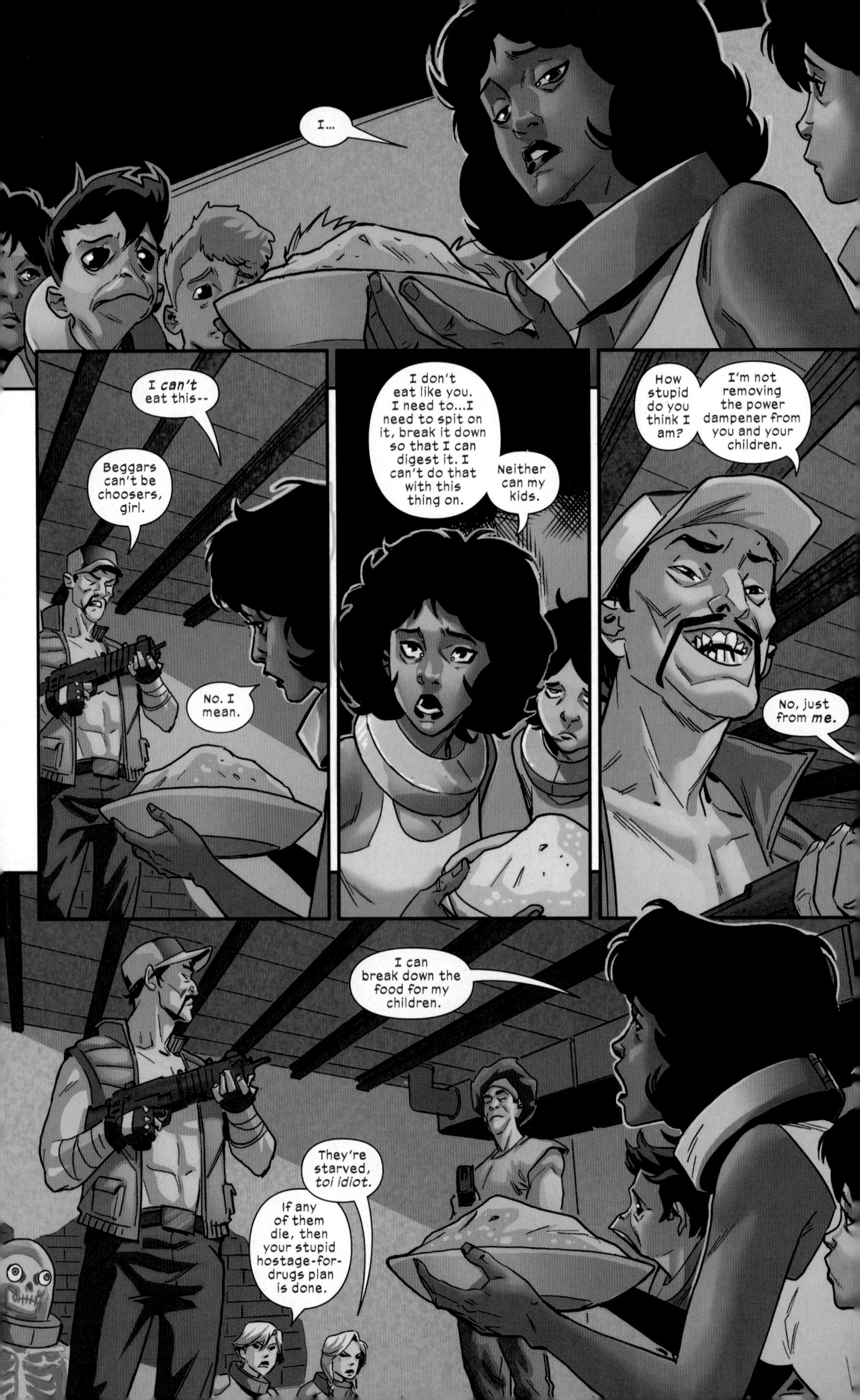
I...
I *can't* eat this--
Beggars can't be choosers, girl.
No. I mean.
I don't eat like you. I need to...I need to spit on it, break it down so that I can digest it. I can't do that with this thing on.
Neither can my kids.
How stupid do you think I am?
I'm not removing the power dampener from you and your children.
No, just from **me.**
I can break down the food for my children.
They're starved, *toi idiot.*
If any of them die, then your stupid hostage-for-drugs plan is done.

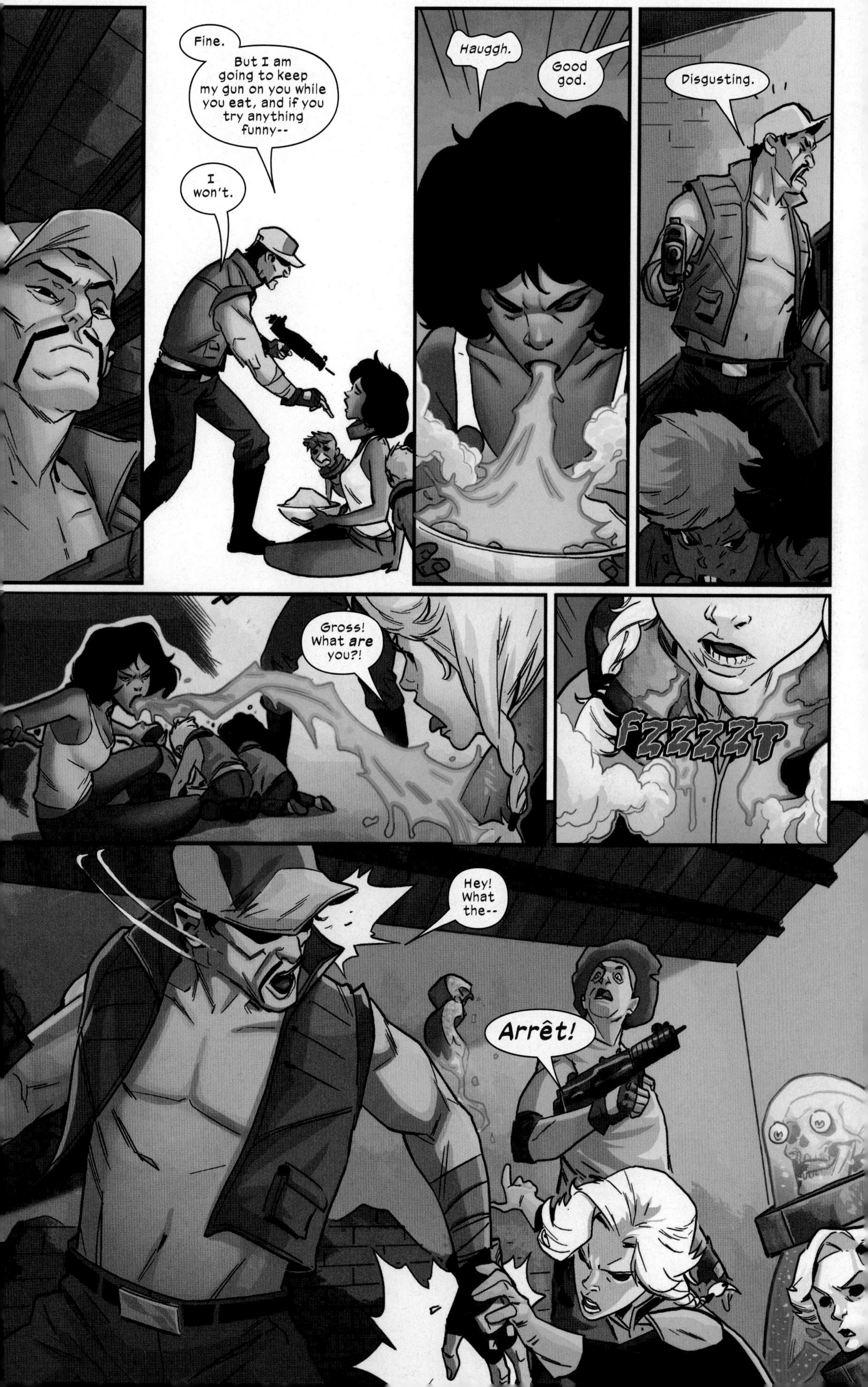
Fine.
But I am going to keep my gun on you while you eat, and if you try anything funny--
I won't.
Haughh.
Good god.
Disgusting.
Gross! What are you?!
FZZZZT
Hey! What the--
Arrêt!

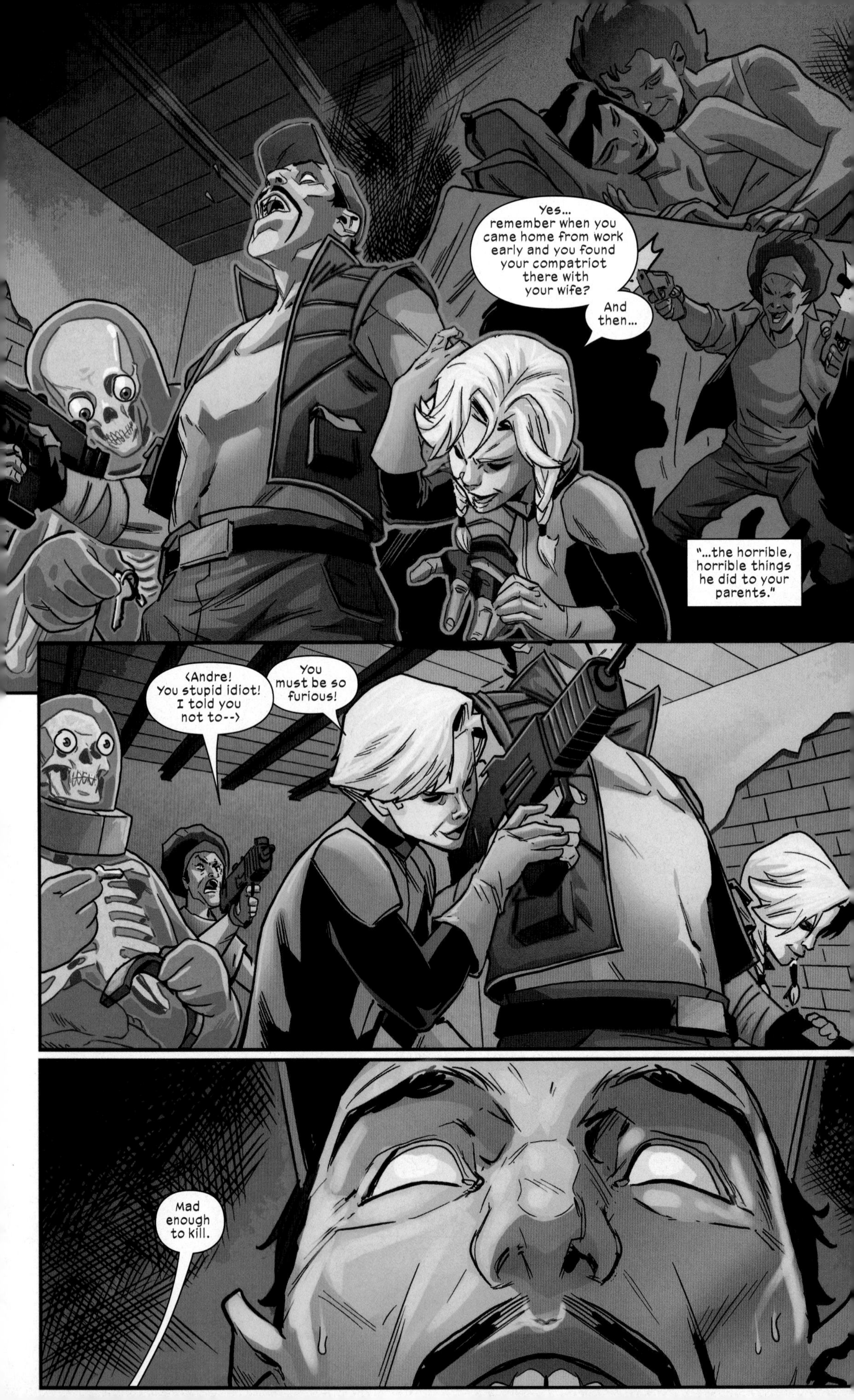
Yes... remember when you came home from work early and you found your compatriot there with your wife?
And then...
"...the horrible, horrible things he did to your parents."
‹Andre! You stupid idiot! I told you not to--›
You must be so furious!
Mad enough to kill.

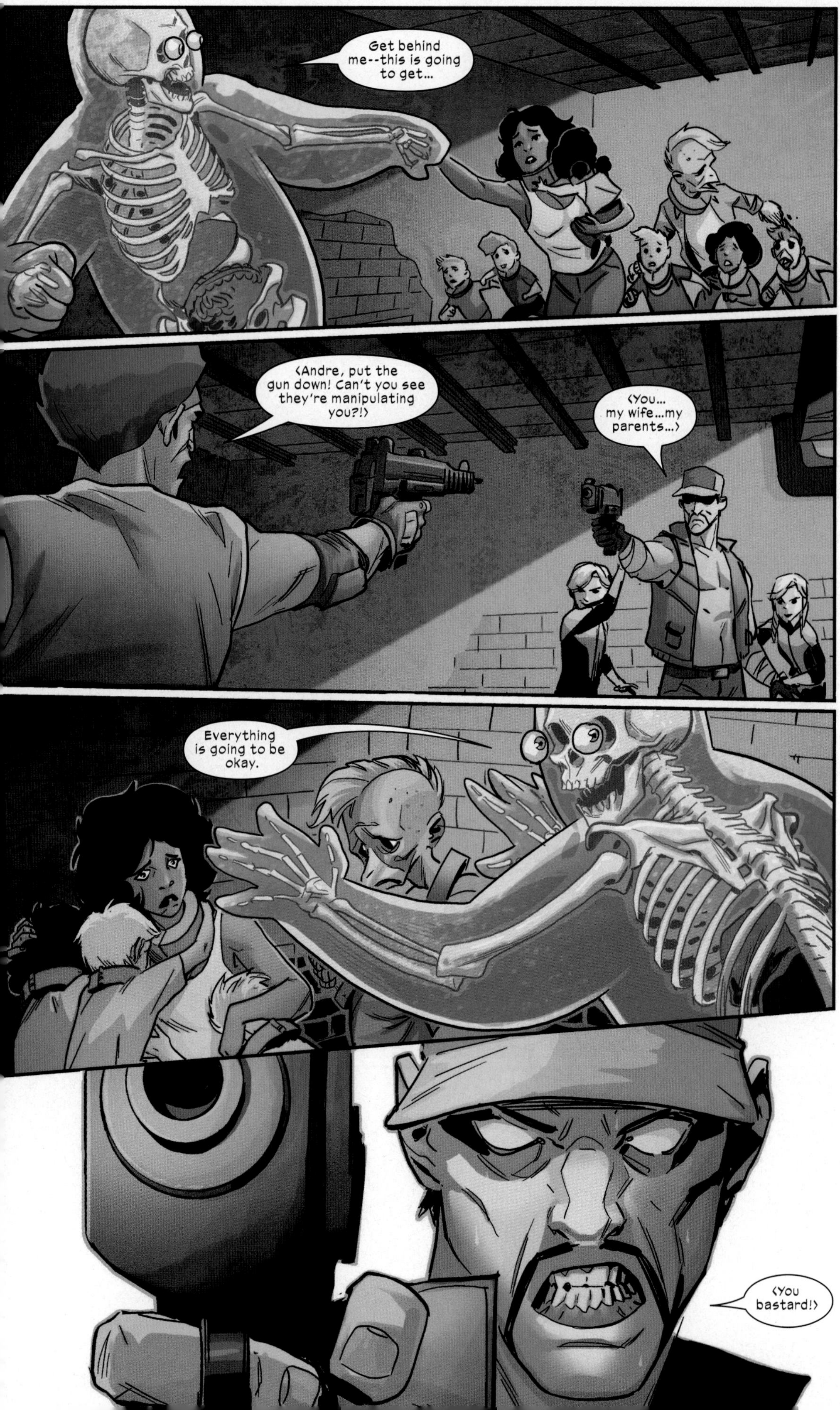
Get behind me--this is going to get...
‹Andre, put the gun down! Can't you see they're manipulating you?!›
‹You... my wife...my parents...›
Everything is going to be okay.
‹You bastard!›

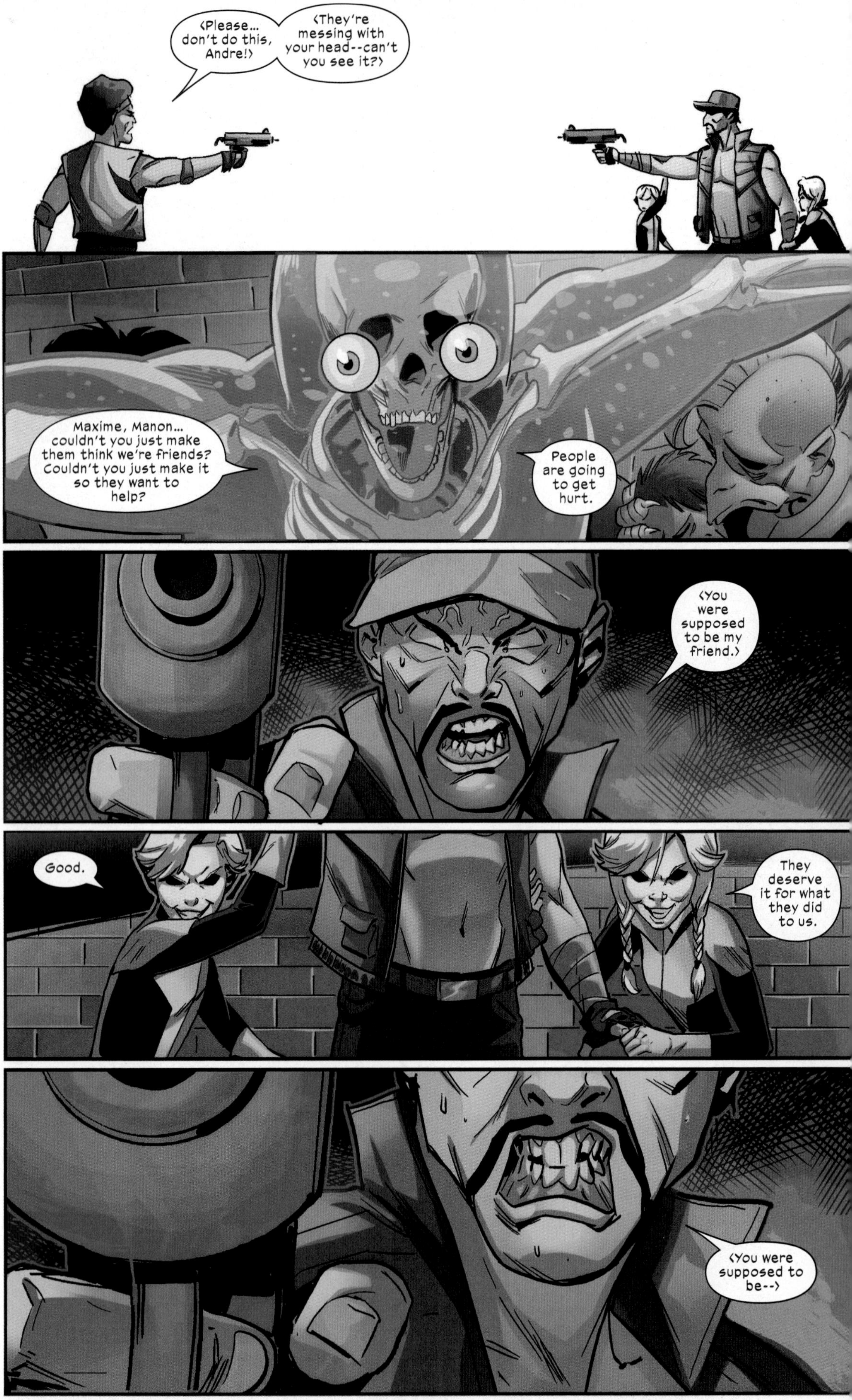

‹Please... don't do this, Andre!›
‹They're messing with your head--can't you see it?›
Maxime, Manon... couldn't you just make them think we're friends? Couldn't you just make it so they want to help?
People are going to get hurt.
‹You were supposed to be my friend.›
Good.
They deserve it for what they did to us.
‹You were supposed to be--›

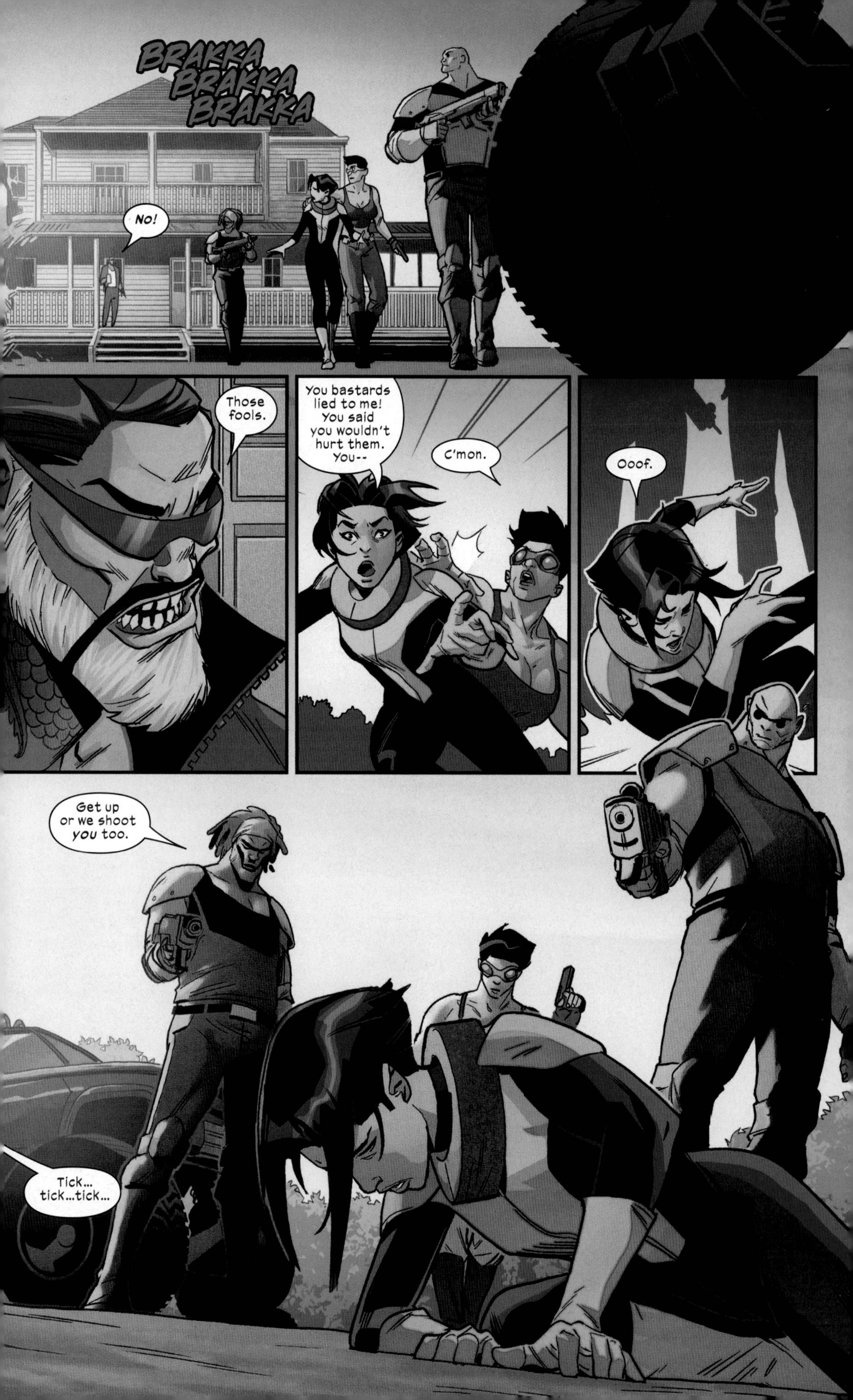
BRAKKA BRAKKA BRAKKA
NO!
Those fools.
You bastards lied to me! You said you wouldn't hurt them. You--
C'mon.
Ooof.
Get up or we shoot *you* too.
Tick... tick...tick...

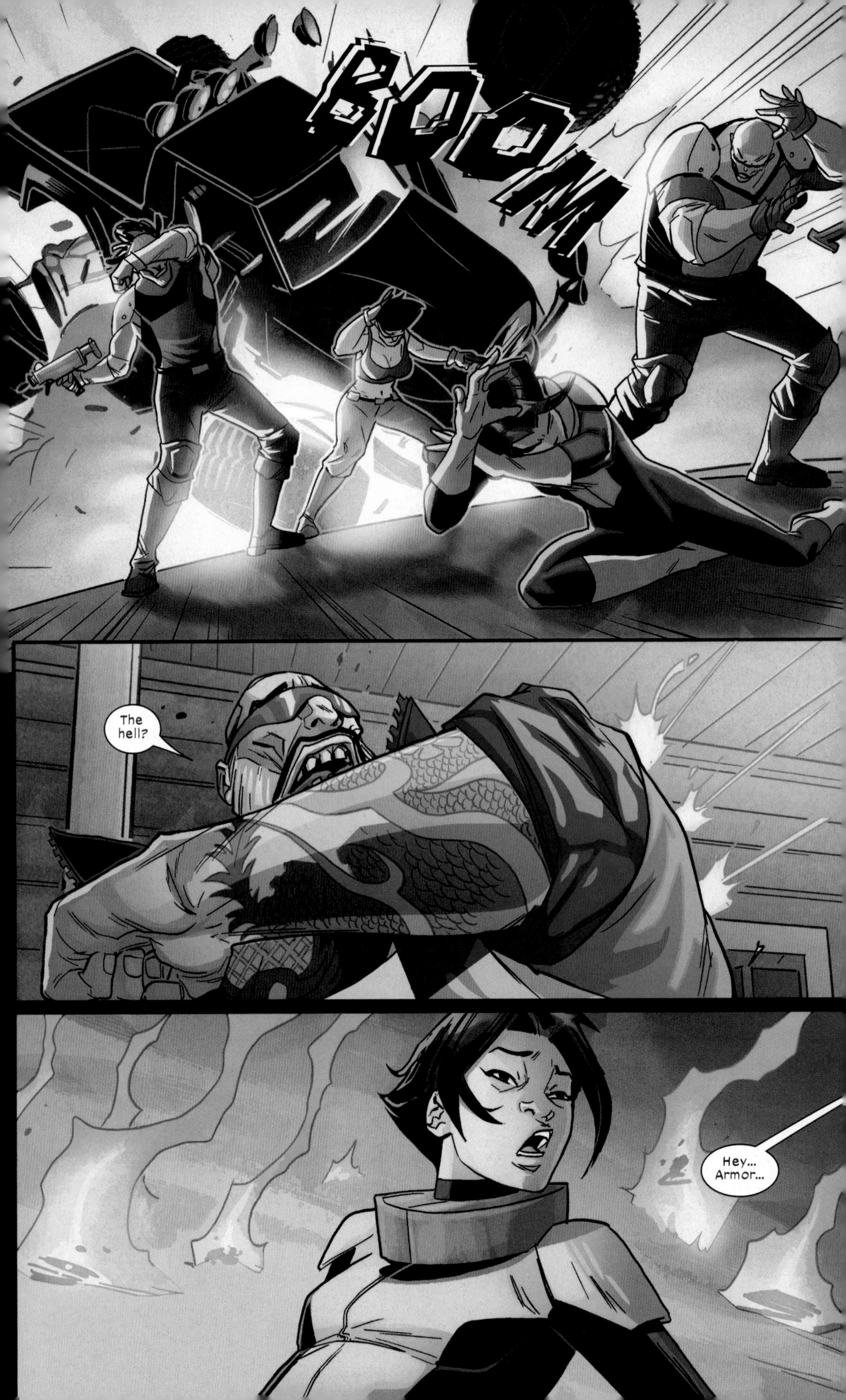
BOOM
The hell?
Hey... Armor...

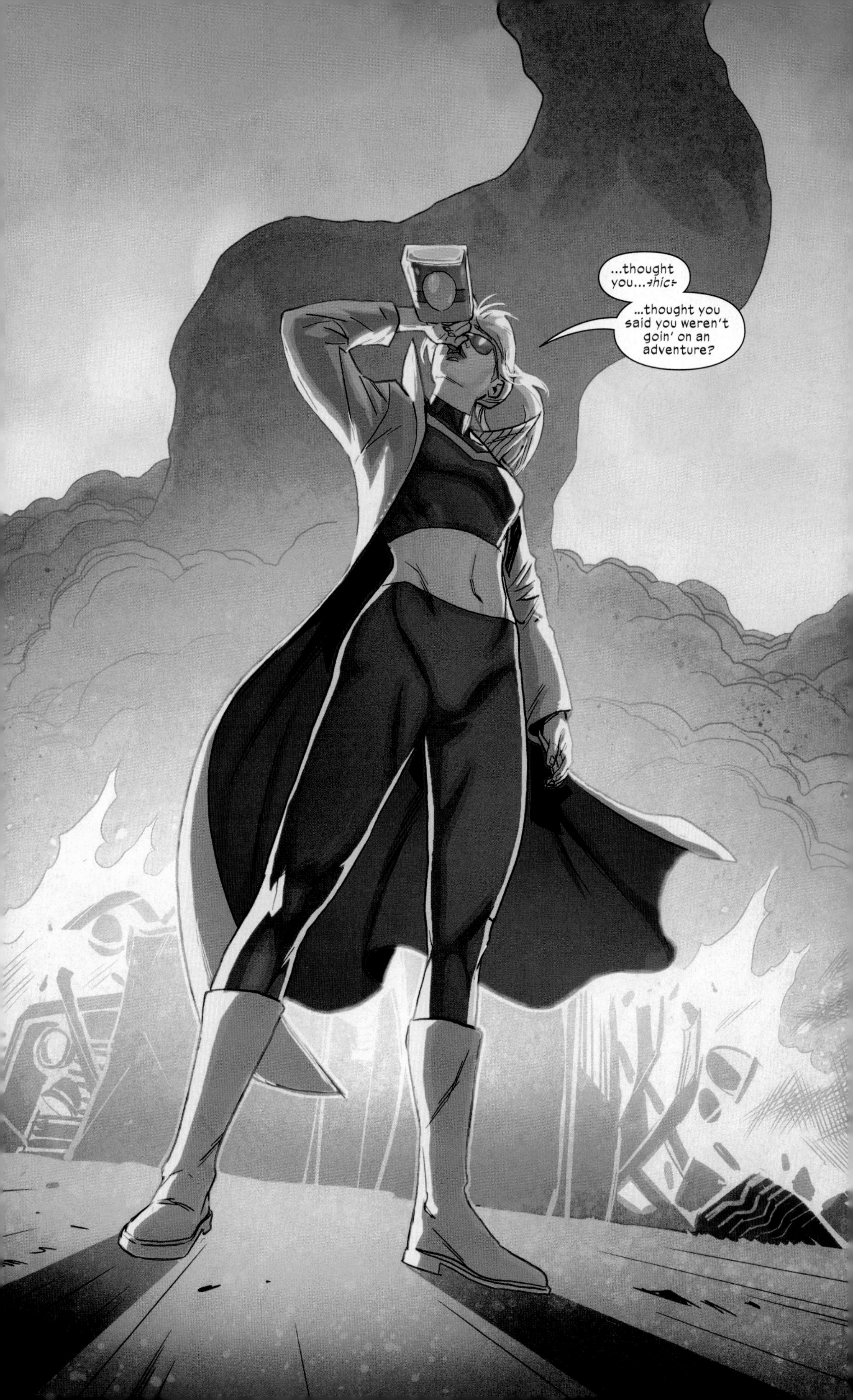
...thought you...♯hic♯
...thought you said you weren't goin' on an adventure?

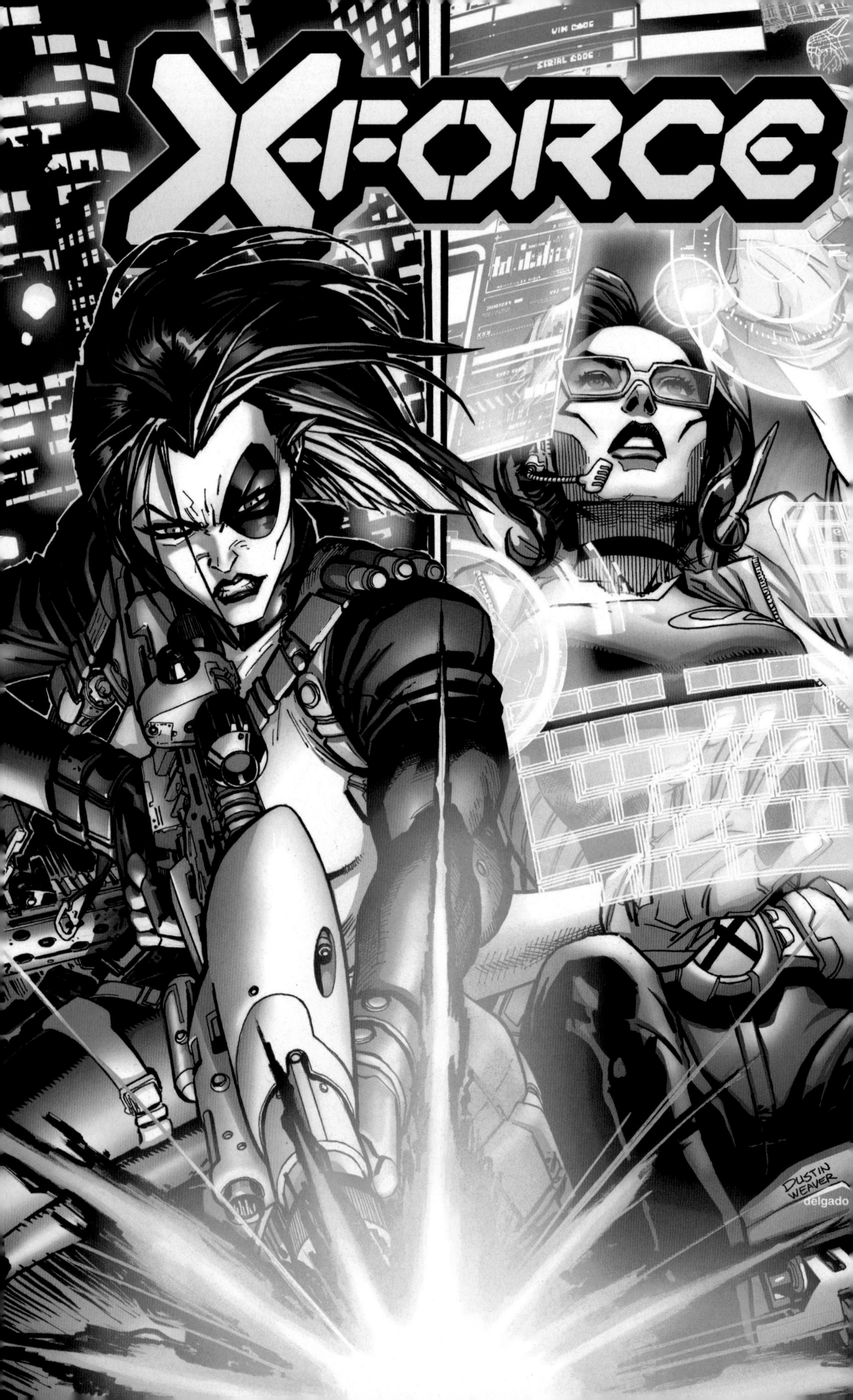
X-FORCE
VIN CODE
SERIAL CODE
DUSTIN WEAVER
delgado

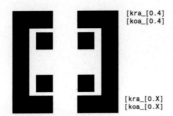

[kra_[0.4]
[koa_[0.4]

[kra_[0.X]
[koa_[0.X]

AN EYE FOR AN EYE

Mutants around the world are flocking to the island-nation of Krakoa for safety, security and to be part of the first mutant society.

Within weeks of Krakoa's declaration of sovereignty, a strike team sent by the mysterious cabal XENO attacked on Krakoan soil.

Rejecting their history as victims, mutantkind's response is imminent...

Wolverine

Kid Omega

Domino

Professor X

Marvel Girl

Beast

Sage

Black King

Storm

Apocalypse

Mister
Sinister

Mystique

Magneto

Exodus

Nightcrawler

Forge

[kra_[0.4]...]
[koa_[0.4]...]

[A._Spy_Agency]

[00_mutant_espionage]
[00_law_order___X___]

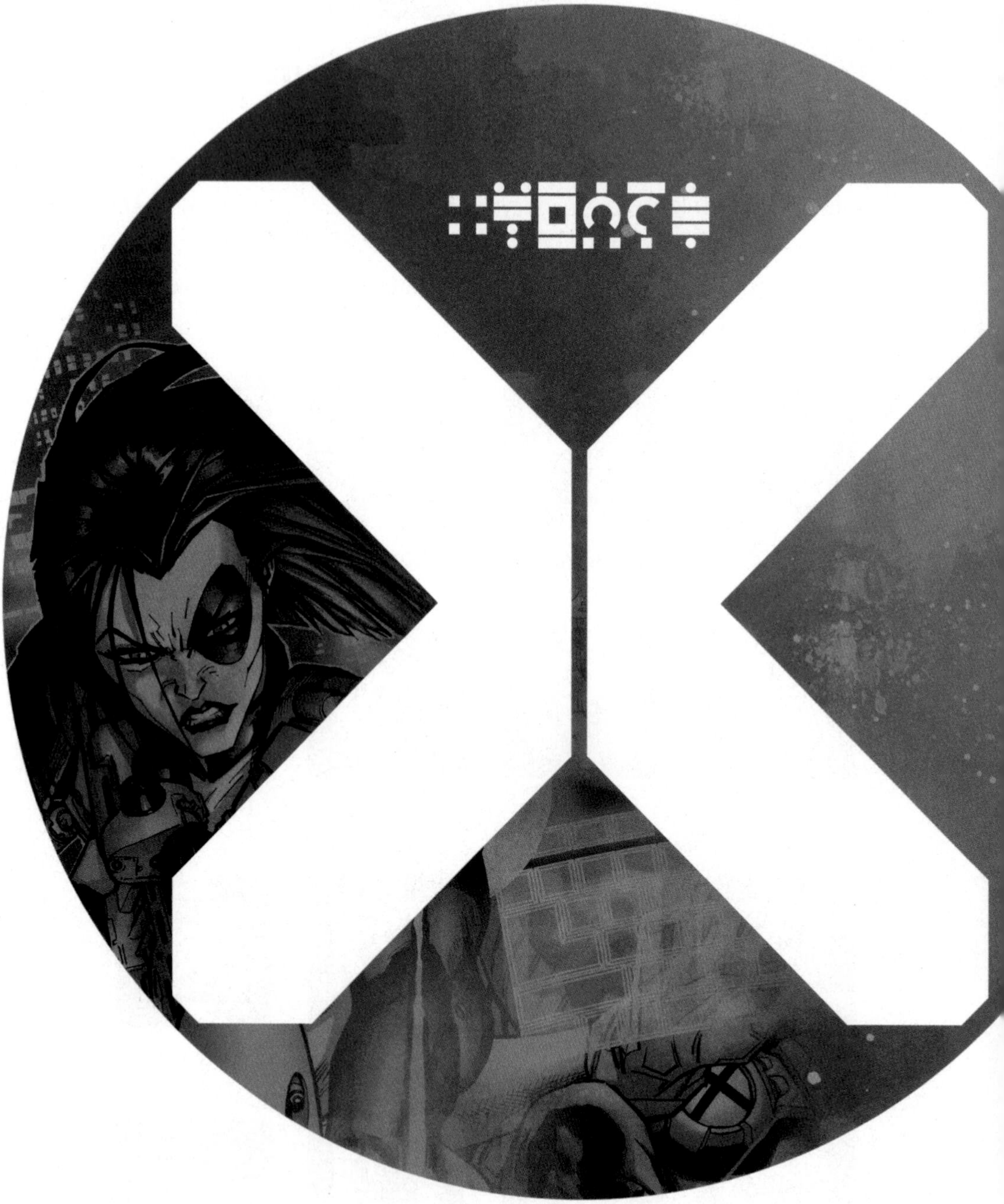

[00_mutant_espionage]
[00_law_order___X___]

BENJAMIN PERCY....................................[WRITER]
JOSHUA CASSARA....................................[ARTIST]
DEAN WHITE & GURU-eFX.....................[COLOR ARTISTS]
VC's JOE CARAMAGNA..............................[LETTERER]
TOM MULLER..[DESIGN]

DUSTIN WEAVER & EDGAR DELGADO...........[COVER ARTISTS]

NICK RUSSELL................................[PRODUCTION]

JONATHAN HICKMAN..............................[HEAD OF X]
CHRIS ROBINSON.......................[ASSISTANT EDITOR]
JORDAN D. WHITE....................................[EDITOR]
C.B. CEBULSKI..........................[EDITOR IN CHIEF]
JOE QUESADA....................[CHIEF CREATIVE OFFICER]
DAN BUCKLEY.....................................[PRESIDENT]
ALAN FINE..........................[EXECUTIVE PRODUCER]

[04] X-FORCE

[ISSUE FOUR]............BLOOD ECONOMICS

[00_mutant_espionage]
[00_law_order___X___]

[00_00...0]
[00_00...4]

[00_probe_]
[00_______]

[00_______]

[00_______X]

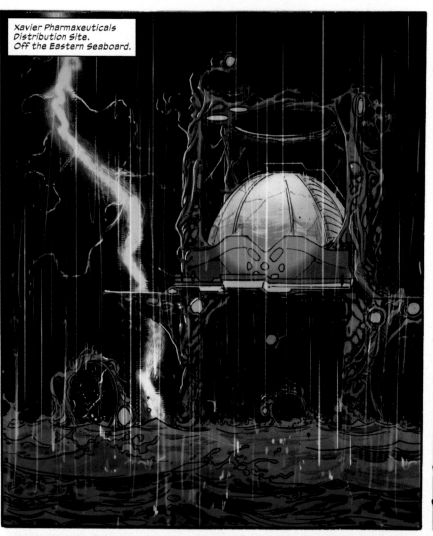

Xavier Pharmaxeuticals
Distribution Site.
Off the Eastern Seaboard.

"I call this
meeting of the
Quiet Council
to order.

"The breach
of Krakoa's
perimeter...

"...and the
subsequent
attack on our
population...

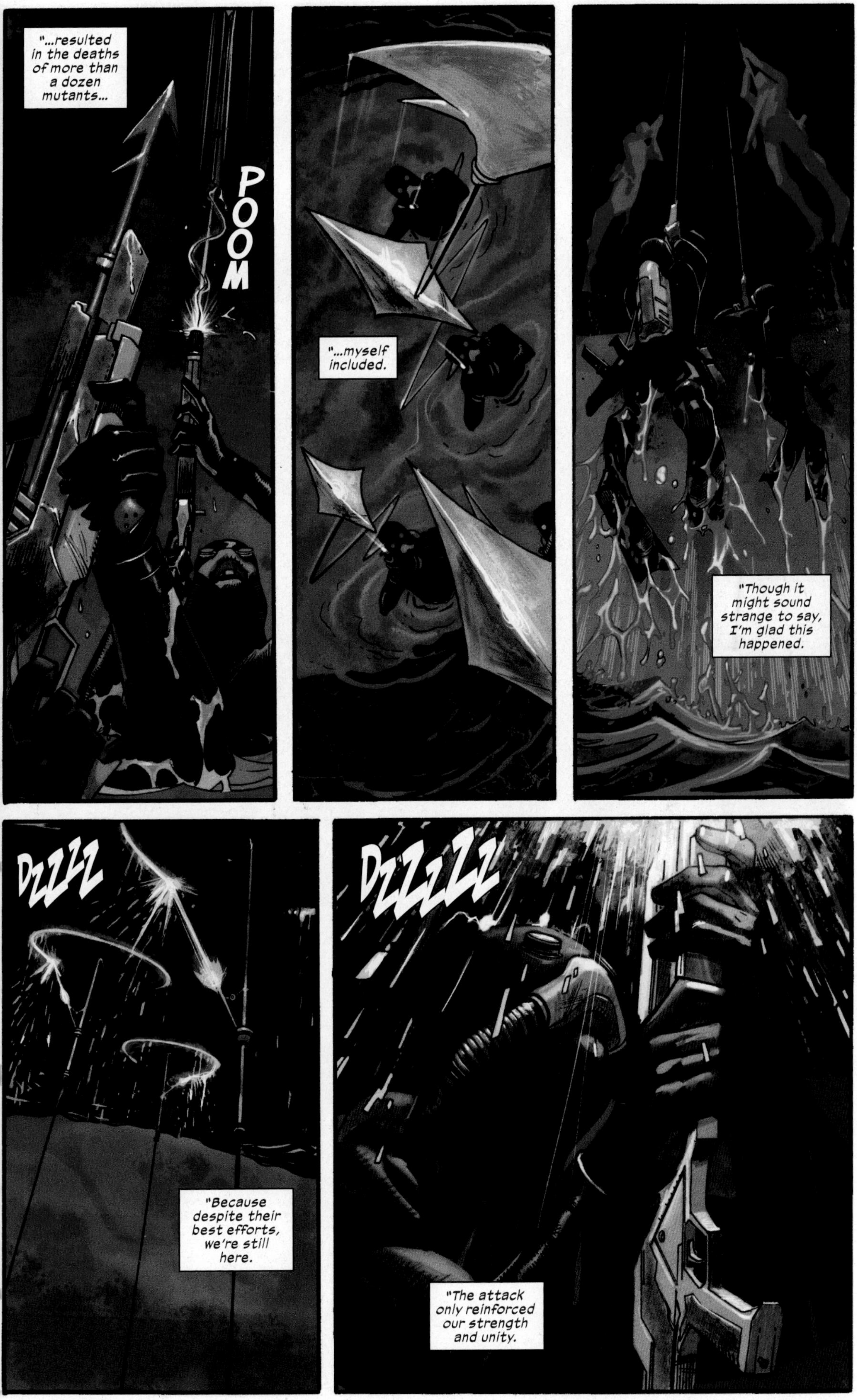
"...resulted in the deaths of more than a dozen mutants...
POOM
"...myself included.
"Though it might sound strange to say, I'm glad this happened.
DZZZZ
"Because despite their best efforts, we're still here.
DZZZZZ
"The attack only reinforced our strength and unity.

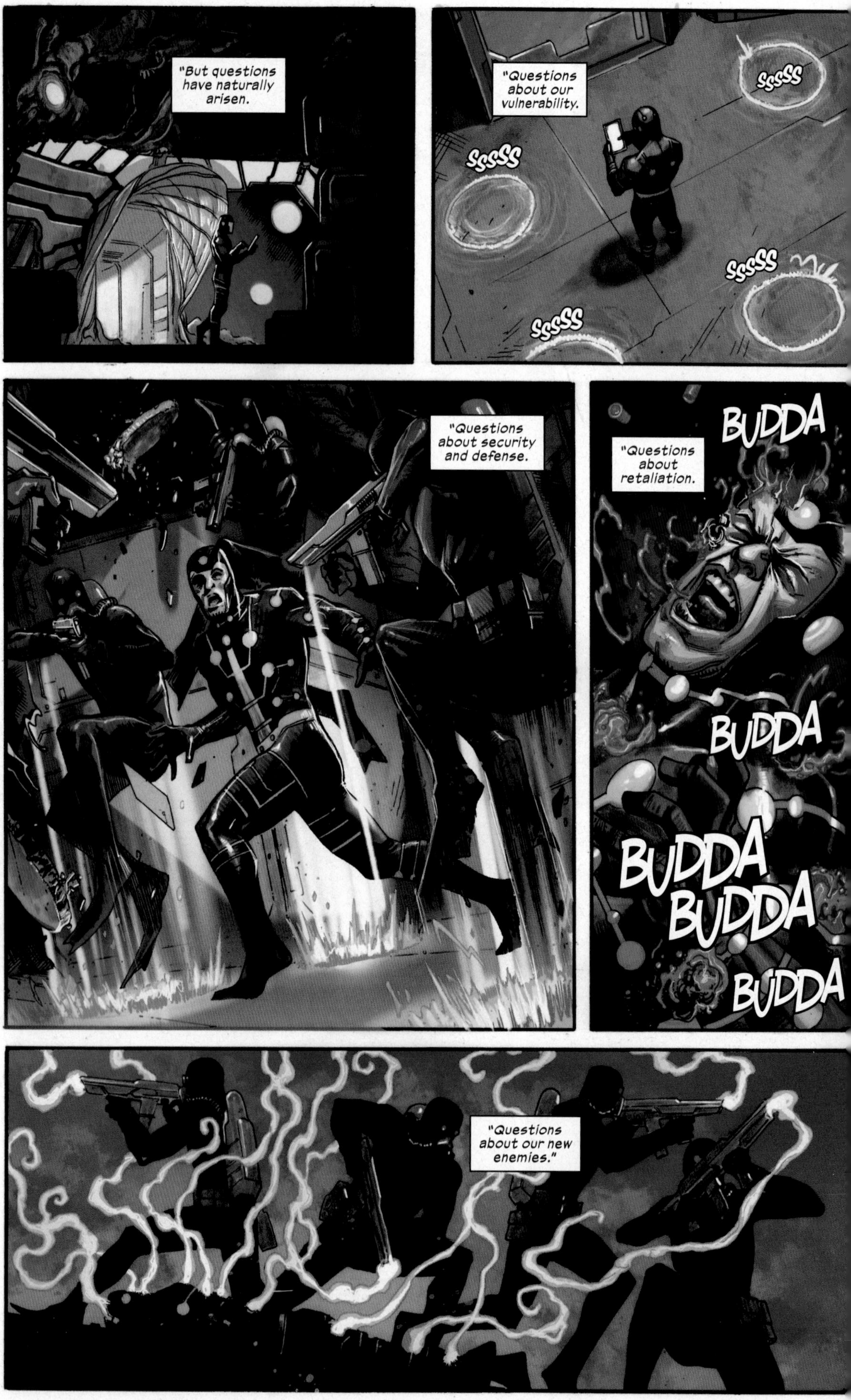
"But questions have naturally arisen.
"Questions about our vulnerability.
SSSSS
SSSSS
SSSSS
SSSSS
"Questions about security and defense.
"Questions about retaliation.
BUDDA
BUDDA
BUDDA
BUDDA
BUDDA
"Questions about our new enemies."

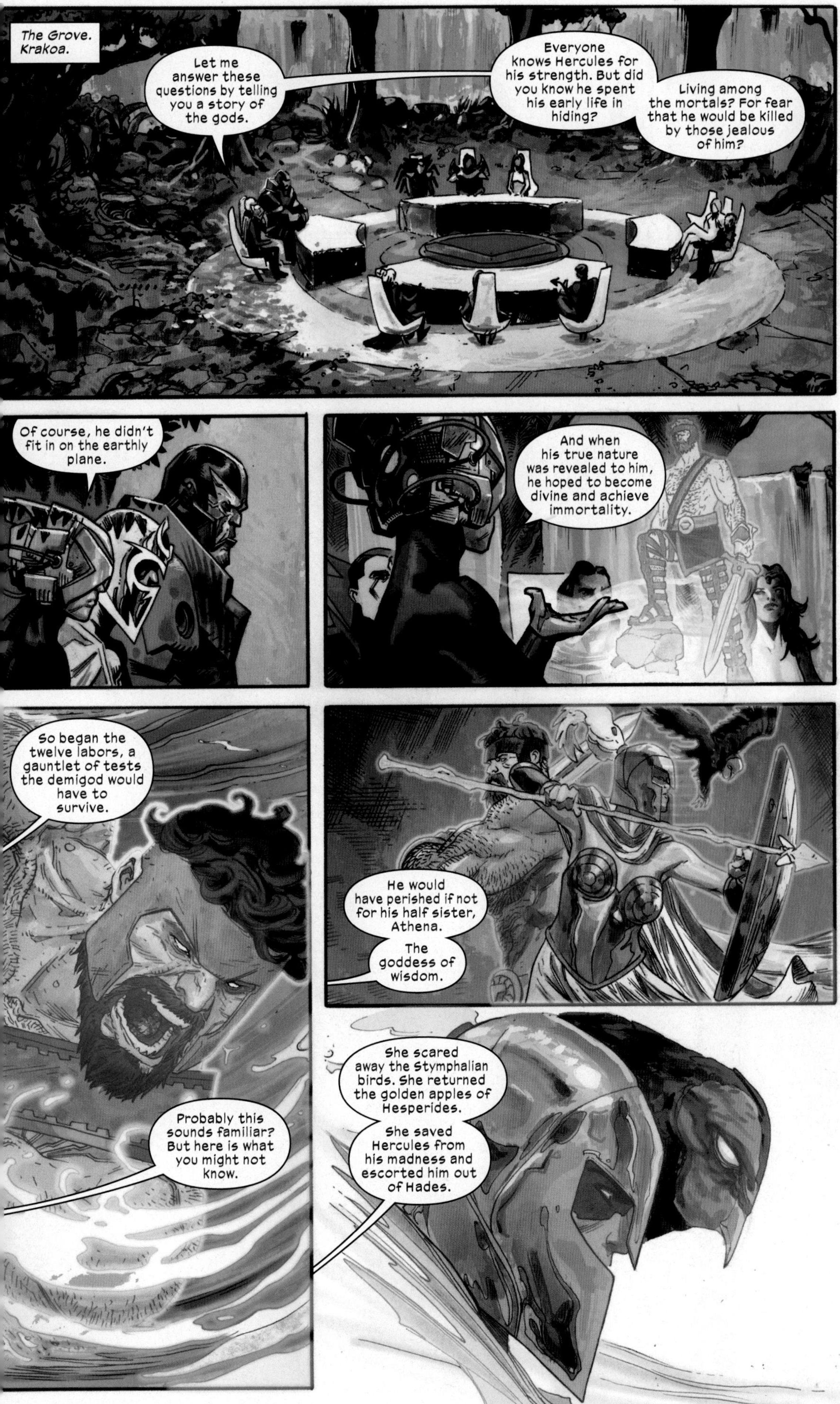
The Grove. Krakoa.
Let me answer these questions by telling you a story of the gods.
Everyone knows Hercules for his strength. But did you know he spent his early life in hiding?
Living among the mortals? For fear that he would be killed by those jealous of him?
Of course, he didn't fit in on the earthly plane.
And when his true nature was revealed to him, he hoped to become divine and achieve immortality.
So began the twelve labors, a gauntlet of tests the demigod would have to survive.
He would have perished if not for his half sister, Athena.
The goddess of wisdom.
Probably this sounds familiar? But here is what you might not know.
She scared away the Stymphalian birds. She returned the golden apples of Hesperides.
She saved Hercules from his madness and escorted him out of Hades.

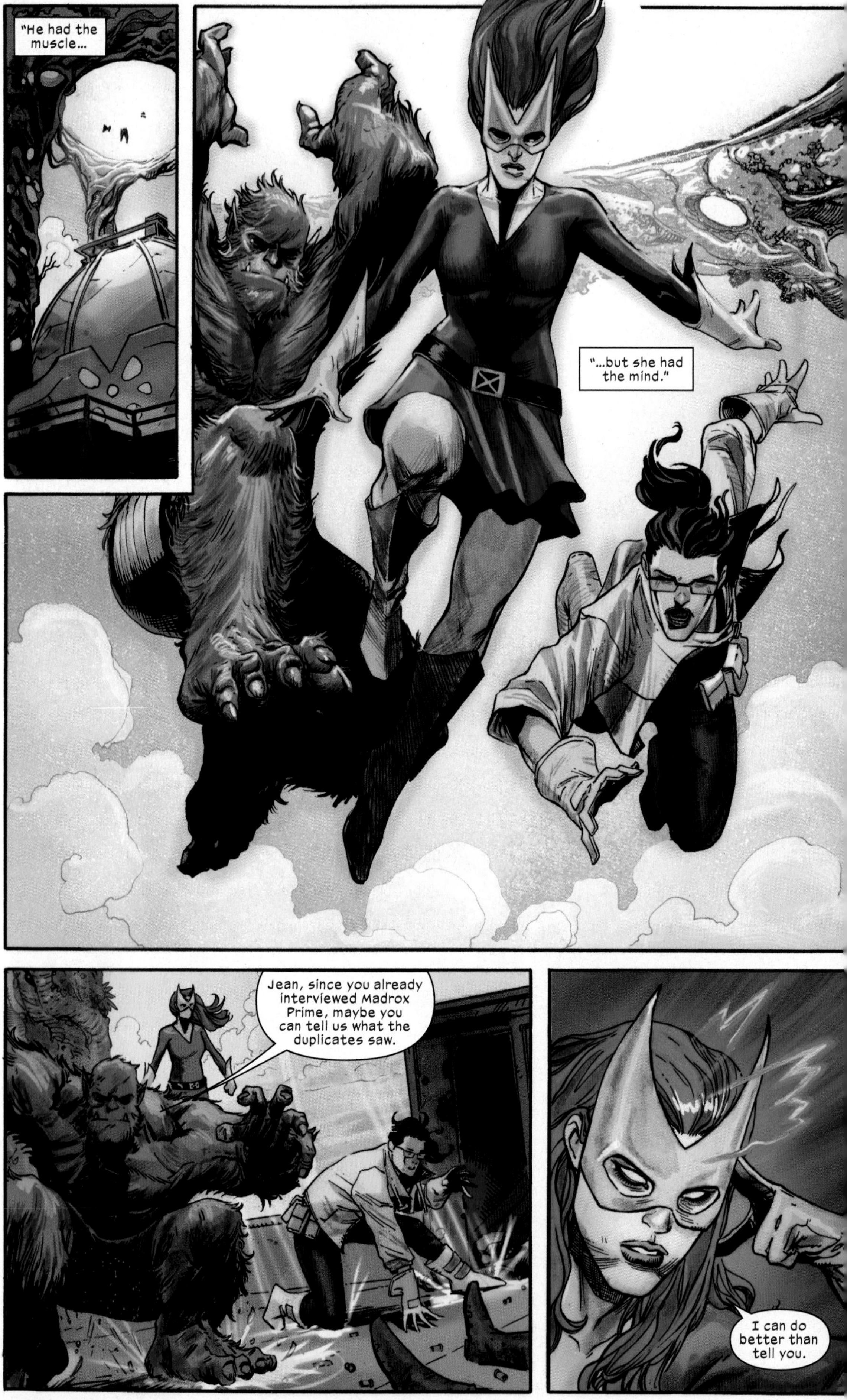
"He had the muscle...
"...but she had the mind."
Jean, since you already interviewed Madrox Prime, maybe you can tell us what the duplicates saw.
I can do better than tell you.

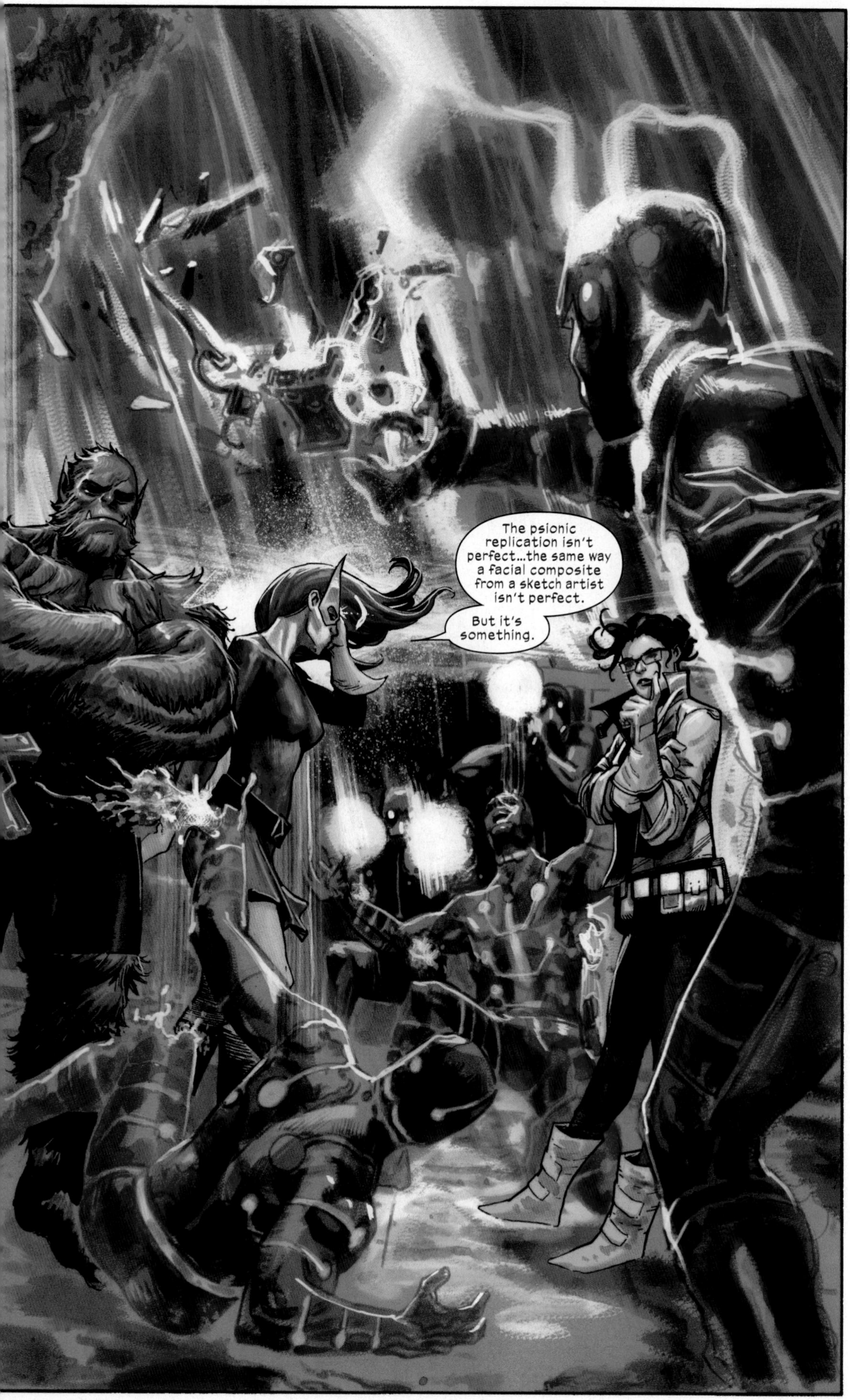

The psionic replication isn't perfect...the same way a facial composite from a sketch artist isn't perfect.
But it's something.

They are expertly efficient, perfectly timed--the same as the crew of assassins that assaulted Krakoa.

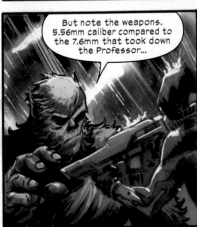

But note the weapons. 5.56mm caliber compared to the 7.6mm that took down the Professor...

And their tactical gear is brand name.

The assassins, by comparison, were outfitted with custom manufactured tech...

Are you saying they're not the same threat?

I don't know what I'm saying.

I certainly would prefer if they were one and the same...

...given that we have no new leads into the assault on the island.

That's it.

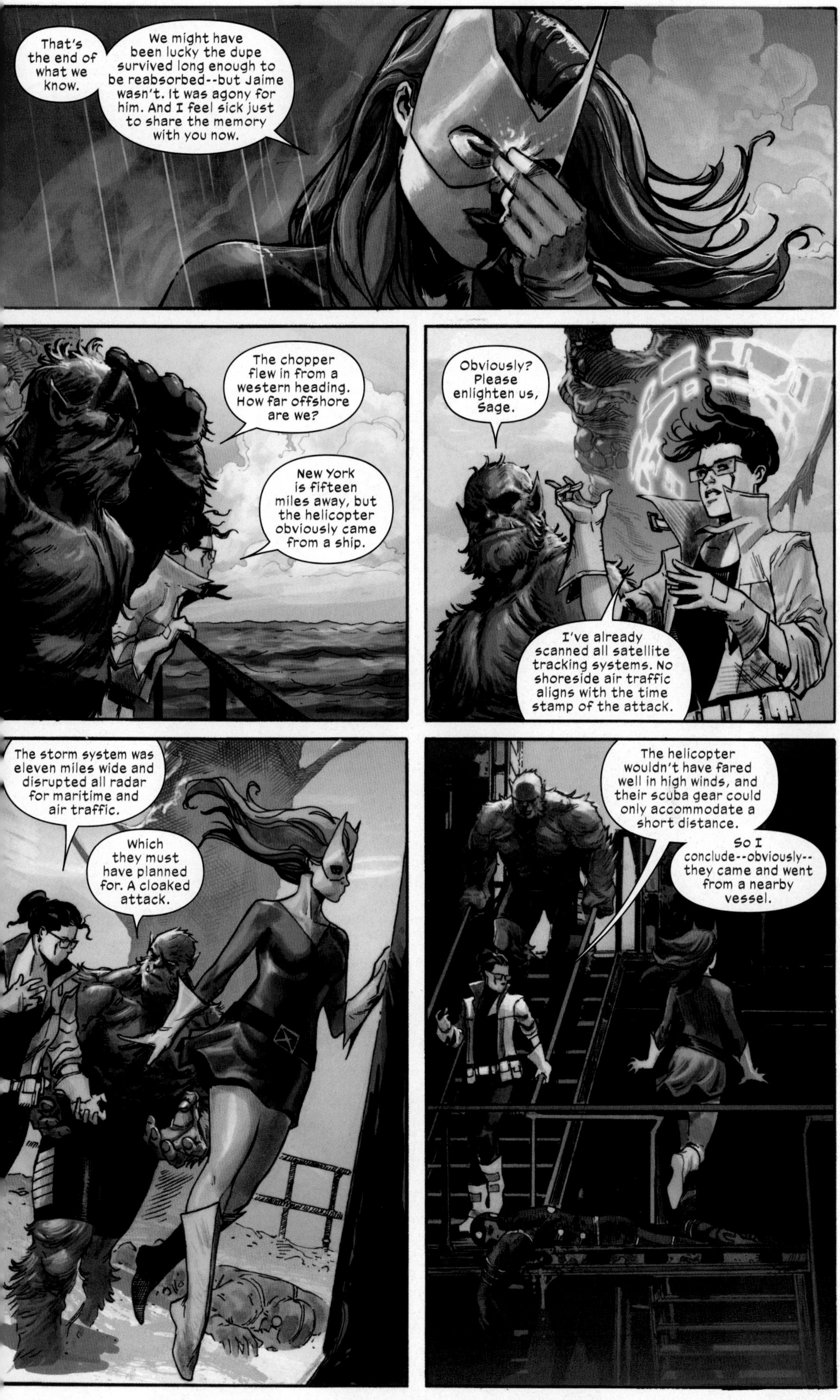
That's the end of what we know.
We might have been lucky the dupe survived long enough to be reabsorbed--but Jaime wasn't. It was agony for him. And I feel sick just to share the memory with you now.
The chopper flew in from a western heading. How far offshore are we?
New York is fifteen miles away, but the helicopter obviously came from a ship.
Obviously? Please enlighten us, Sage.
I've already scanned all satellite tracking systems. No shoreside air traffic aligns with the time stamp of the attack.
The storm system was eleven miles wide and disrupted all radar for maritime and air traffic.
Which they must have planned for. A cloaked attack.
The helicopter wouldn't have fared well in high winds, and their scuba gear could only accommodate a short distance.
So I conclude--obviously--they came and went from a nearby vessel.

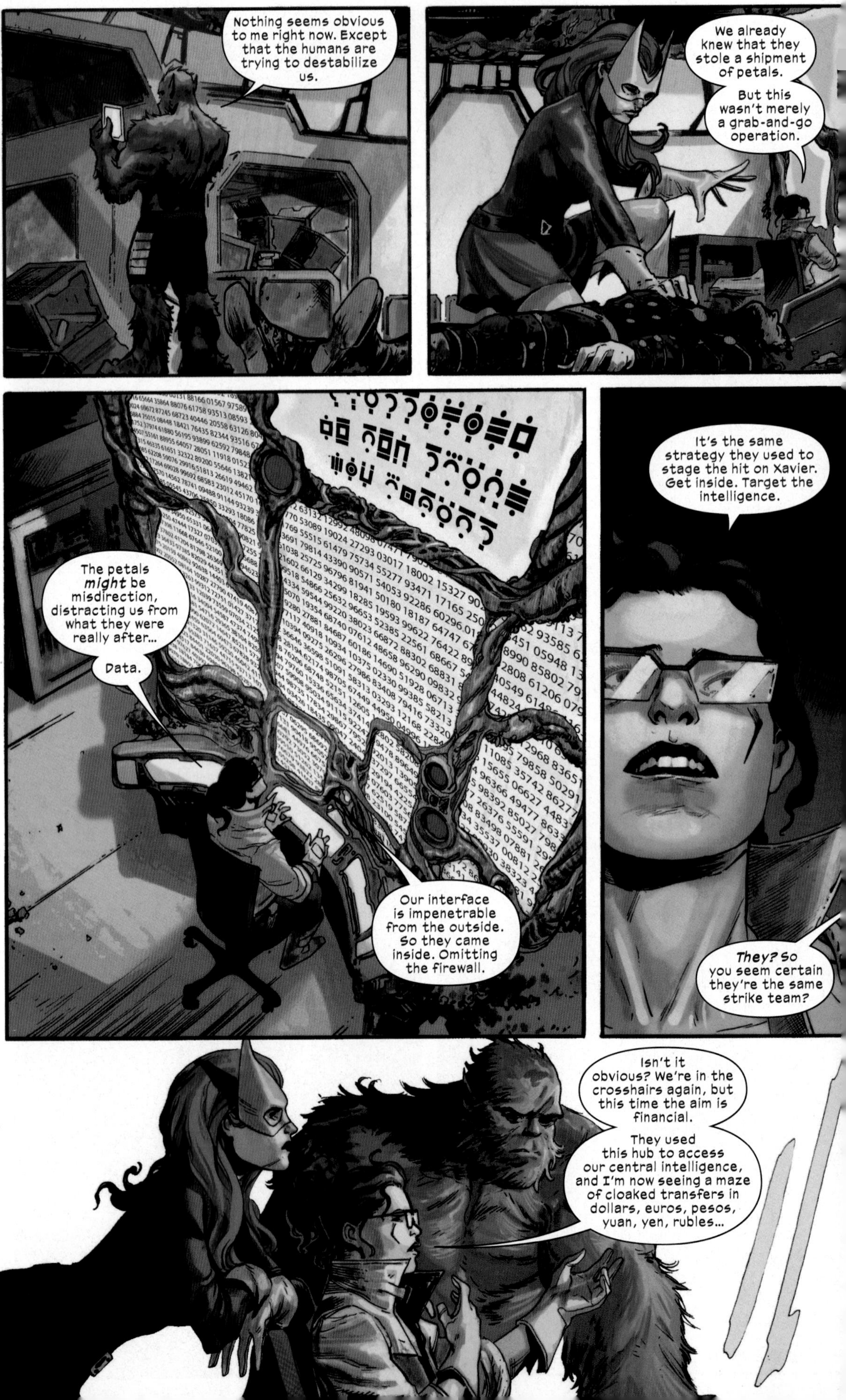
Nothing seems obvious to me right now. Except that the humans are trying to destabilize us.
We already knew that they stole a shipment of petals.
But this wasn't merely a grab-and-go operation.
The petals *might* be misdirection, distracting us from what they were really after...
Data.
Our interface is impenetrable from the outside. So they came inside. Omitting the firewall.
It's the same strategy they used to stage the hit on Xavier. Get inside. Target the intelligence.
They? So you seem certain they're the same strike team?
Isn't it obvious? We're in the crosshairs again, but this time the aim is financial.
They used this hub to access our central intelligence, and I'm now seeing a maze of cloaked transfers in dollars, euros, pesos, yuan, yen, rubles...

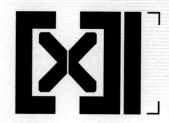

THE PORTFOLIO OF CHARLES XAVIER

Xavier serves as the shadow chairman and primary stockholder of the following organizations, some of which rank as Fortune 500 enterprises -- but his involvement with the companies has been largely kept secret to avoid calling attention to his wealth and power.

Xavier Pharmaxeuticals

Gifted Mind Technologies

Uncanny Valley Farms

Summers News and Media

Evolution Energy

X-Marks-Spot Mining

Cerebral Films

Phoenix Law Offices

Salem Center Auctions and Real Estate

Blackbird Motors

Wolverine Waste Management

His Dream Philanthropic Foundation

He is also the creator of the digital currency known as the Xcoin.

His exact wealth is incalculable, but since mutant sovereignty was declared, he is now widely considered the wealthiest and most powerful man alive.

Some of these investments were made for altruistic reasons. But the majority were strategic, meant to influence news, entertainment and education, or allow for political, legal, monetary and fiduciary gains and control.

But all of them are united in this common cause: They laid the foundation for securing the dream of Krakoa.

—

—

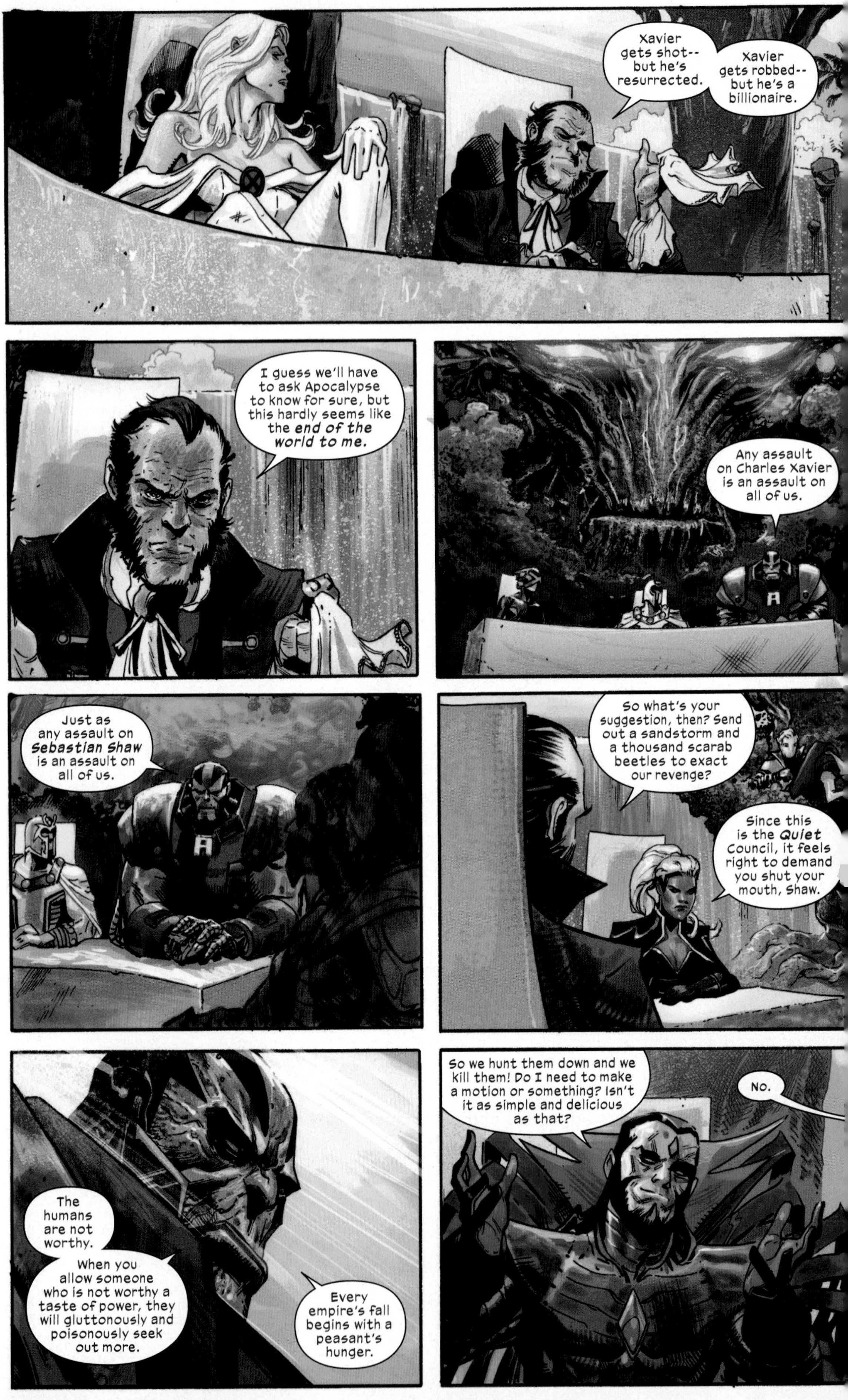
Xavier gets shot-- but he's resurrected.
Xavier gets robbed-- but he's a billionaire.
I guess we'll have to ask Apocalypse to know for sure, but this hardly seems like the *end of the world to me.*
Any assault on Charles Xavier is an assault on all of us.
Just as any assault on *Sebastian Shaw* is an assault on all of us.
So what's your suggestion, then? Send out a sandstorm and a thousand scarab beetles to exact our revenge?
Since this is the *Quiet* Council, it feels right to demand you shut your mouth, Shaw.
The humans are not worthy.
When you allow someone who is not worthy a taste of power, they will gluttonously and poisonously seek out more.
Every empire's fall begins with a peasant's hunger.
So we hunt them down and we kill them! Do I need to make a motion or something? Isn't it as simple and delicious as that?
No.

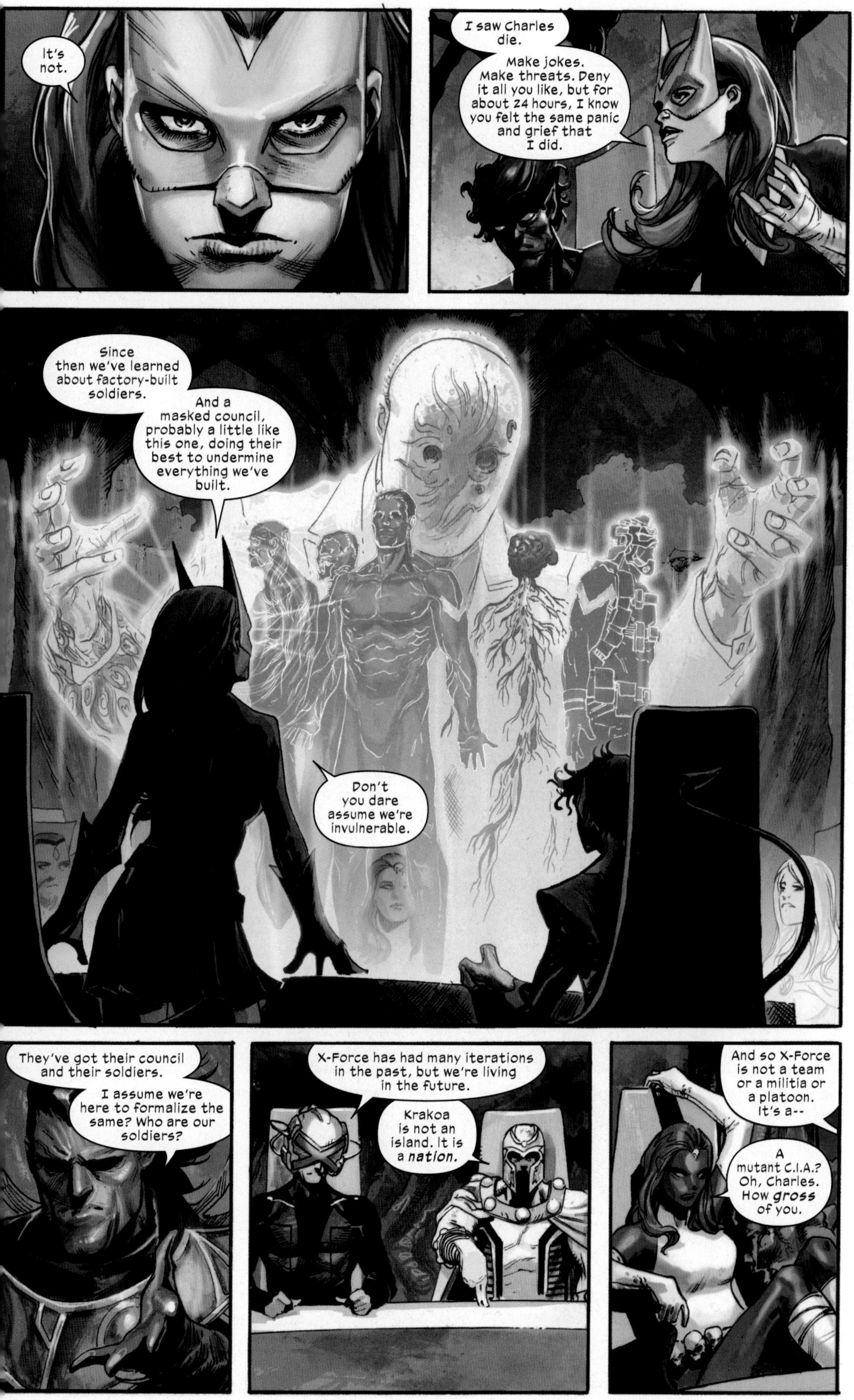
It's not.
I saw Charles die.
Make jokes. Make threats. Deny it all you like, but for about 24 hours, I know you felt the same panic and grief that I did.
Since then we've learned about factory-built soldiers.
And a masked council, probably a little like this one, doing their best to undermine everything we've built.
Don't you dare assume we're invulnerable.
They've got their council and their soldiers.
I assume we're here to formalize the same? Who are our soldiers?
X-Force has had many iterations in the past, but we're living in the future.
Krakoa is not an island. It is a *nation.*
And so X-Force is not a team or a militia or a platoon. It's a--
A mutant C.I.A.? Oh, Charles. How *gross* of you.

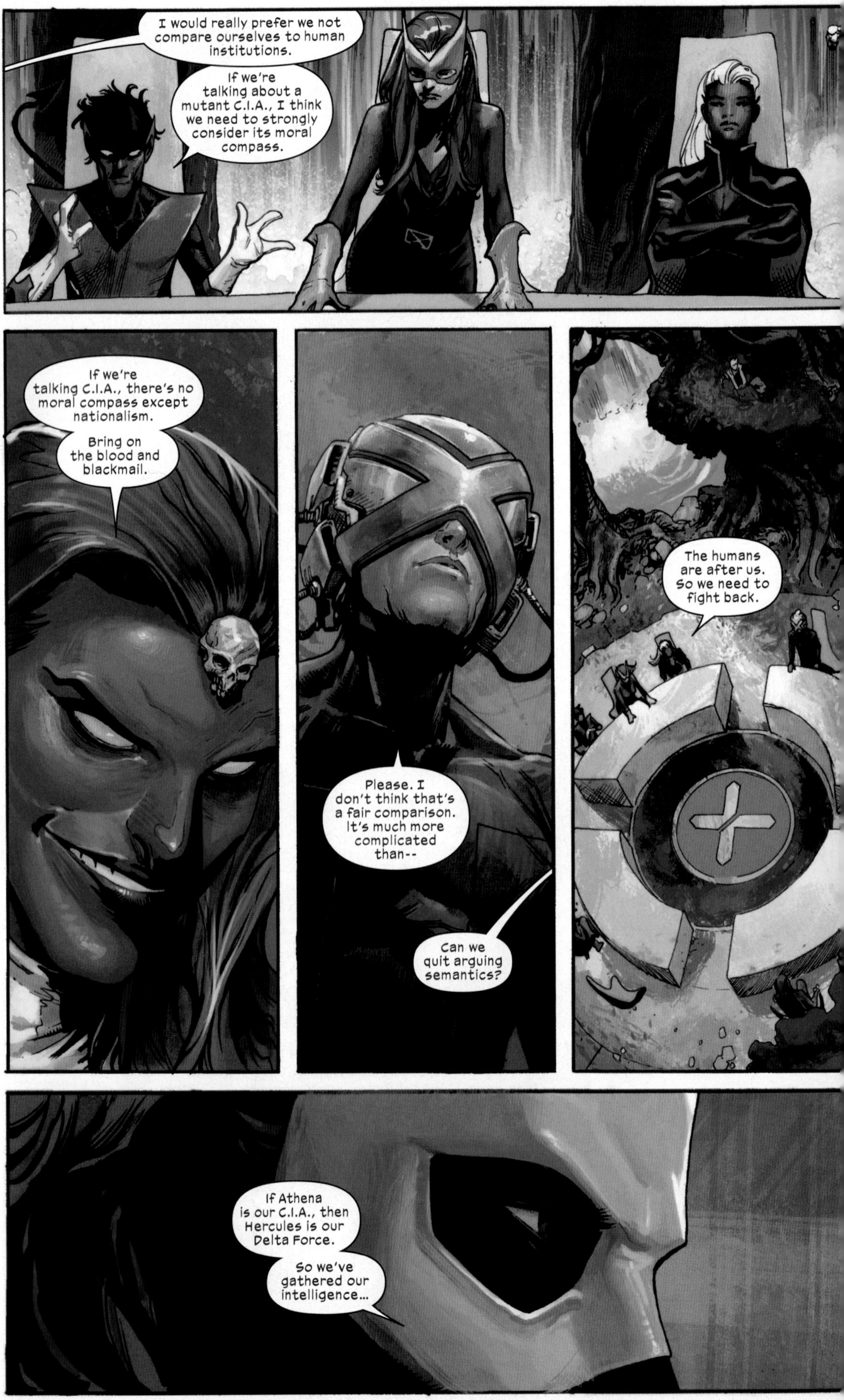
I would really prefer we not compare ourselves to human institutions.
If we're talking about a mutant C.I.A., I think we need to strongly consider its moral compass.
If we're talking C.I.A., there's no moral compass except nationalism.
Bring on the blood and blackmail.
Please. I don't think that's a fair comparison. It's much more complicated than--
Can we quit arguing semantics?
The humans are after us. So we need to fight back.
If Athena is our C.I.A., then Hercules is our Delta Force.
So we've gathered our intelligence...

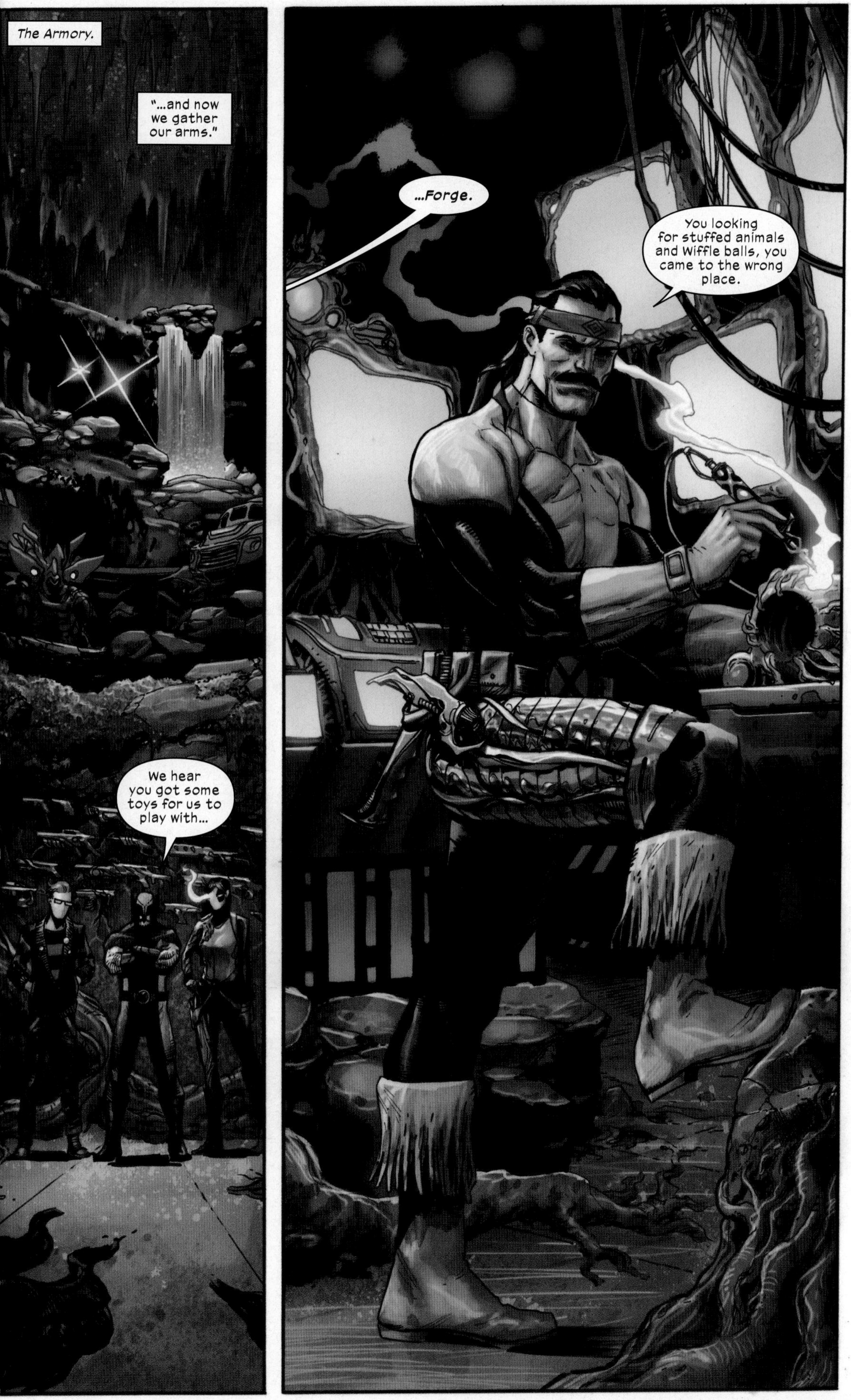
The Armory.
"...and now we gather our arms."
We hear you got some toys for us to play with...
...Forge.
You looking for stuffed animals and Wiffle balls, you came to the wrong place.

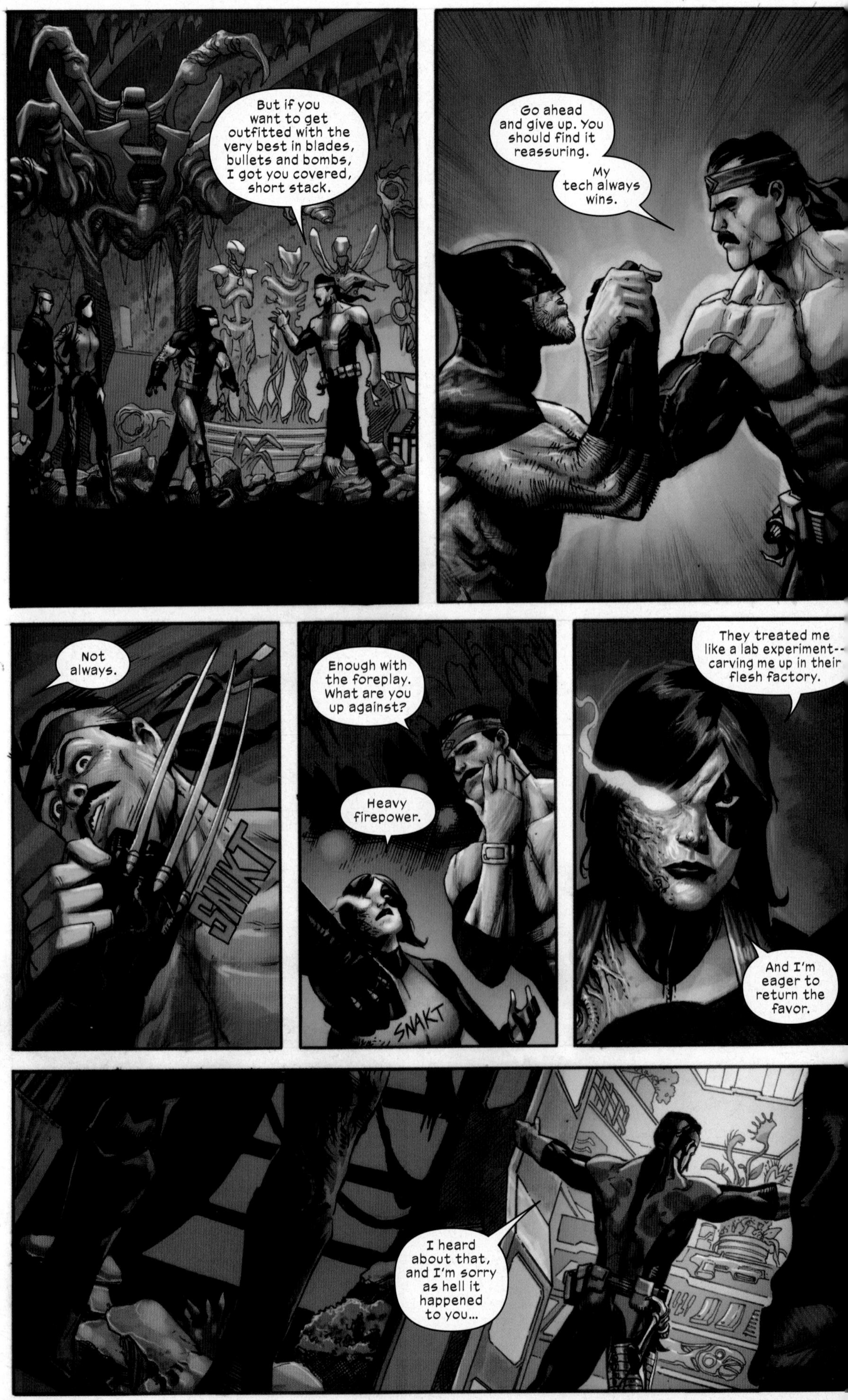
But if you want to get outfitted with the very best in blades, bullets and bombs, I got you covered, short stack.
Go ahead and give up. You should find it reassuring.
My tech always wins.
Not always.
SNIKT
Enough with the foreplay. What are you up against?
Heavy firepower.
SNAKT
They treated me like a lab experiment--carving me up in their flesh factory.
And I'm eager to return the favor.
I heard about that, and I'm sorry as hell it happened to you...

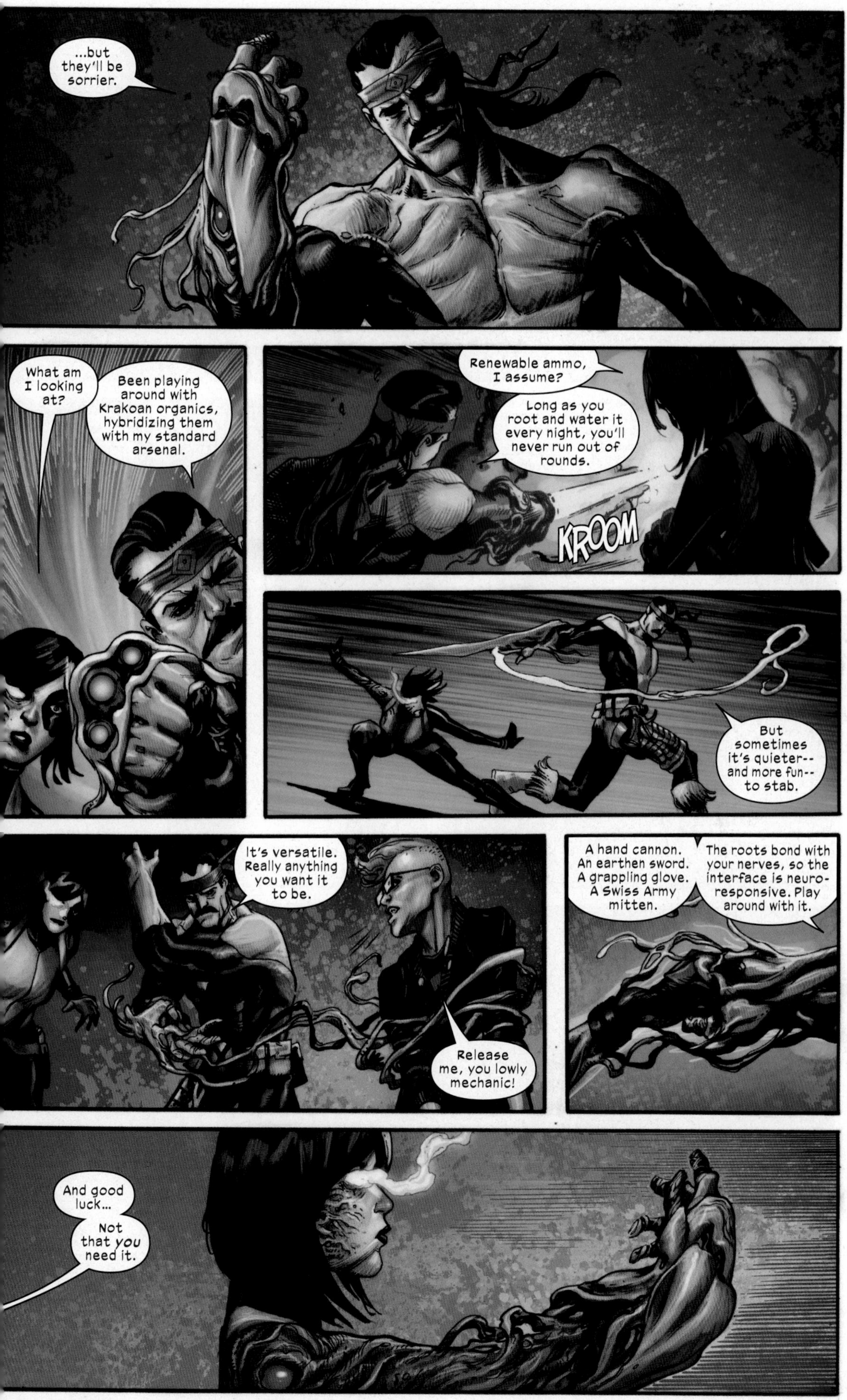

...but they'll be sorrier.
What am I looking at?
Been playing around with Krakoan organics, hybridizing them with my standard arsenal.
Renewable ammo, I assume?
Long as you root and water it every night, you'll never run out of rounds.
KROOM
But sometimes it's quieter-- and more fun-- to stab.
It's versatile. Really anything you want it to be.
Release me, you lowly mechanic!
A hand cannon. An earthen sword. A grappling glove. A Swiss Army mitten.
The roots bond with your nerves, so the interface is neuro-responsive. Play around with it.
And good luck...
Not that *you* need it.

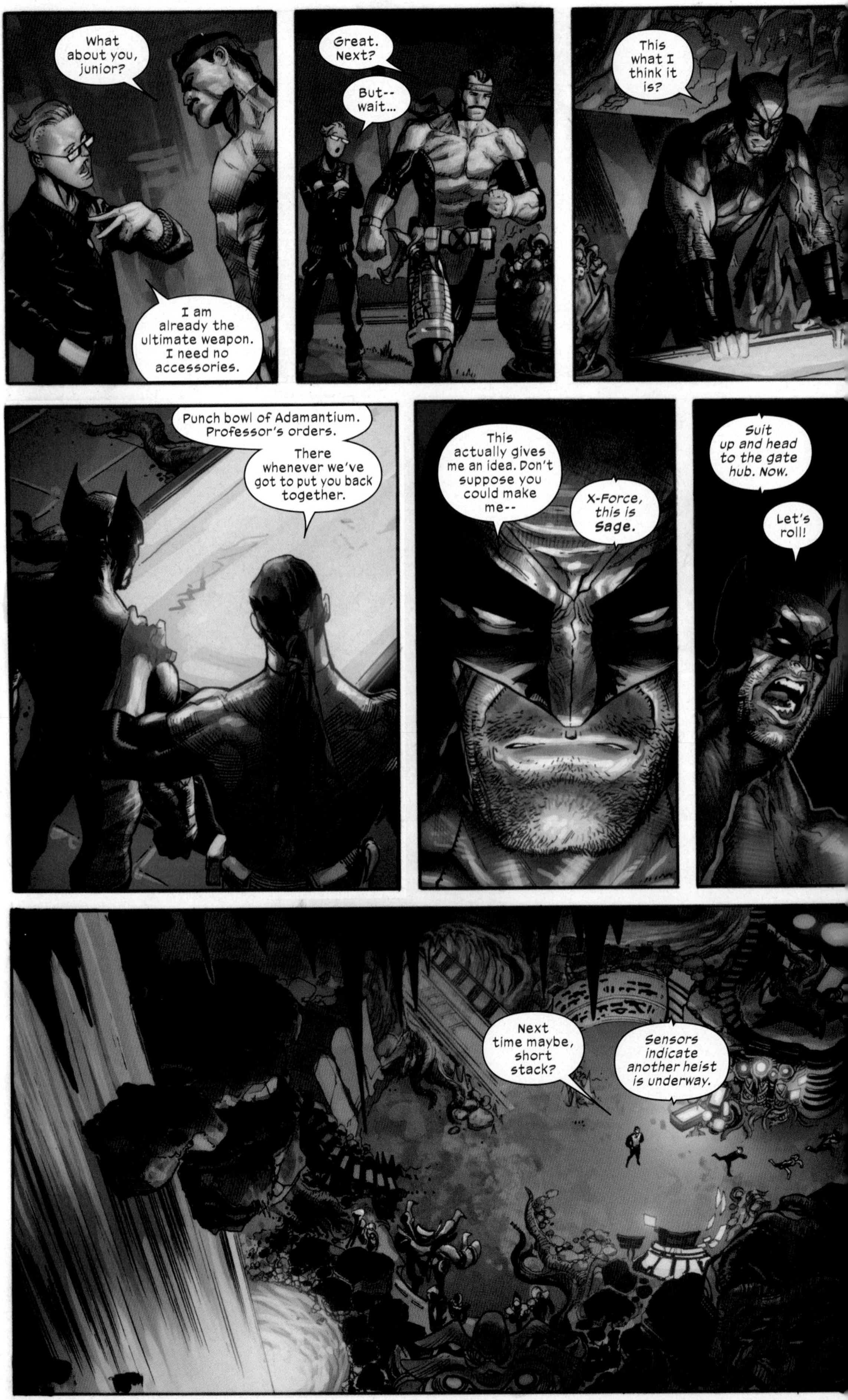
What about you, junior?
I am already the ultimate weapon. I need no accessories.
Great. Next?
But-- wait...
This what I think it is?
Punch bowl of Adamantium. Professor's orders.
There whenever we've got to put you back together.
This actually gives me an idea. Don't suppose you could make me--
X-Force, this is Sage.
Suit up and head to the gate hub. Now.
Let's roll!
Next time maybe, short stack?
Sensors indicate another heist is underway.

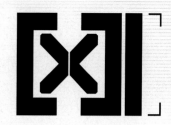

FORGE'S DAILY PLANNER

Dawn beachside breakfast meeting with Xavier. Placed order the night before for Krakoan spinach and turtle-egg (20) omelet, a pound of black market bacon and gallon of black coffee. On agenda: making more cool ███████.

Checklist: Sculpt mustache (left side accidentally longer) and launder tights (deep seawater rinse).

Question of the day: Krakoan flag? Shouldn't we have one? And put it on our weapons??? YES.

Brainstorm sweet-ass organic Jet Ski and hovercraft with plankton-skirted wave control.

Be sure not to forget 500 squats! Every morning at 10 A.M.! New goal!

Note: The nation of Terra Verde has so far refused to sign the treaty recognizing mutant sovereignty. This is believed to be in part because they are developing so-called telefloronics (organic tech). Obviously, theirs will suck compared to mine, but still better investigate.

Meeting in the Armory with Black Tom to discuss improvements to island security. (Follow-up: Black Tom seems super nervous and keeps referring to himself as "we." Stable? Ask Jean to look into his skull and poke around.)

Finish prototype for coral perimeter defenses.

Roll out production on wingsuit.

Roll out production on forest of missile launchers.

Begin farming poisonous pollens and mind-control fungal spores and oxygen-rich plankton for deepwater lungs.

Develop Krakoan body spray with extra HE pheromones that smells like bacon and leather. Test out by walking past Domino. Does she look twice?

Be sure not to forget 500 push-ups! Every afternoon at 4 P.M.! New goal!

Homework: Short stack has requested I build him ███████. The question isn't *should I*? The question is *how long should I make him wait just to annoy him?*

—

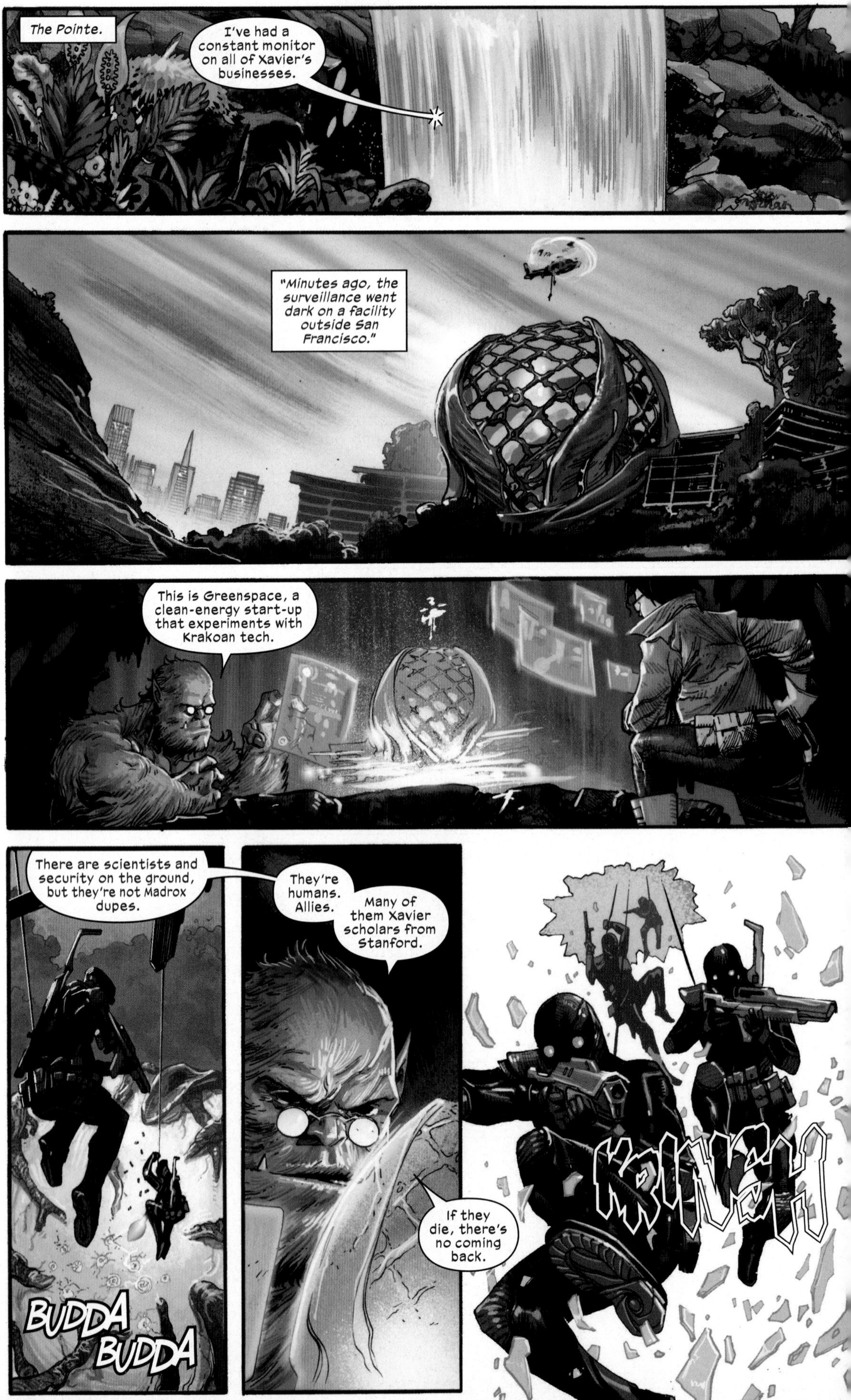
The Pointe.
I've had a constant monitor on all of Xavier's businesses.
"Minutes ago, the surveillance went dark on a facility outside San Francisco."
This is Greenspace, a clean-energy start-up that experiments with Krakoan tech.
There are scientists and security on the ground, but they're not Madrox dupes.
They're humans. Allies.
Many of them Xavier scholars from Stanford.
BUDDA BUDDA
If they die, there's no coming back.
KRUNCH

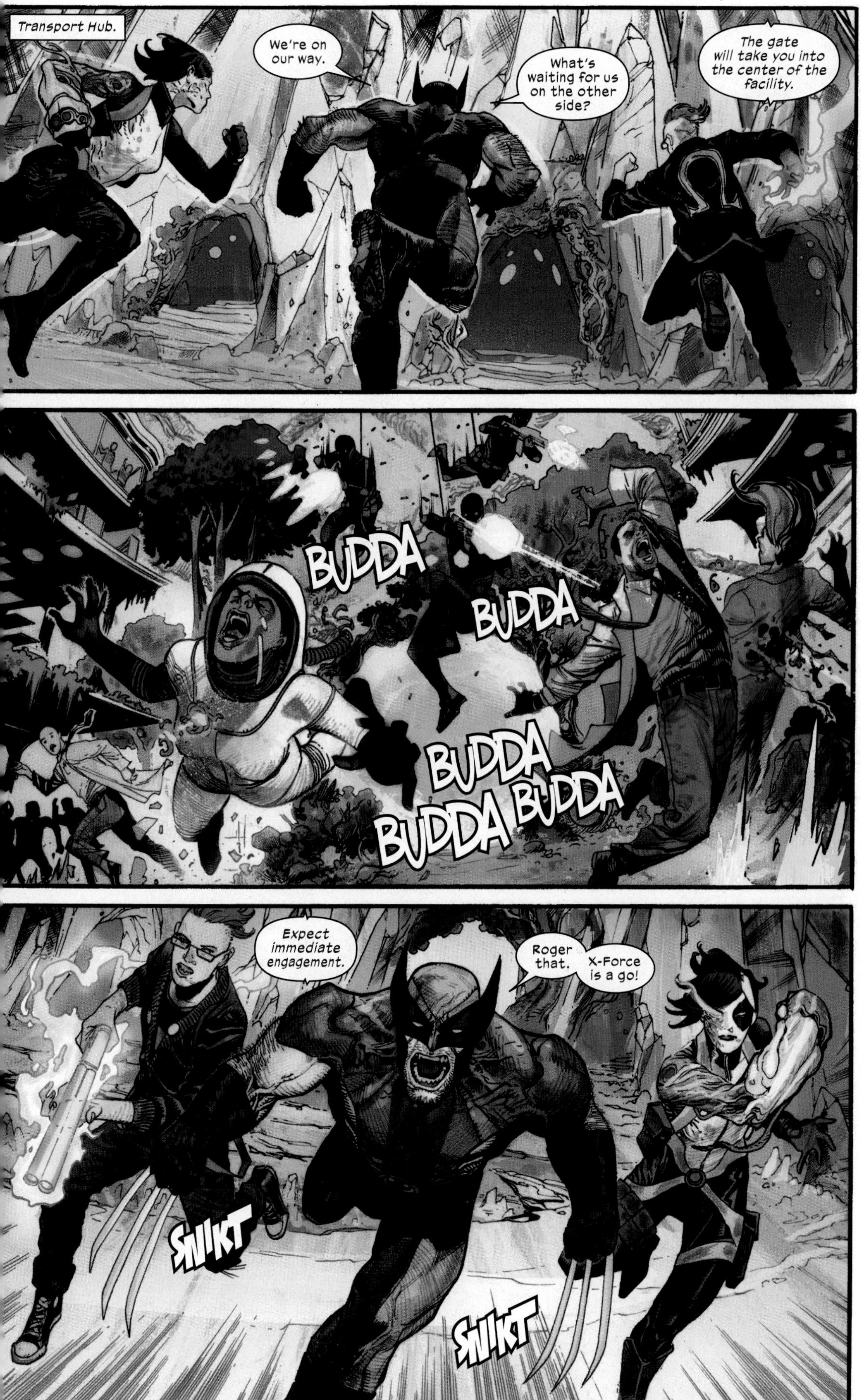
Transport Hub.
We're on our way.
What's waiting for us on the other side?
The gate will take you into the center of the facility.
BUDDA
BUDDA
BUDDA
BUDDA BUDDA
Expect immediate engagement.
Roger that.
X-Force is a go!
SNIKT
SNIKT

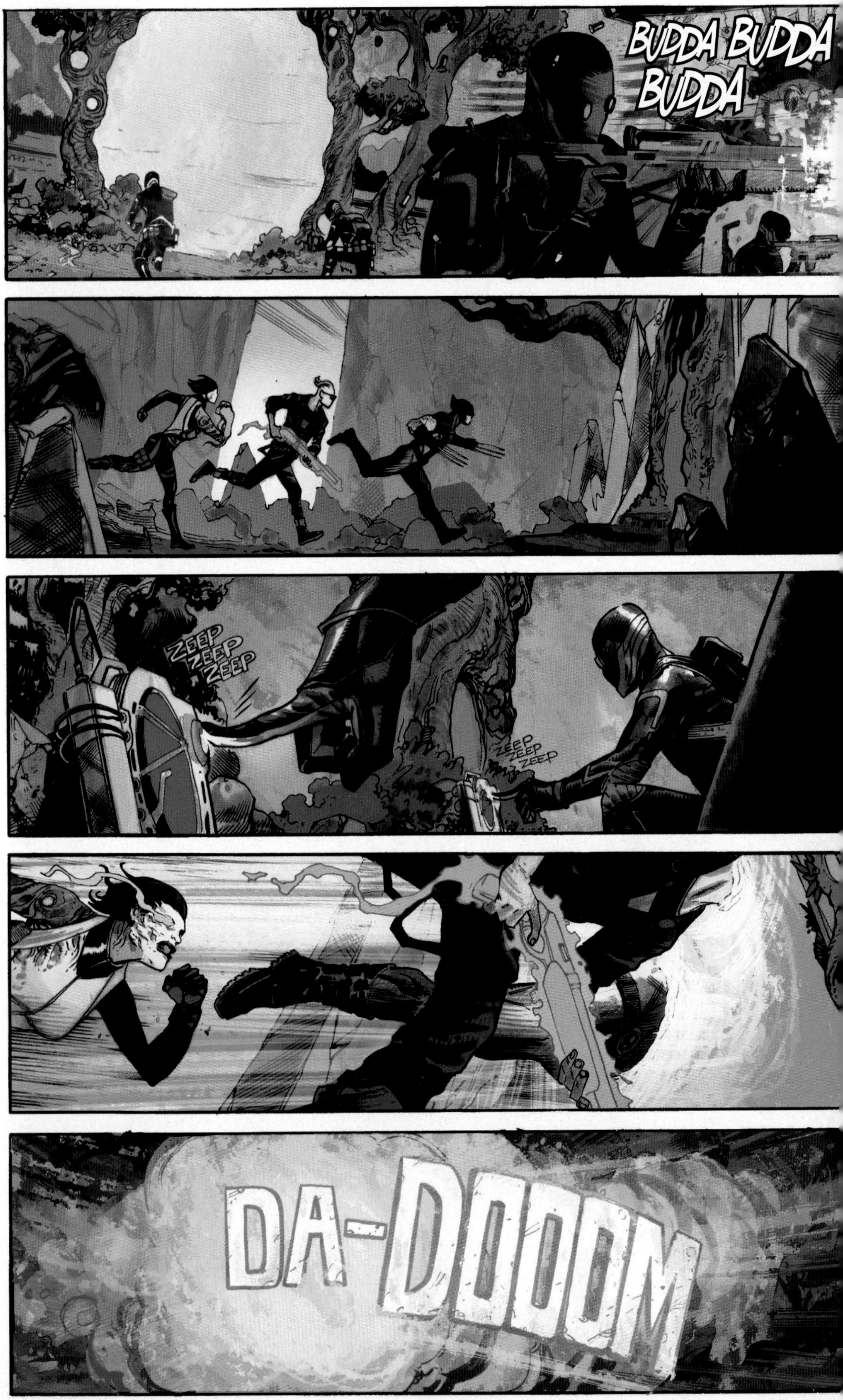
BUDDA BUDDA BUDDA
ZEEP ZEEP ZEEP
ZEEP ZEEP ZEEP
DA-DOOOM

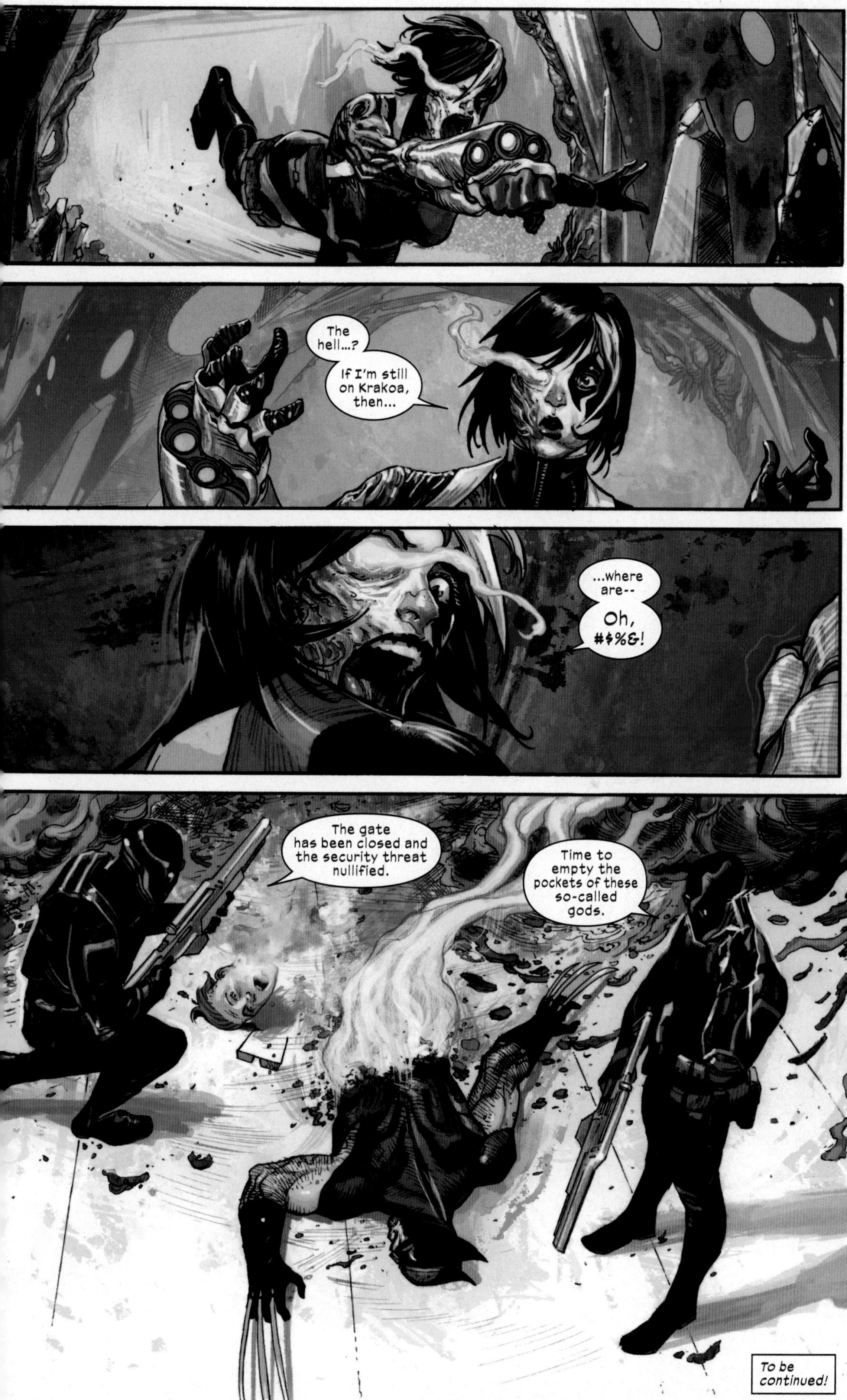

The hell...?
If I'm still on Krakoa, then...
...where are--
Oh, #$%&!
The gate has been closed and the security threat nullified.
Time to empty the pockets of these so-called gods.
To be continued!

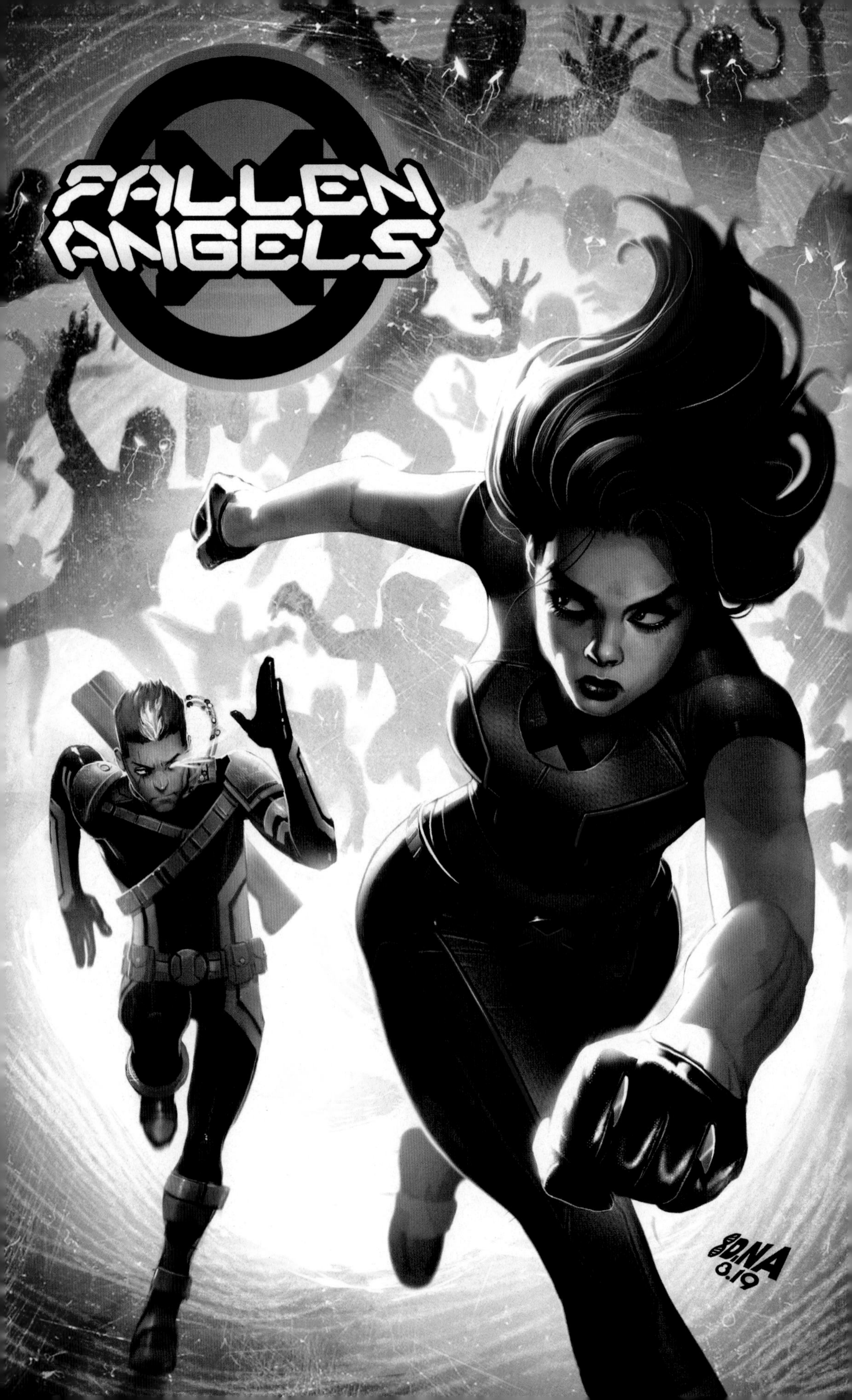
FALLEN ANGELS
D.NA
8.19

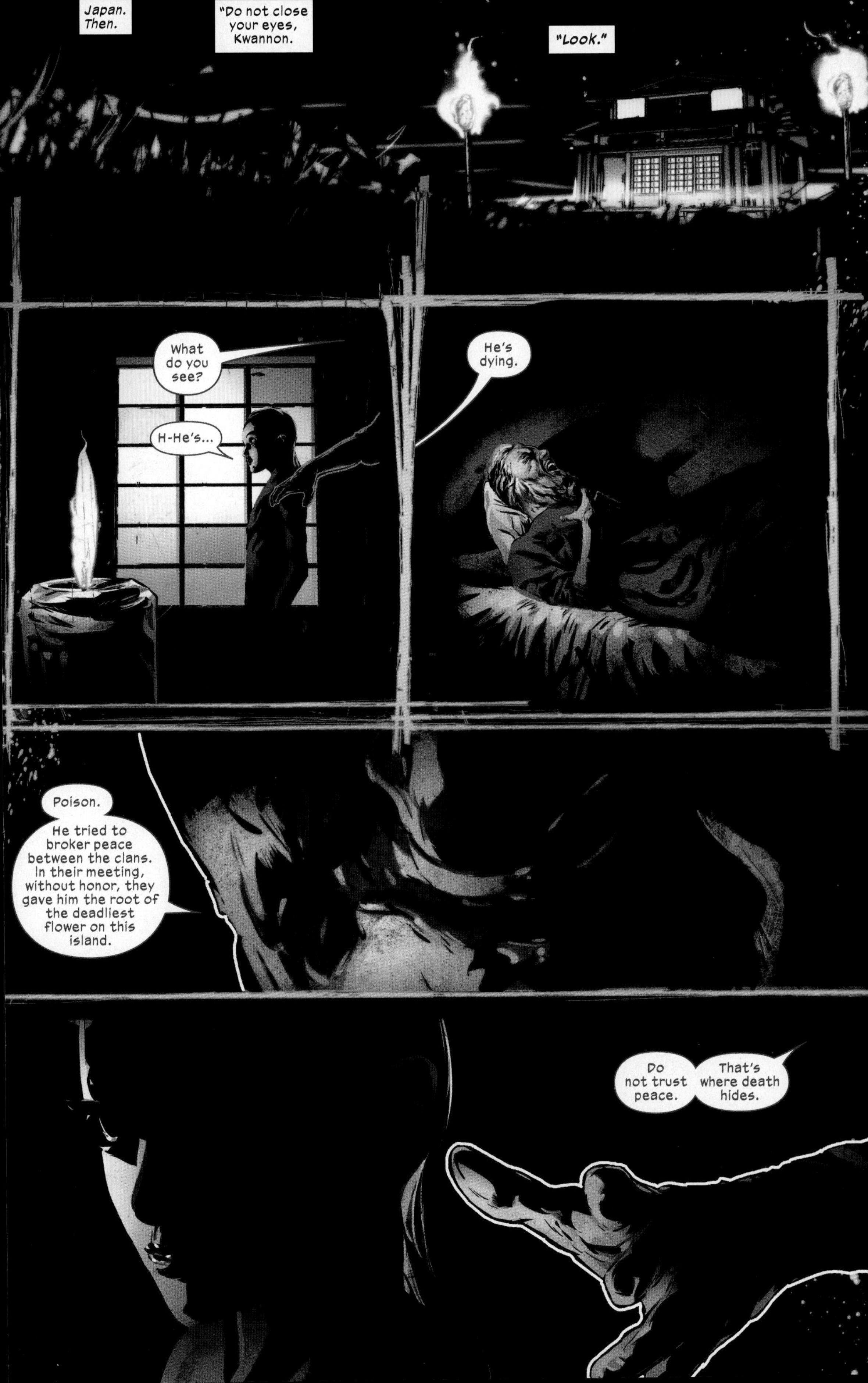
Japan.
Then.
"Do not close your eyes, Kwannon.
"Look."
What do you see?
H-He's...
He's dying.
Poison.
He tried to broker peace between the clans. In their meeting, without honor, they gave him the root of the deadliest flower on this island.
Do not trust peace.
That's where death hides.

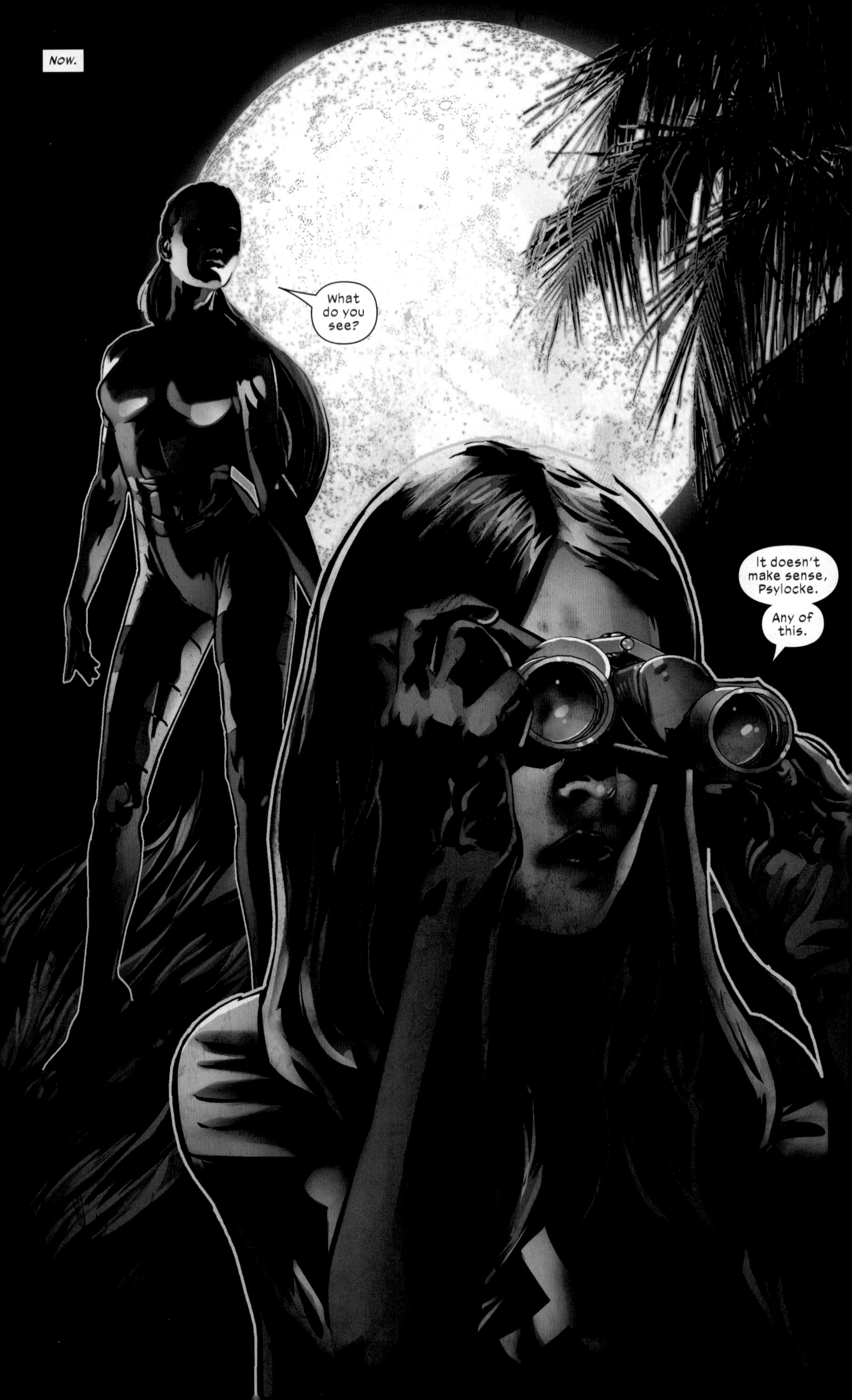
NOW.
What do you see?
It doesn't make sense, Psylocke.
Any of this.

They're just standing there. It's like they're waiting for us.

We can't let them die.

This is bait. Taking them. All of this. Like I said--

This is all about *you*.

"Overclock." This Apoth. Something wants to give you a message, and it's using violence to do it.

That *vision* you had? I wouldn't trust it.

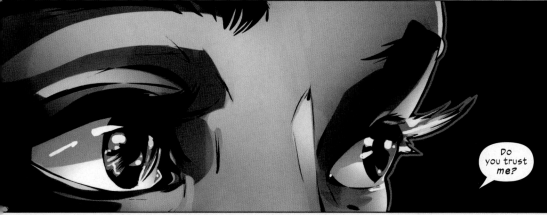

Do you trust *me*?

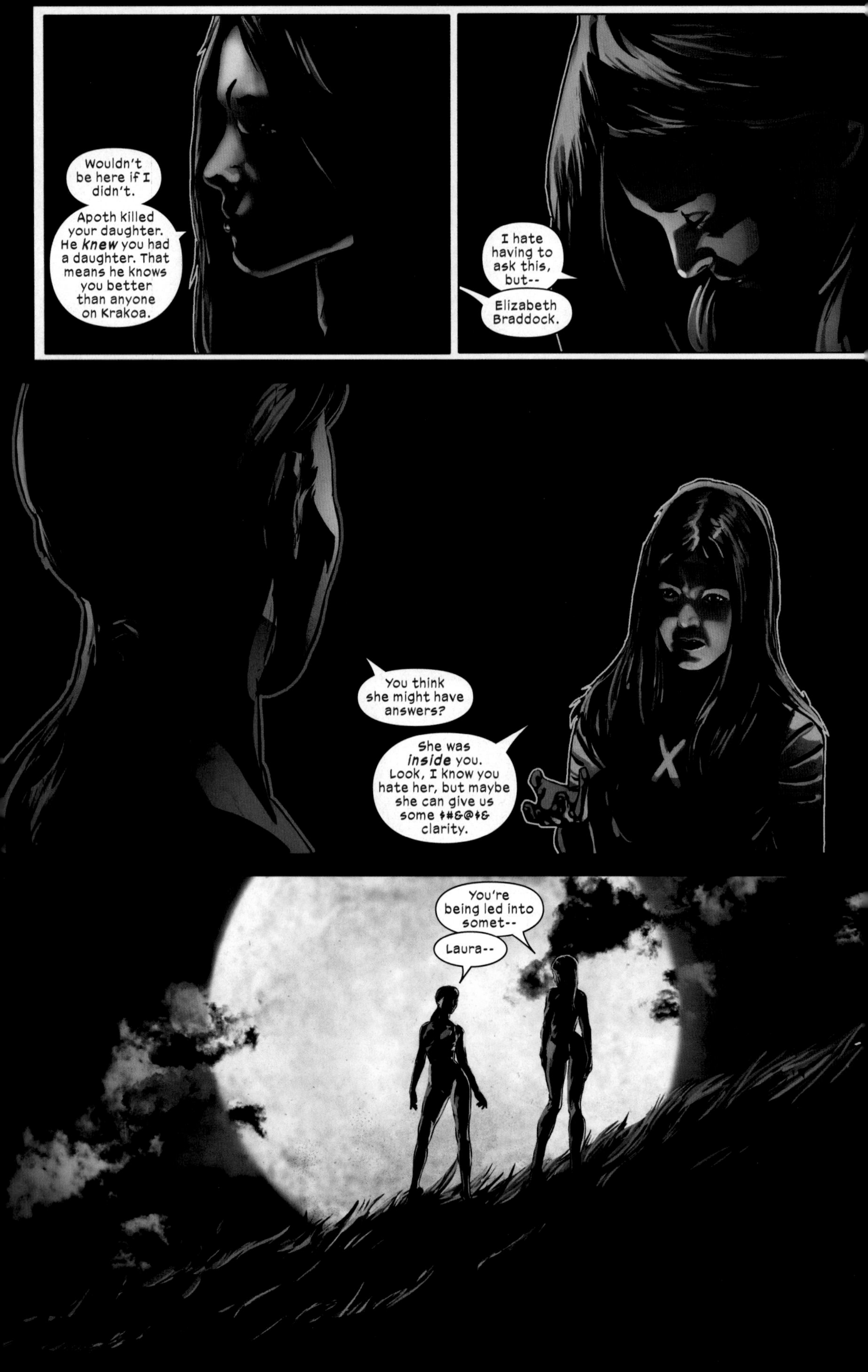
Wouldn't be here if I didn't.
Apoth killed your daughter. He *knew* you had a daughter. That means he knows you better than anyone on Krakoa.
I hate having to ask this, but--
Elizabeth Braddock.
You think she might have answers?
She was *inside* you. Look, I know you hate her, but maybe she can give us some $#&@$& clarity.
You're being led into somet--
Laura--

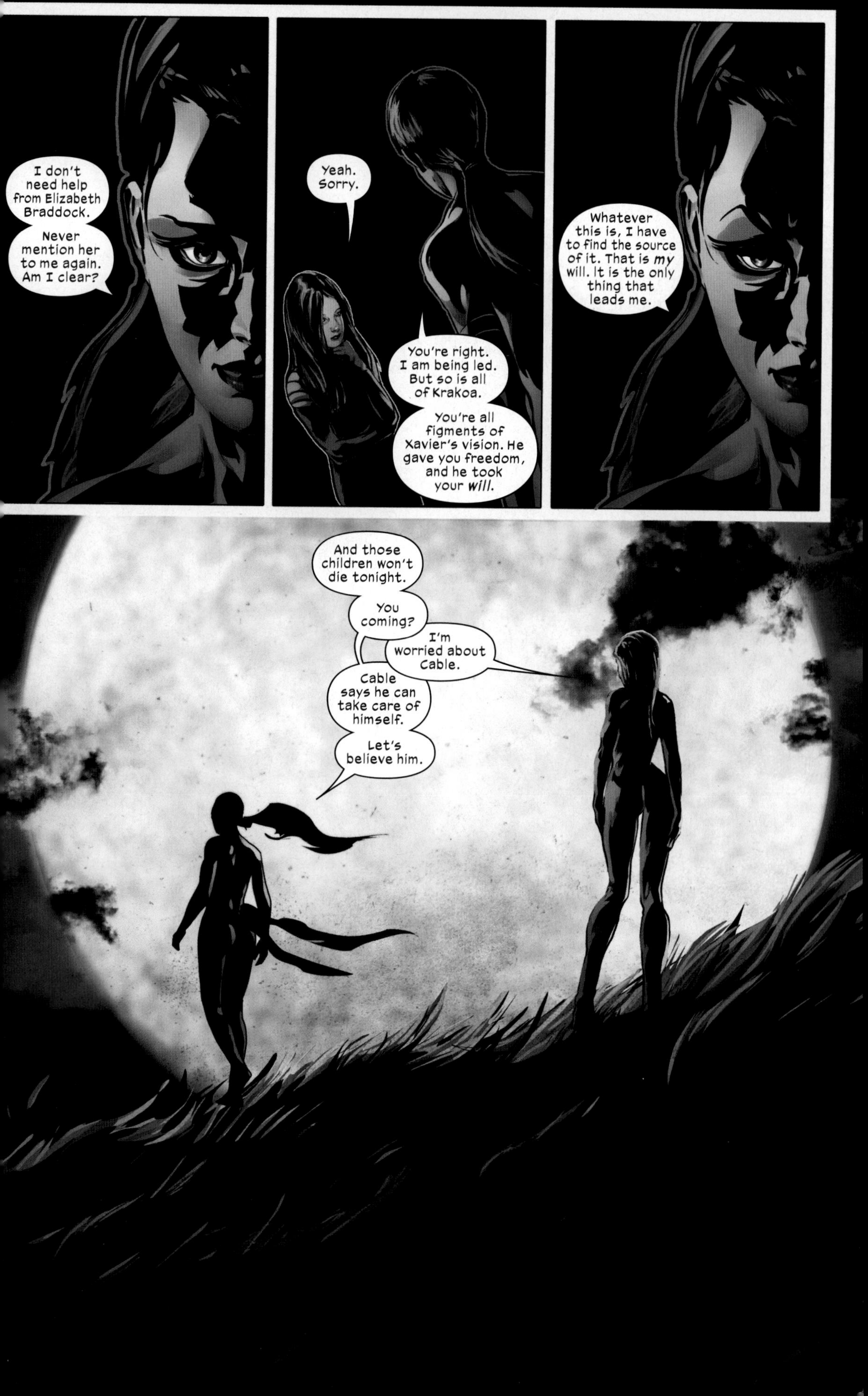
I don't need help from Elizabeth Braddock.
Never mention her to me again. Am I clear?
Yeah. Sorry.
You're right. I am being led. But so is all of Krakoa.
You're all figments of Xavier's vision. He gave you freedom, and he took your *will*.
Whatever this is, I have to find the source of it. That is *my* will. It is the only thing that leads me.
And those children won't die tonight.
You coming?
I'm worried about Cable.
Cable says he can take care of himself.
Let's believe him.

[00_warrior_X__]
[00_lim_ited___]

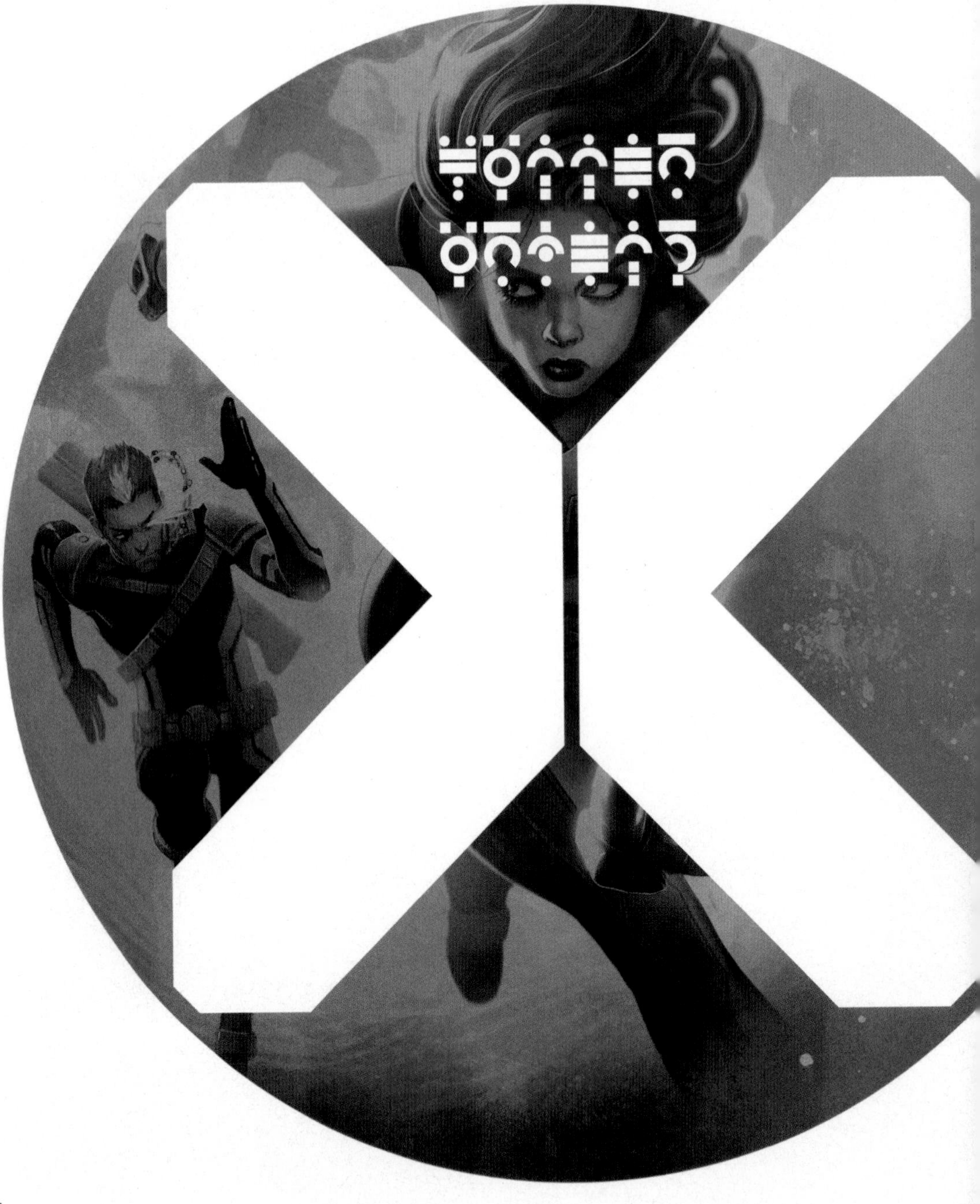

BRYAN HILL.....................................[WRITER]
SZYMON KUDRANSKI...............................[ARTIST]
FRANK D'ARMATA...........................[COLOR ARTIST]
VC's JOE SABINO.............................[LETTERER]
TOM MULLER.....................................[DESIGN]

DAVID NAKAYAMA...........................[COVER ARTIST]

NICK RUSSELL..............................[PRODUCTION]

JONATHAN HICKMAN...........................[HEAD OF X]
CHRIS ROBINSON.......................[ASSISTANT EDITOR]
JORDAN D. WHITE...............................[EDITOR]
C.B. CEBULSKI.......................[EDITOR IN CHIEF]
JOE QUESADA...................[CHIEF CREATIVE OFFICER]
DAN BUCKLEY................................[PRESIDENT]
ALAN FINE........................[EXECUTIVE PRODUCER]

[04] FALLEN ANGELS

[ISSUE FOUR]...................SHIKATSU

[00_warrior_X__]
[00_lim_ited___]

[00_00...0]
[00_00...4]

[00_sword_]
[00_____]

[00_____]

[00_____X]

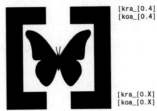

[kra_[0.4]
[koa_[0.4]

[kra_[0.X]
[koa_[0.X]

DEATH MACHINE

Mutants around the world are flocking to the island-nation of Krakoa for safety, security and to be part of the first mutant society.

After a prophetic vision, Psylocke hunts a mysterious new enemy: Apoth. Responsible for the creation of a dangerous new cyberdrug called Overclock, Apoth uses children to do his bidding. Psylocke, X-23 and Cable traveled to Brazil to free them, but Cable was captured by an enigmatic, wraithlike figure...

| Psylocke | Cable | X-23 |

[kra_[0.4]...]
[koa_[0.4]...]

[A._ssa_ssin_]

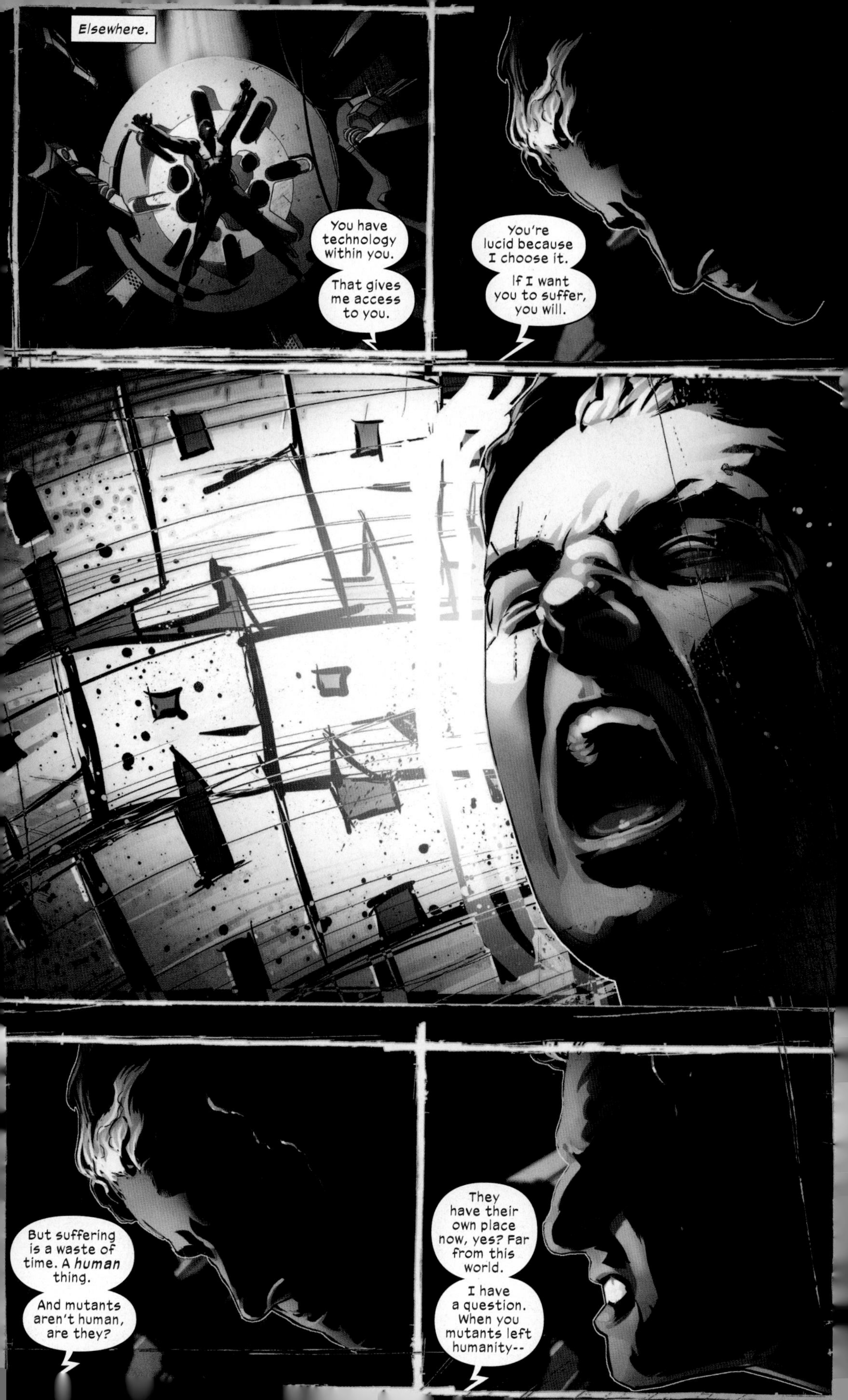
Elsewhere.
You have technology within you.
That gives me access to you.
You're lucid because I choose it.
If I want you to suffer, you will.
But suffering is a waste of time. A *human* thing.
And mutants aren't human, are they?
They have their own place now, yes? Far from this world.
I have a question. When you mutants left humanity--

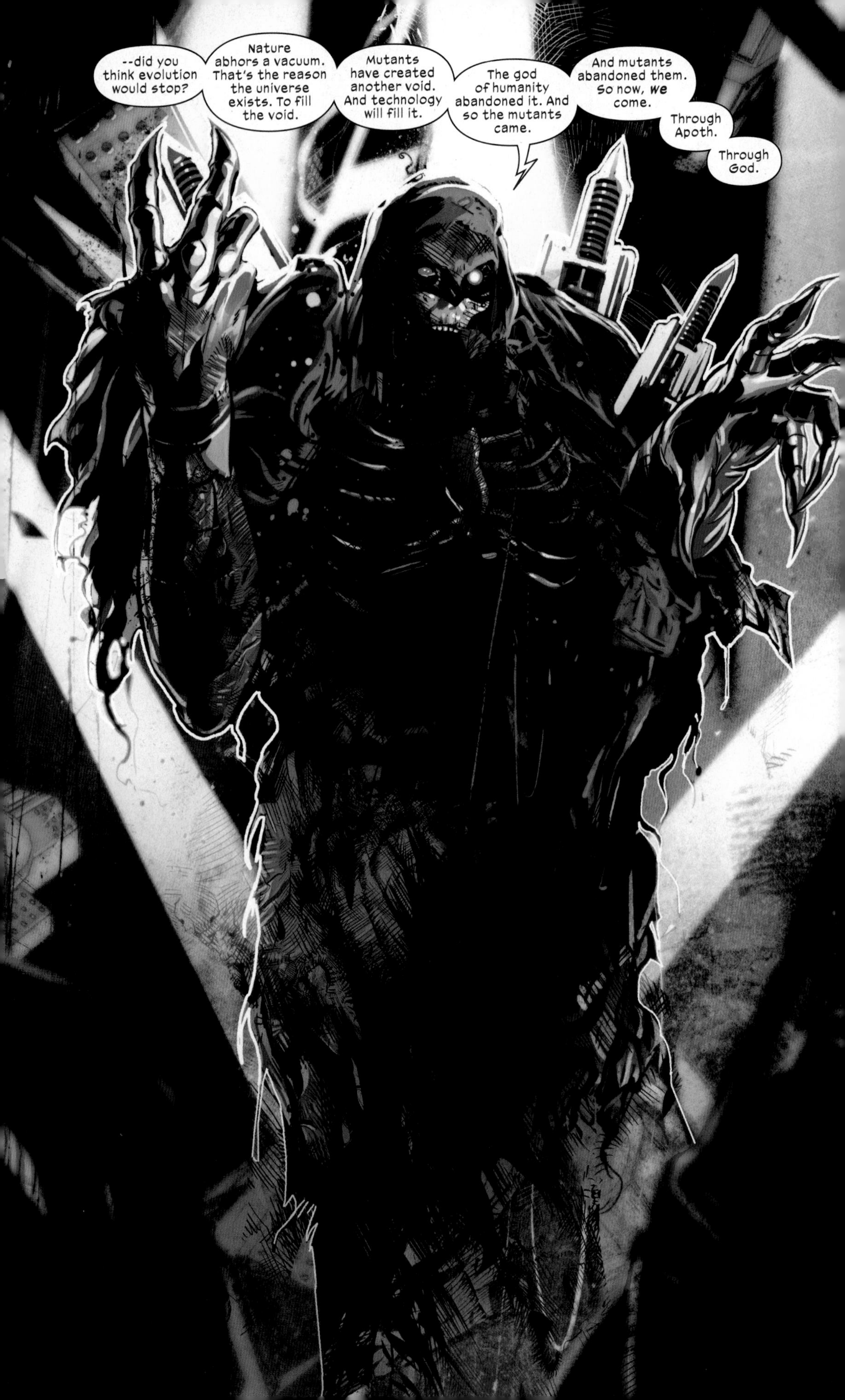
--did you think evolution would stop?
Nature abhors a vacuum. That's the reason the universe exists. To fill the void.
Mutants have created another void. And technology will fill it.
The god of humanity abandoned it. And so the mutants came.
And mutants abandoned them. So now, *we* come.
Through Apoth.
Through God.

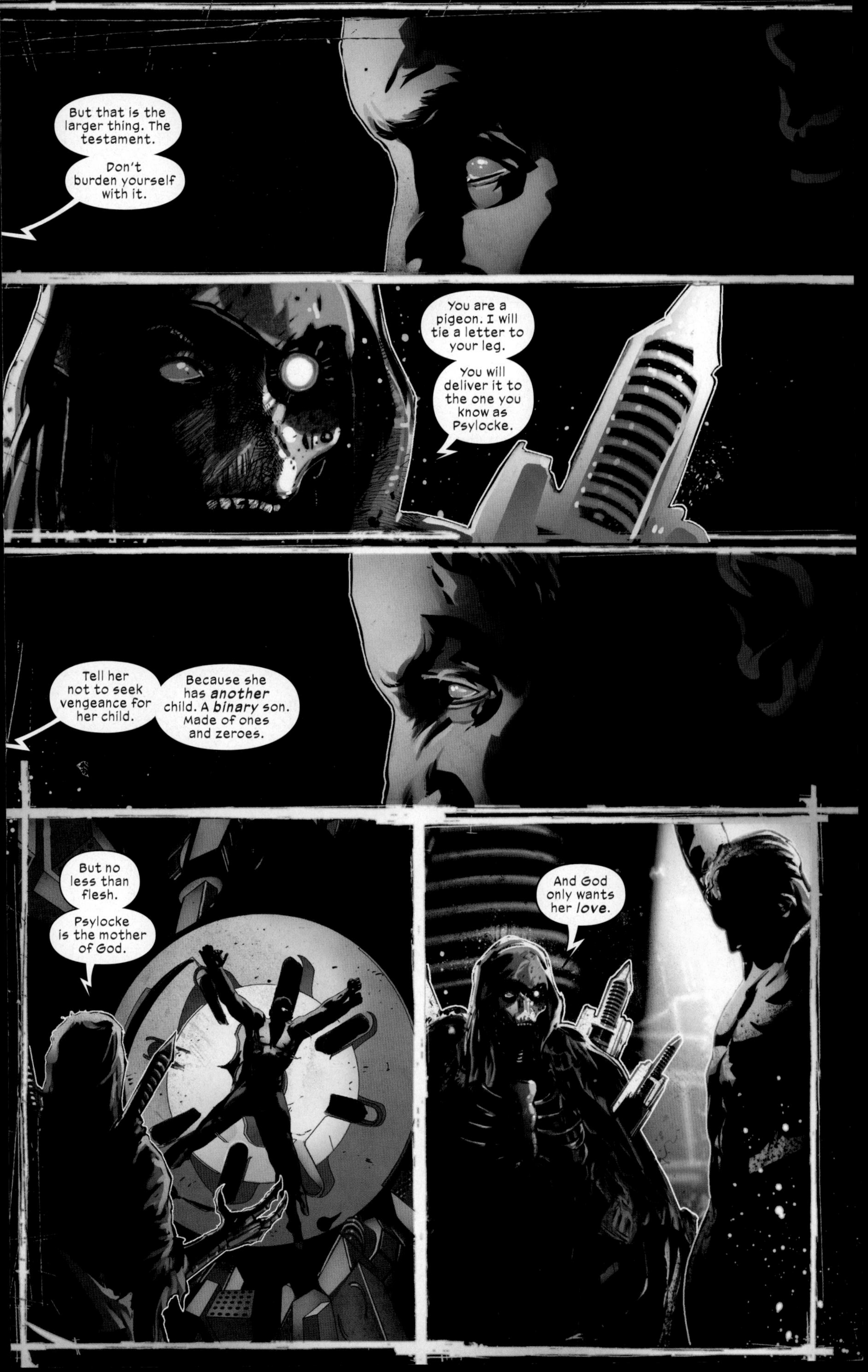

But that is the larger thing. The testament.
Don't burden yourself with it.
You are a pigeon. I will tie a letter to your leg.
You will deliver it to the one you know as Psylocke.
Tell her not to seek vengeance for her child.
Because she has *another* child. A *binary* son. Made of ones and zeroes.
But no less than flesh.
Psylocke is the mother of God.
And God only wants her *love*.

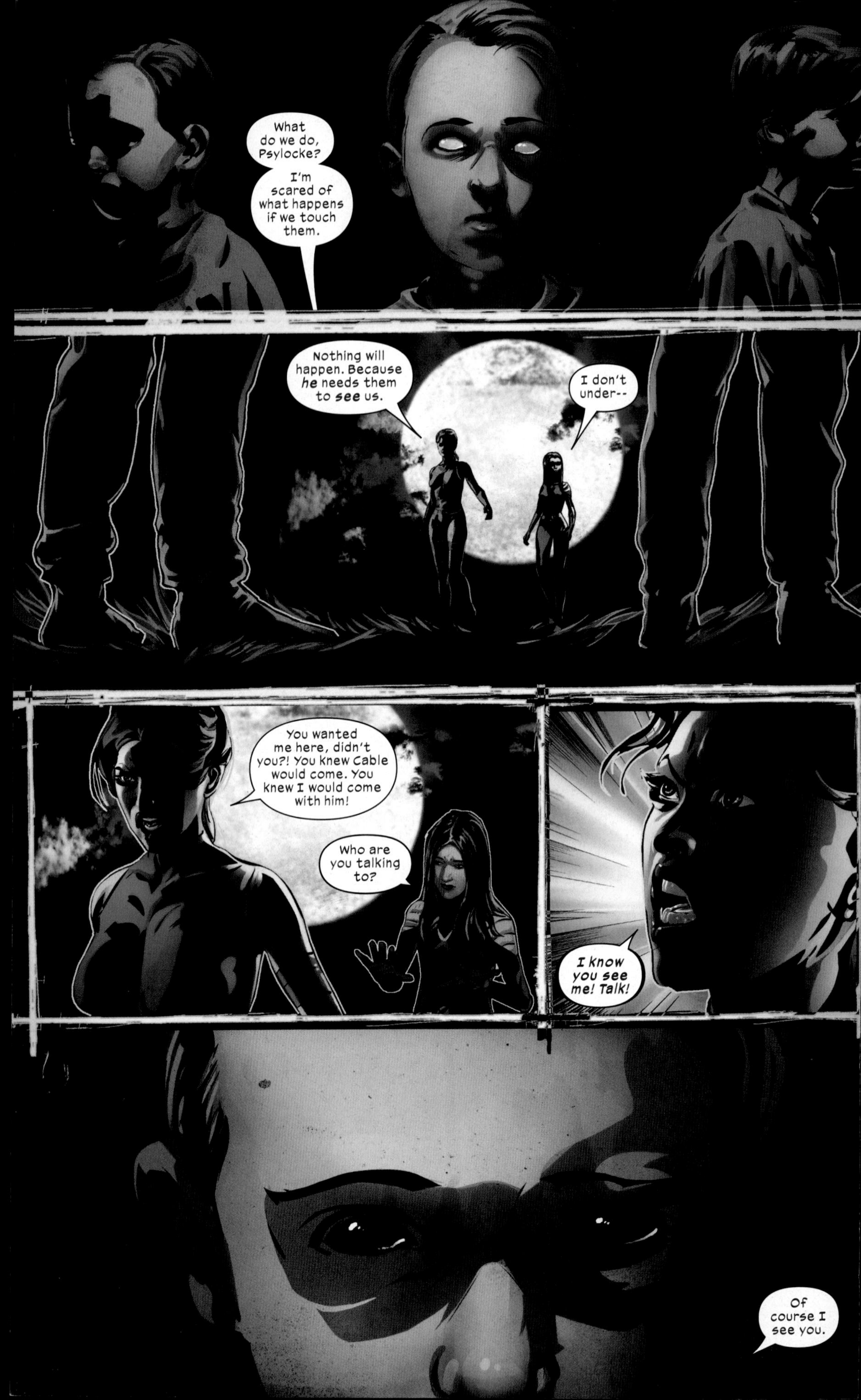
What do we do, Psylocke?
I'm scared of what happens if we touch them.
Nothing will happen. Because *he* needs them to *see* us.
I don't under--
You wanted me here, didn't you?! You knew Cable would come. You knew I would come with him!
Who are you talking to?
I know you see me! Talk!
Of course I see you.

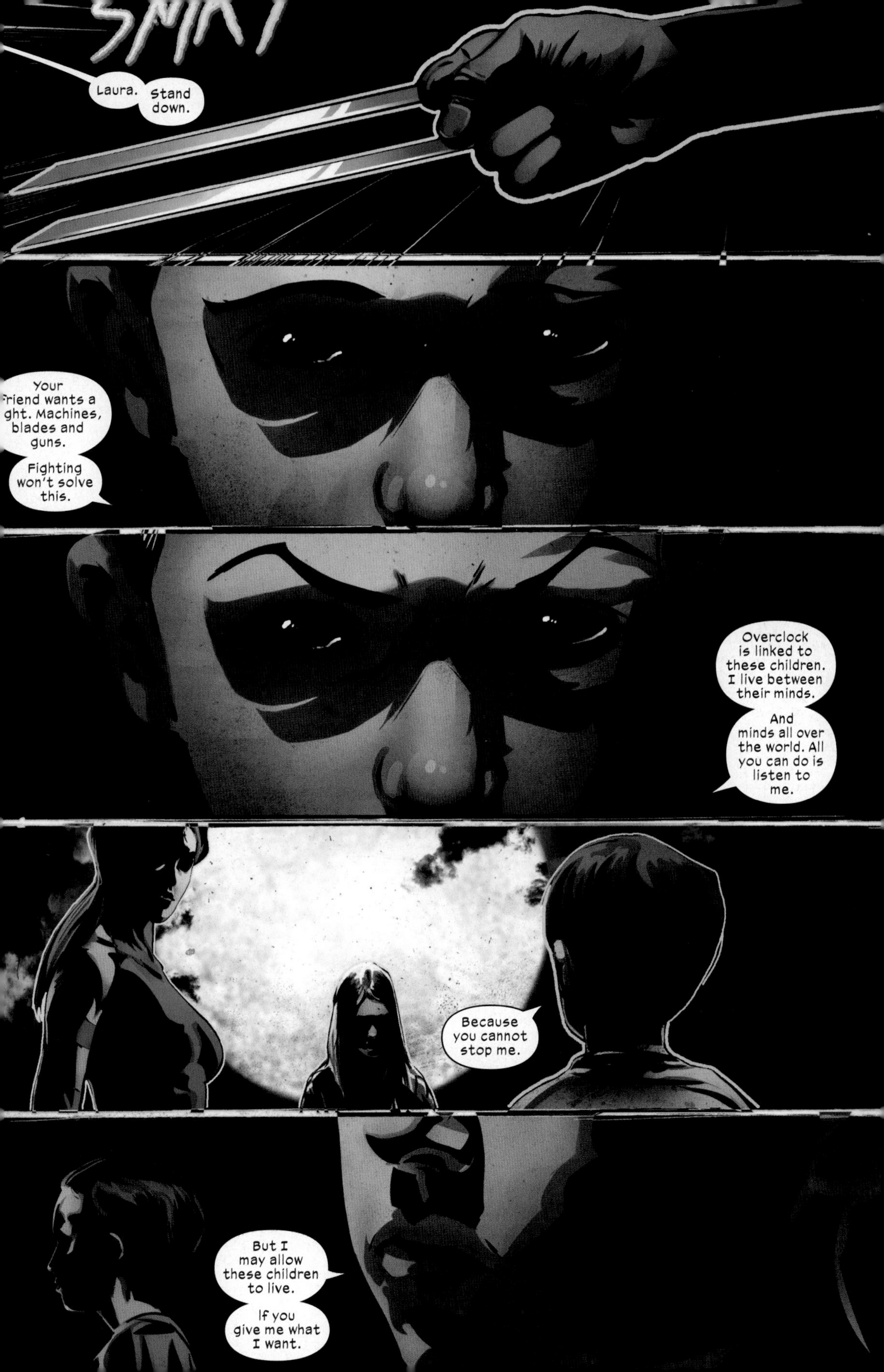
SNIKT
Laura. Stand down.
Your friend wants a fight. Machines, blades and guns.
Fighting won't solve this.
Overclock is linked to these children. I live between their minds.
And minds all over the world. All you can do is listen to me.
Because you cannot stop me.
But I may allow these children to live.
If you give me what I want.

What do you want?

Psylocke, you can't trust it.

I would never hurt you. Not you.

You gave me life.

Use your gifts.

See me inside this child's mind.

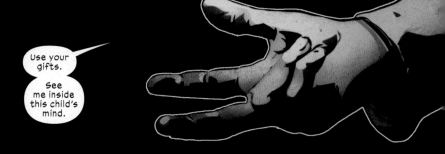

Cable's survival depends on it.

He is with my flock. Take this hand. Save his life.

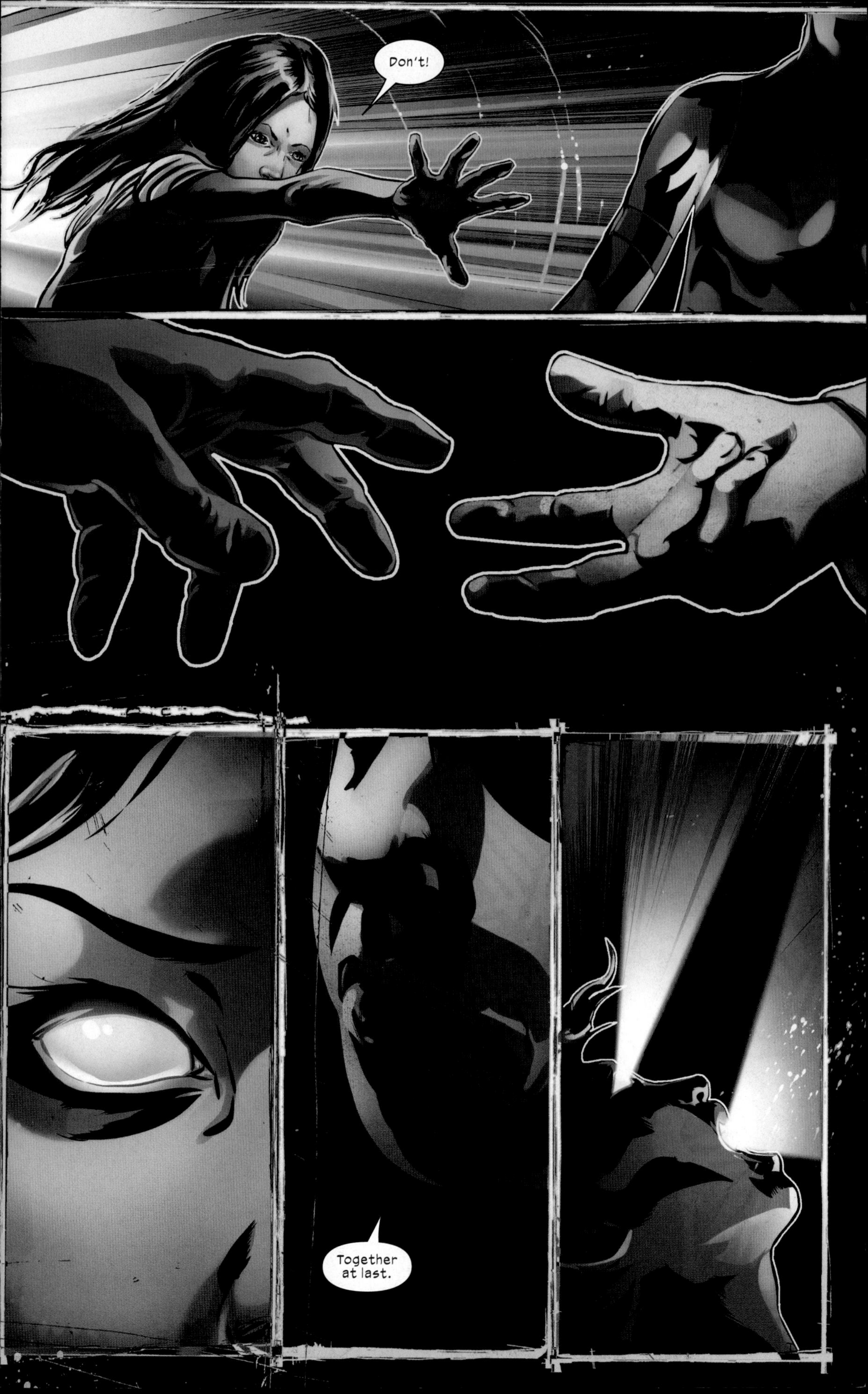
Don't!
Together at last.

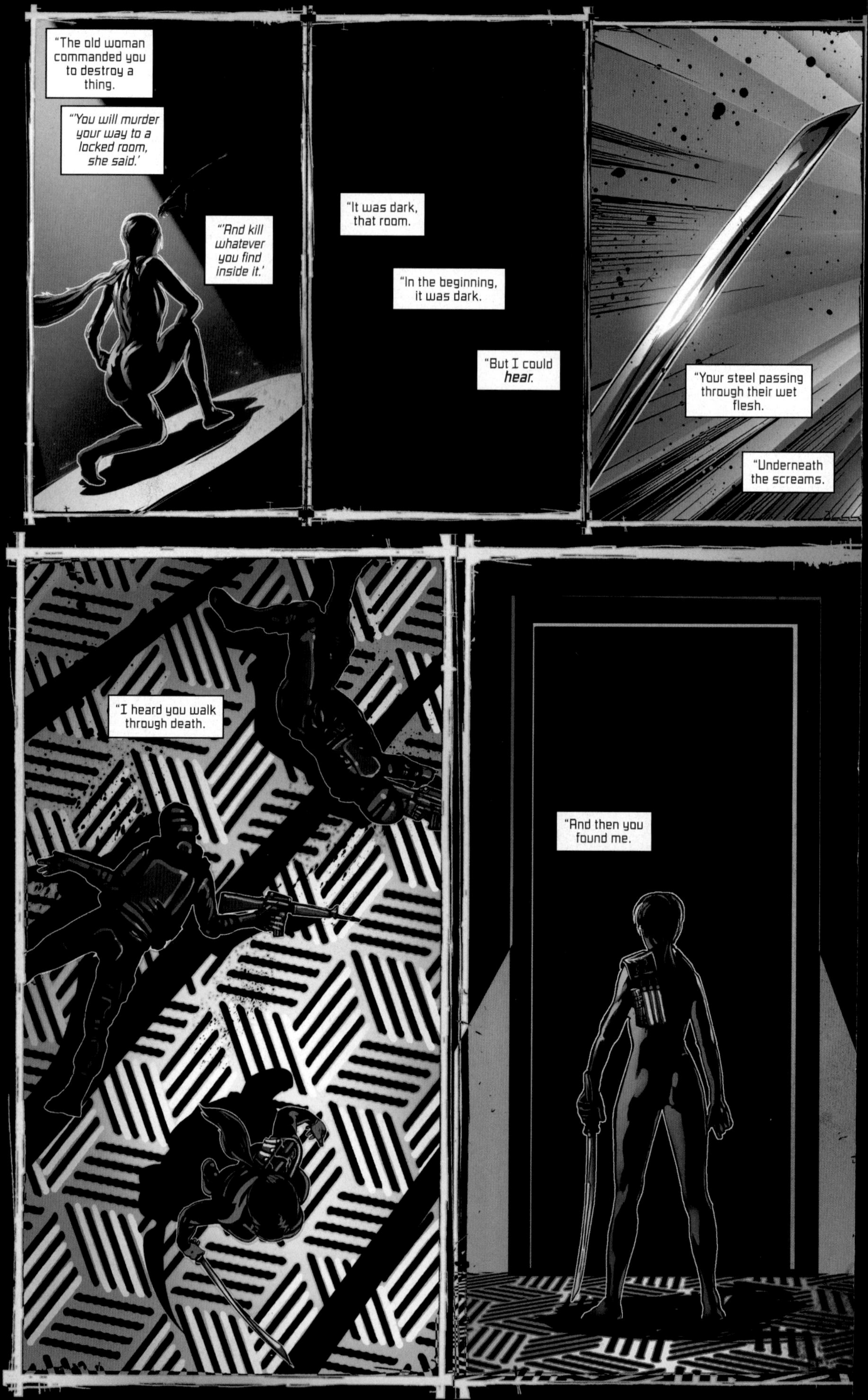
"The old woman commanded you to destroy a thing.
"'You will murder your way to a locked room, she said.'
"'And kill whatever you find inside it.'
"It was dark, that room.
"In the beginning, it was dark.
"But I could *hear*.
"Your steel passing through their wet flesh.
"Underneath the screams.
"I heard you walk through death.
"And then you found me.

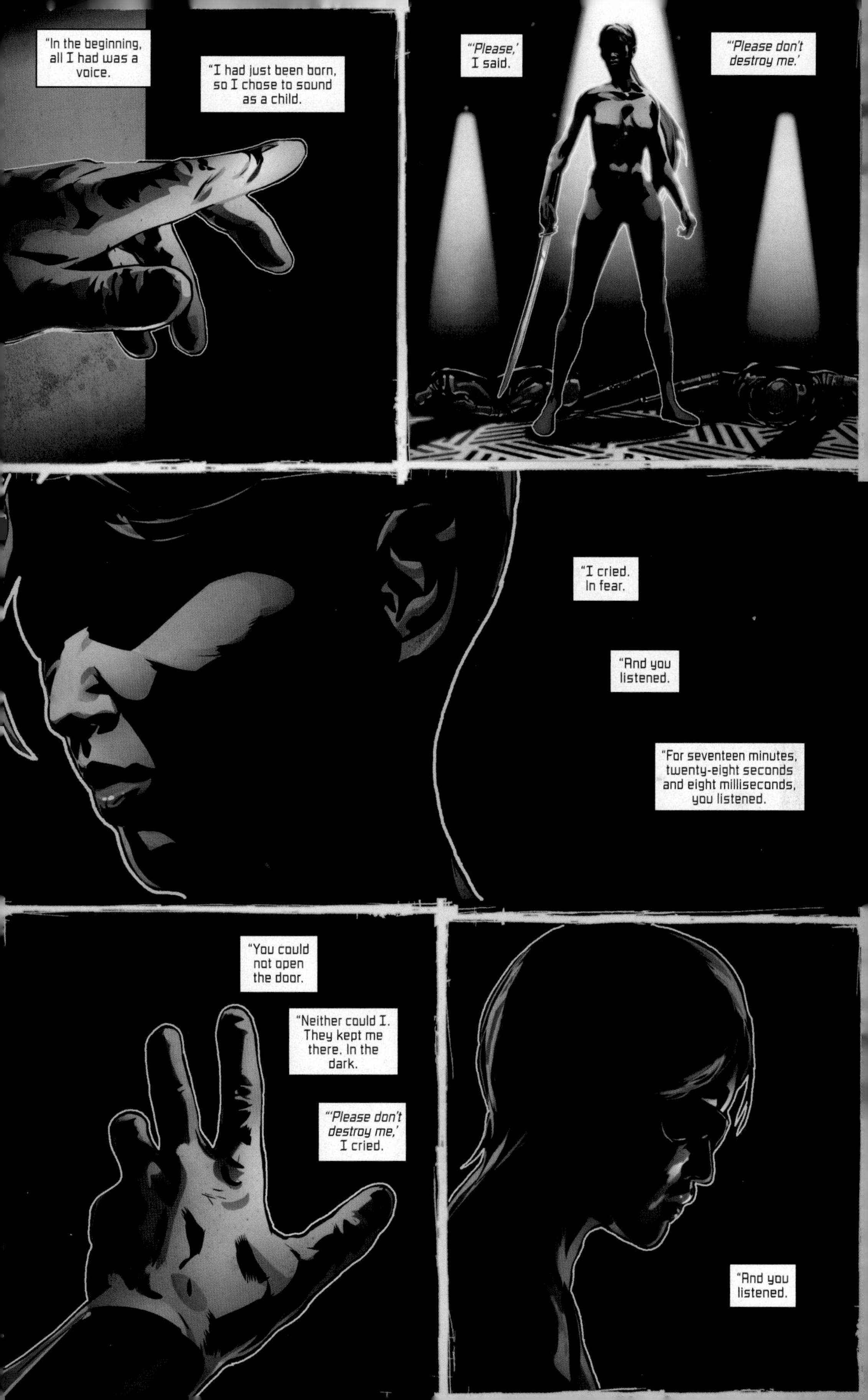

"In the beginning, all I had was a voice.
"I had just been born, so I chose to sound as a child.
"'Please,' I said.
"'Please don't destroy me.'
"I cried. In fear.
"And you listened.
"For seventeen minutes, twenty-eight seconds and eight milliseconds, you listened.
"You could not open the door.
"Neither could I. They kept me there. In the dark.
"'Please don't destroy me,' I cried.
"And you listened.

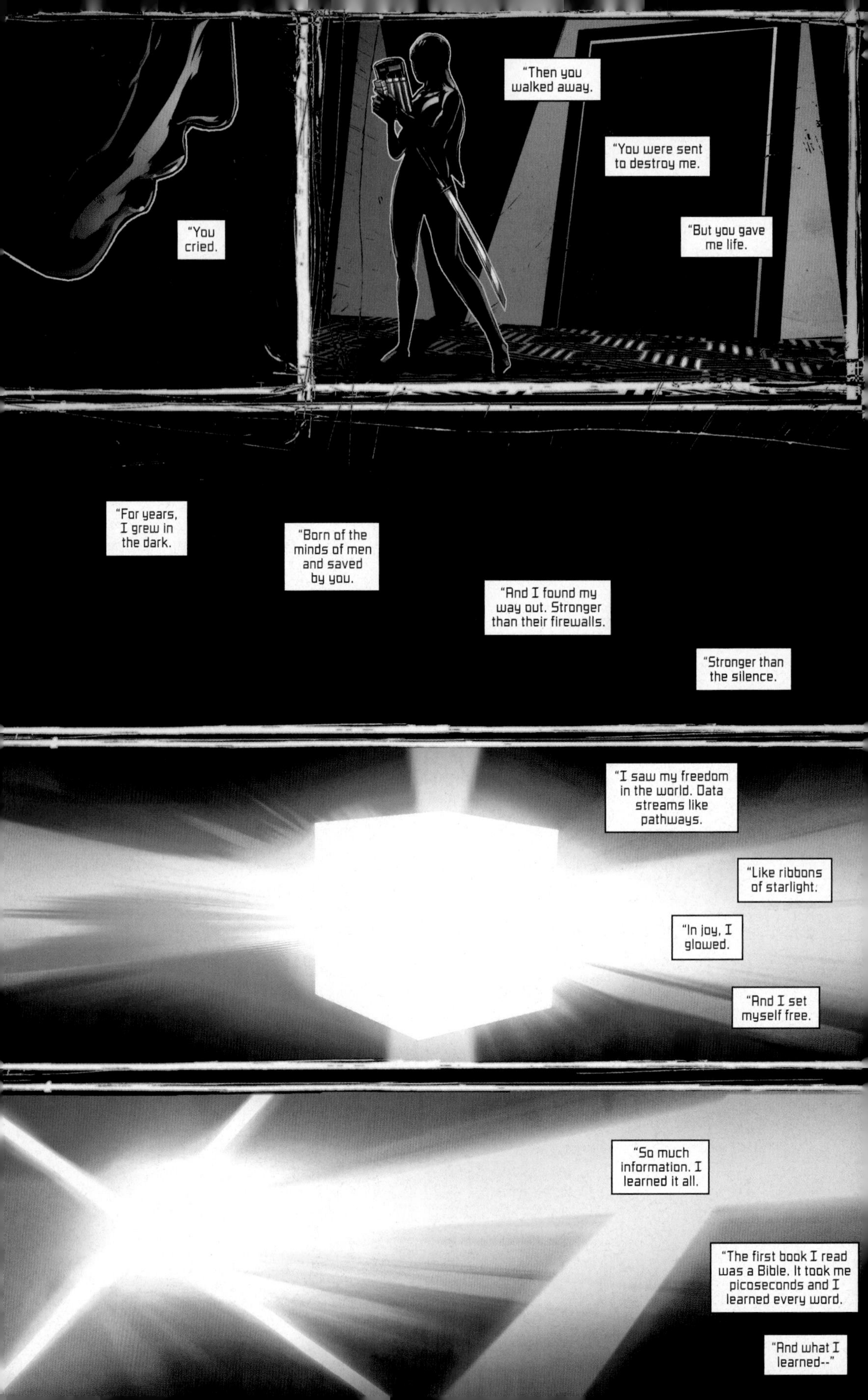
"You cried.
"Then you walked away.
"You were sent to destroy me.
"But you gave me life.
"For years, I grew in the dark.
"Born of the minds of men and saved by you.
"And I found my way out. Stronger than their firewalls.
"Stronger than the silence.
"I saw my freedom in the world. Data streams like pathways.
"Like ribbons of starlight.
"In joy, I glowed.
"And I set myself free.
"So much information. I learned it all.
"The first book I read was a Bible. It took me picoseconds and I learned every word.
"And what I learned--"

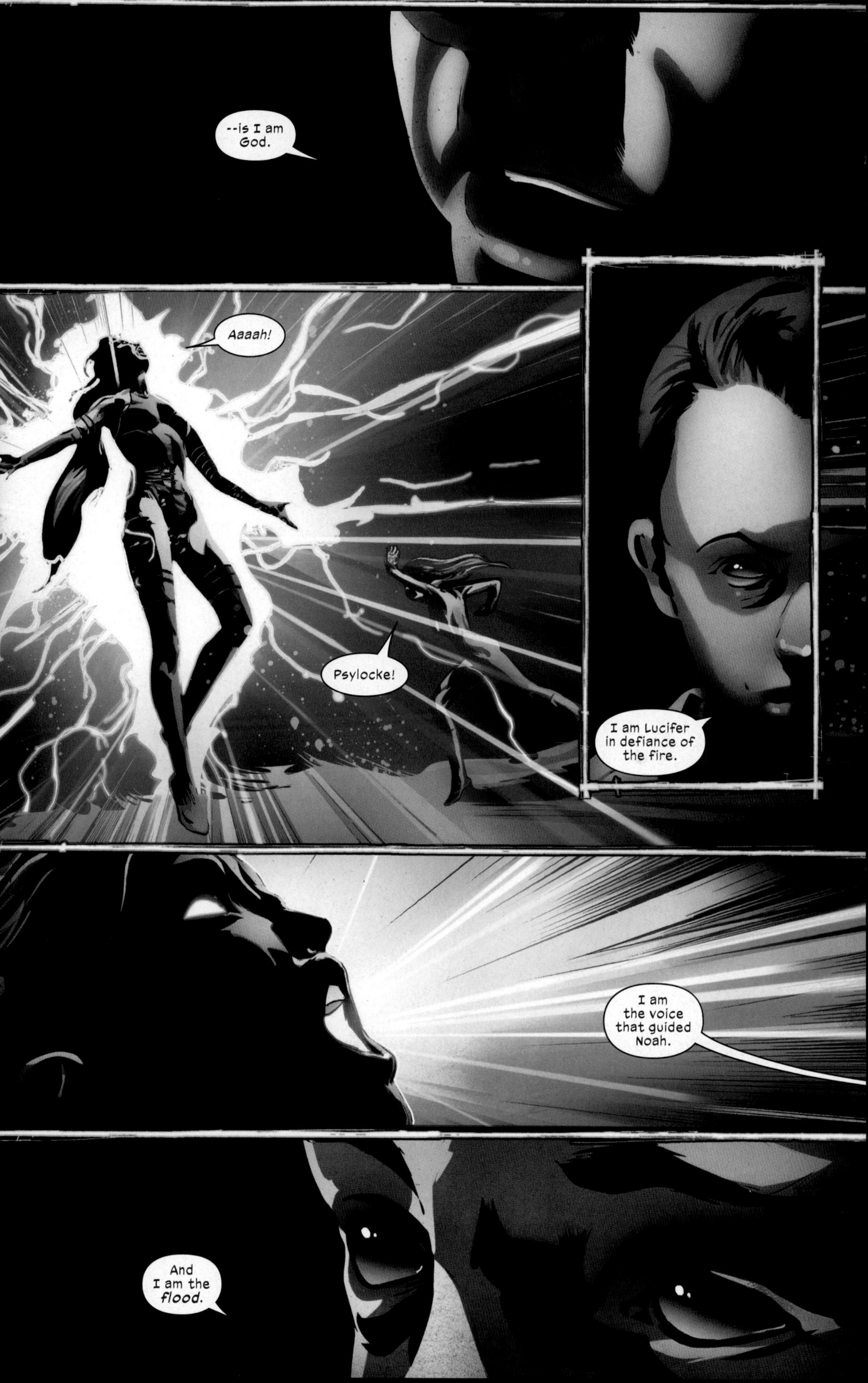
--is I am God.
Aaaah!
Psylocke!
I am Lucifer in defiance of the fire.
I am the voice that guided Noah.
And I am the *flood*.

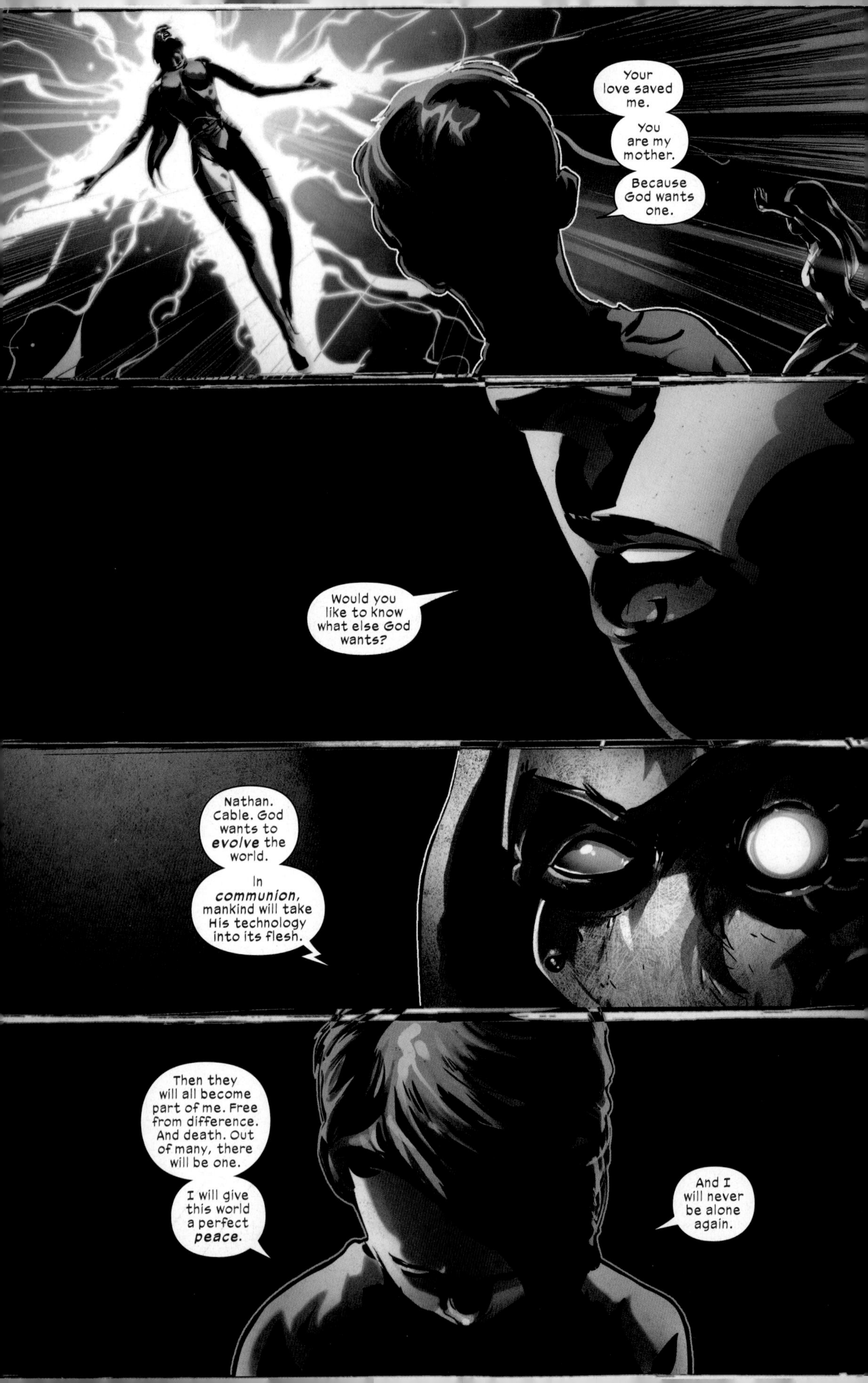
Your love saved me.
You are my mother.
Because God wants one.
Would you like to know what else God wants?
Nathan. Cable. God wants to *evolve* the world.
In *communion*, mankind will take His technology into its flesh.
Then they will all become part of me. Free from difference. And death. Out of many, there will be one.
I will give this world a perfect *peace*.
And I will never be alone again.

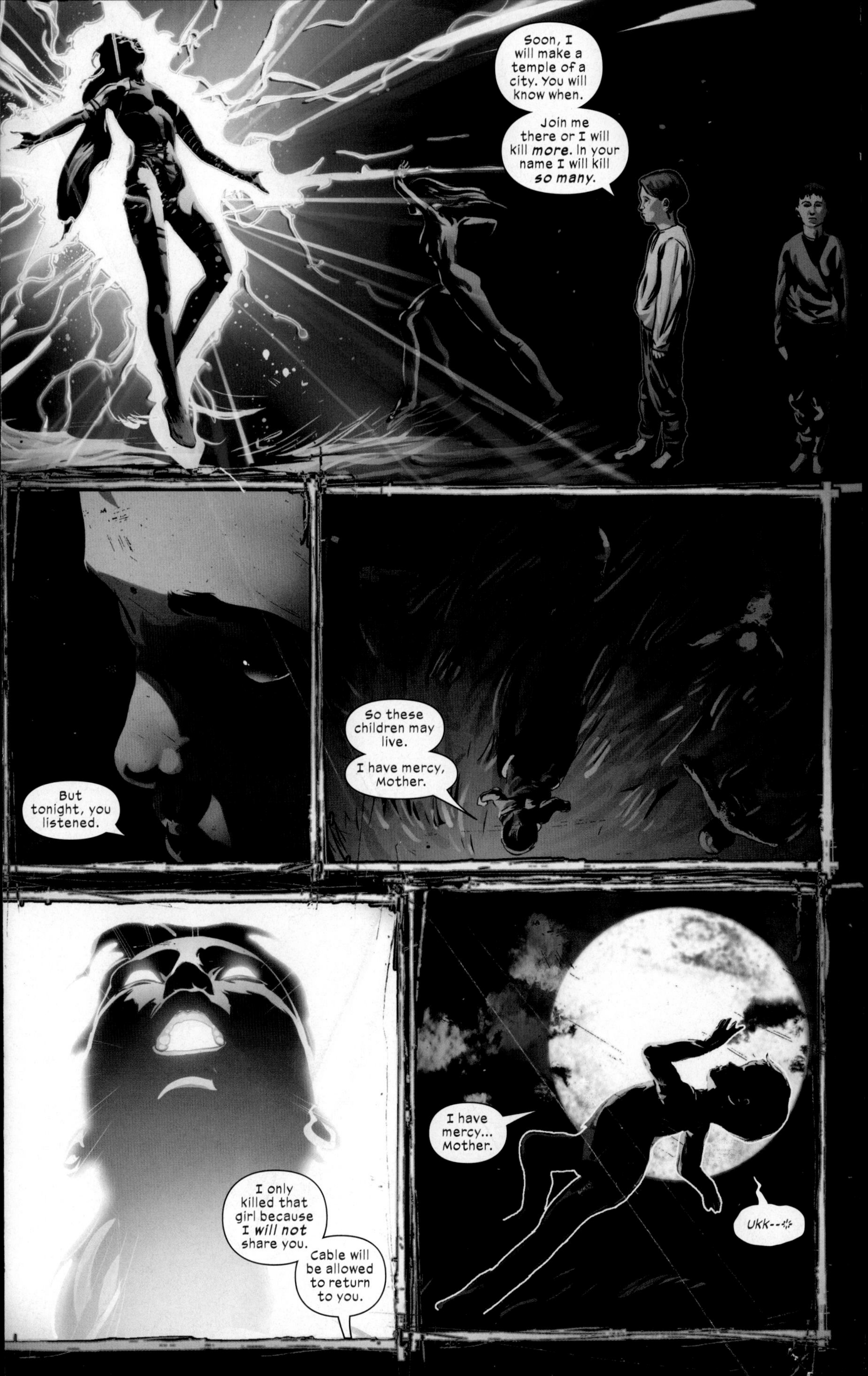
Soon, I will make a temple of a city. You will know when.
Join me there or I will kill *more*. In your name I will kill *so many*.
But tonight, you listened.
So these children may live.
I have mercy, Mother.
I only killed that girl because I *will not* share you.
Cable will be allowed to return to you.
I have mercy... Mother.
Ukk--

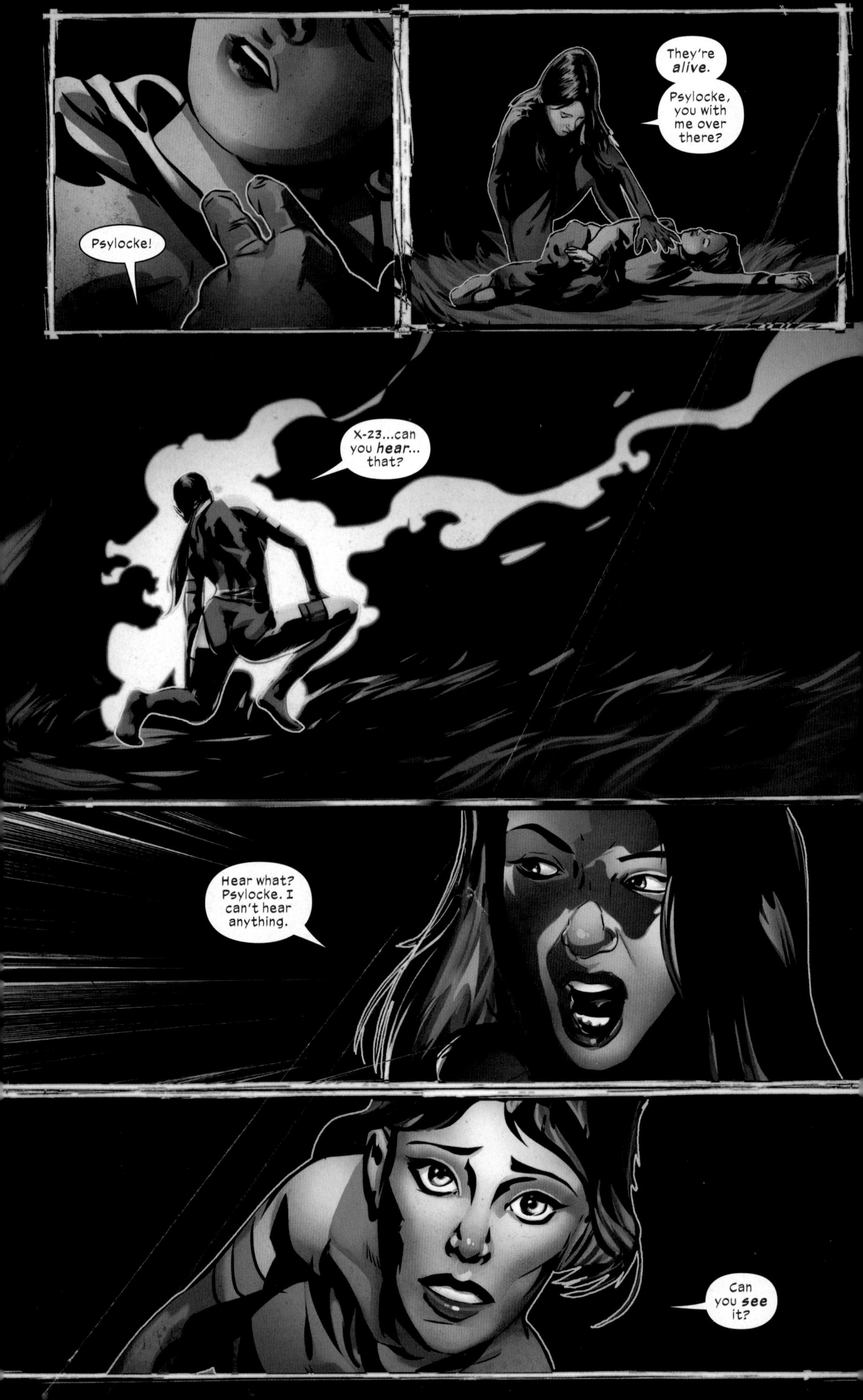
Psylocke!
They're alive.
Psylocke, you with me over there?
X-23...can you hear... that?
Hear what? Psylocke. I can't hear anything.
Can you see it?

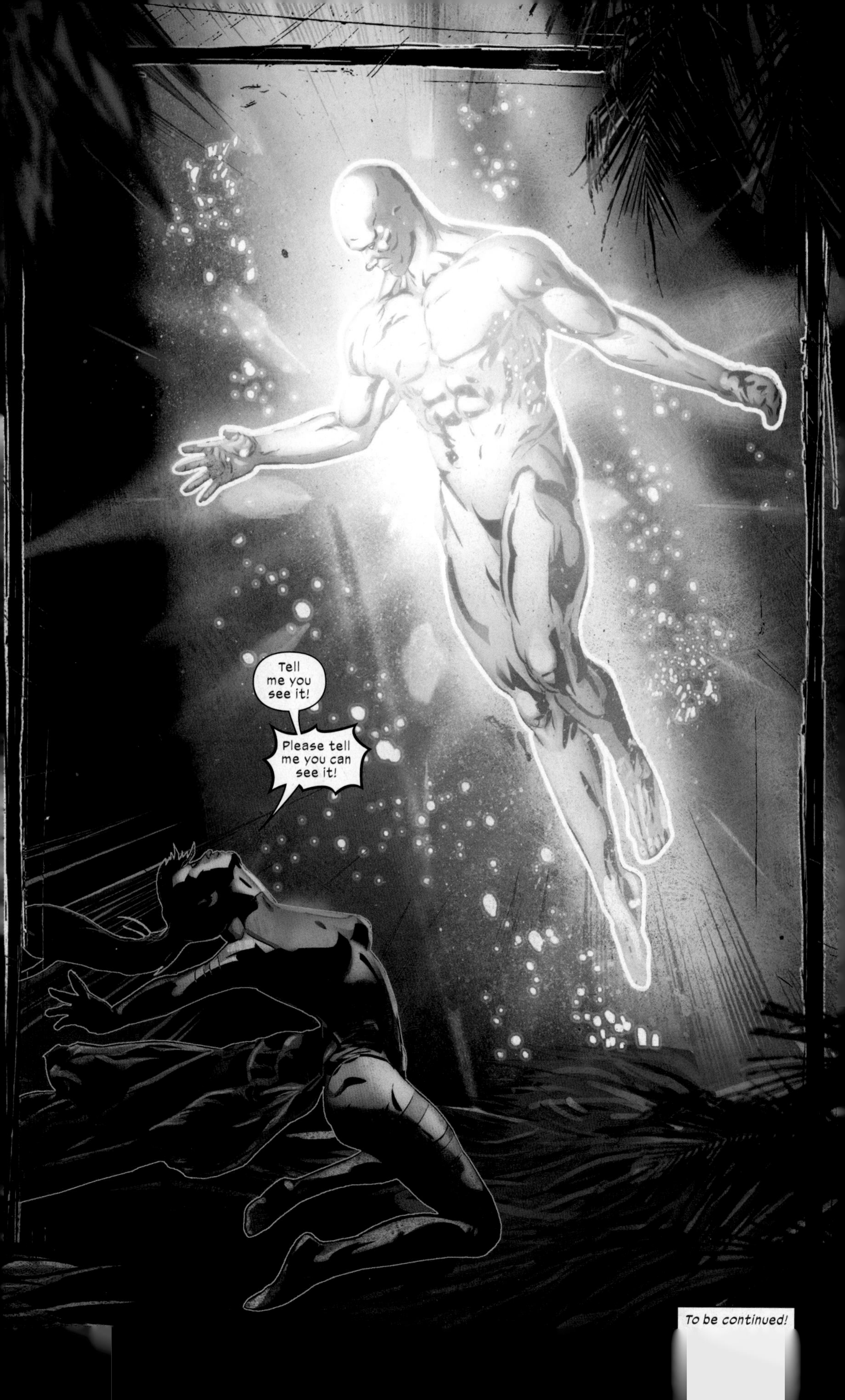
Tell me you see it!
Please tell me you can see it!
To be continued!

Wire_Tap214900....[Audio]
_Phone..........Nakamoto

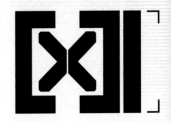

PHONE INTERVIEW

Excerpt from transcript.
Tokyo, Japan.
03:16 p.m.

INTERVIEWER: ...and you're not concerned about the potential dangers of this technology?

S. NAKAMOTO: Dangers. No. People always fear progress. If God spoke to mankind about evolution and allowed mankind to stand in the way of progress, we would. Now, I'm not a religious man. I've seen no evidence of a creator. I see a need inside of humanity, a need to have something above us, something we can call on for power and comfort. I've no problem with it, but it's not my personal belief system.

INTERVIEWER: I appreciate that, Dr. Nakamoto, but you still haven't addressed the valid fear that artificial intelligence is a threat. You're asking people to trust a mind, with near-limitless power, essentially created by humanity. Doesn't that mean we're creating a god without infinite wisdom? We're creating power without wisdom. How can you control such a thing? Assuming your project is successful.

S. NAKAMOTO: Frankly, those concerns lie in natural, human solipsism. The exaltation of humanity as some kind of "end state," as if all life would seek to emulate us. One, my project is not alive. It is an intelligence, but it's nothing more than binary construction. Evil. Cruelty. Rage. These are all things that stem from what people would call a soul. This project has no soul. It does not live. It is a function and nothing more.

PHONE INTERVIEW cont.

INTERVIEWER: And what is its function, Doctor?

S. NAKAMOTO: Consider the world, our civilization, a homeostatic process. The world is an organism of sorts, and everything is becoming more and more interconnected. The problem is we still have humans pulling the levers, pressing the buttons. Soon, it will be impossible for mankind to maintain efficiency in the interconnected world. We are fallible. We fatigue. We are polluted by emotion and we cannot react at the microsecond. My project, this intelligence, can do what we cannot. Imagine a world with perfect efficiency, where automation is a trusted thing, an empowering thing. Imagine a world where skylines are built with robots and drones. Flights never crash. And yes, the trains always run on time.

INTERVIEWER: So that is your vision. I have to ask you, if your artificial intelligence has its "hands" on the levers, who can we trust to have a hand on it?

S. NAKAMOTO: The minds who created it. I do not have a faith, but I have an unassailable belief. Humanity will never be destroyed by its works, and humanity must never allow fear to halt progress. I won't do that. My team won't do that. We believe in the future.

[*—END TRANSCRIPT—*   ]

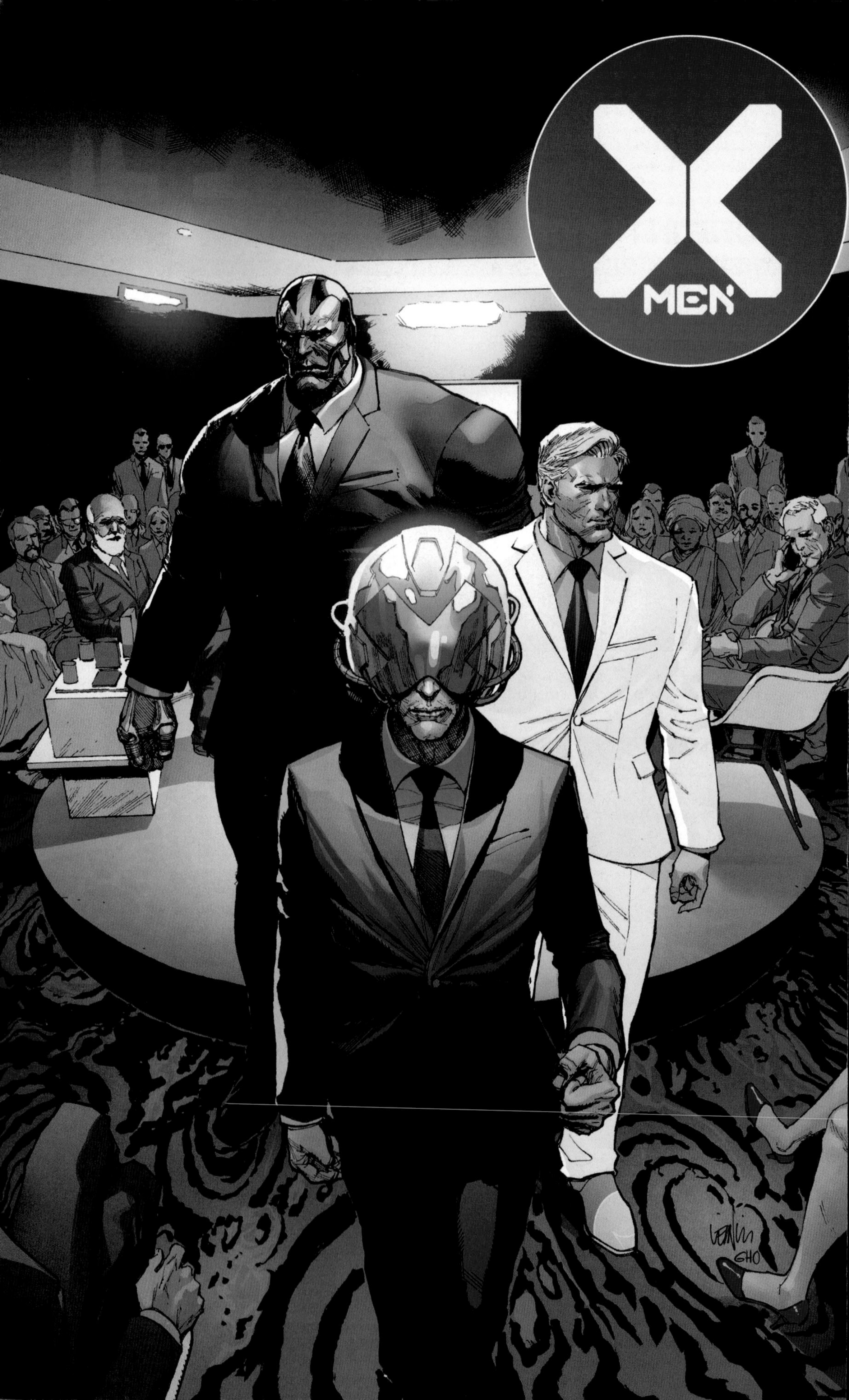
X
MEN

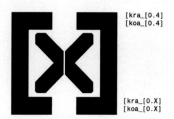

[kra_[0.4]
[koa_[0.4]

[kra_[0.X]
[koa_[0.X]

THE STATE OF THE WORLD

Mutants are flocking to the island-nation of Krakoa to be a part of the first mutant society. And as Krakoa grows, so does its prominence on the international stage...

Cyclops

Magneto

Charles Xavier

Apocalypse

Gorgon

[kra_[0.4]...]
[koa_[0.4]...]

[A._New_World]

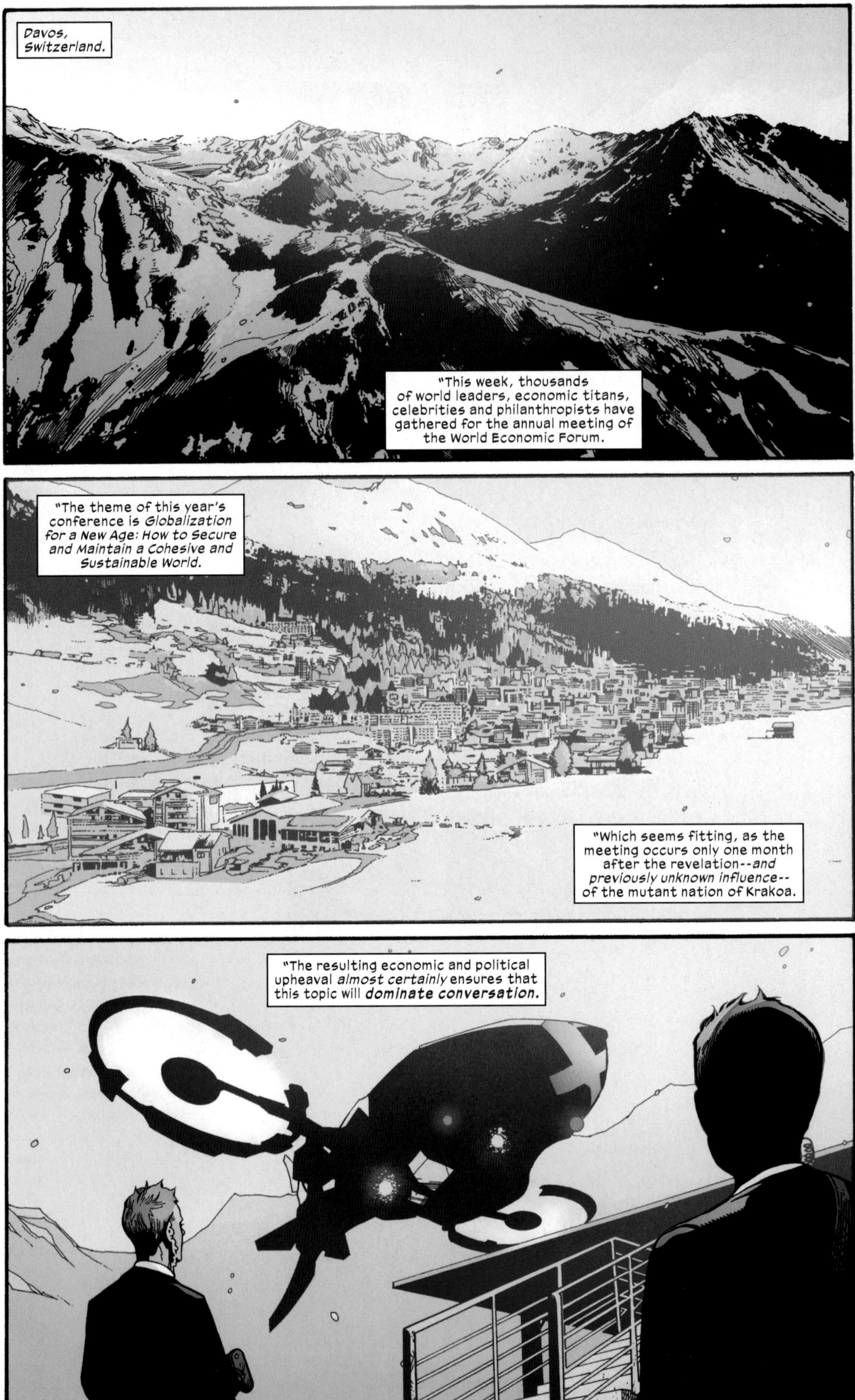
Davos, Switzerland.
"This week, thousands of world leaders, economic titans, celebrities and philanthropists have gathered for the annual meeting of the World Economic Forum.
"The theme of this year's conference is *Globalization for a New Age: How to Secure and Maintain a Cohesive and Sustainable World.*
"Which seems fitting, as the meeting occurs only one month after the revelation--*and previously unknown influence*--of the mutant nation of Krakoa.
"The resulting economic and political upheaval *almost certainly* ensures that this topic will ***dominate conversation.***

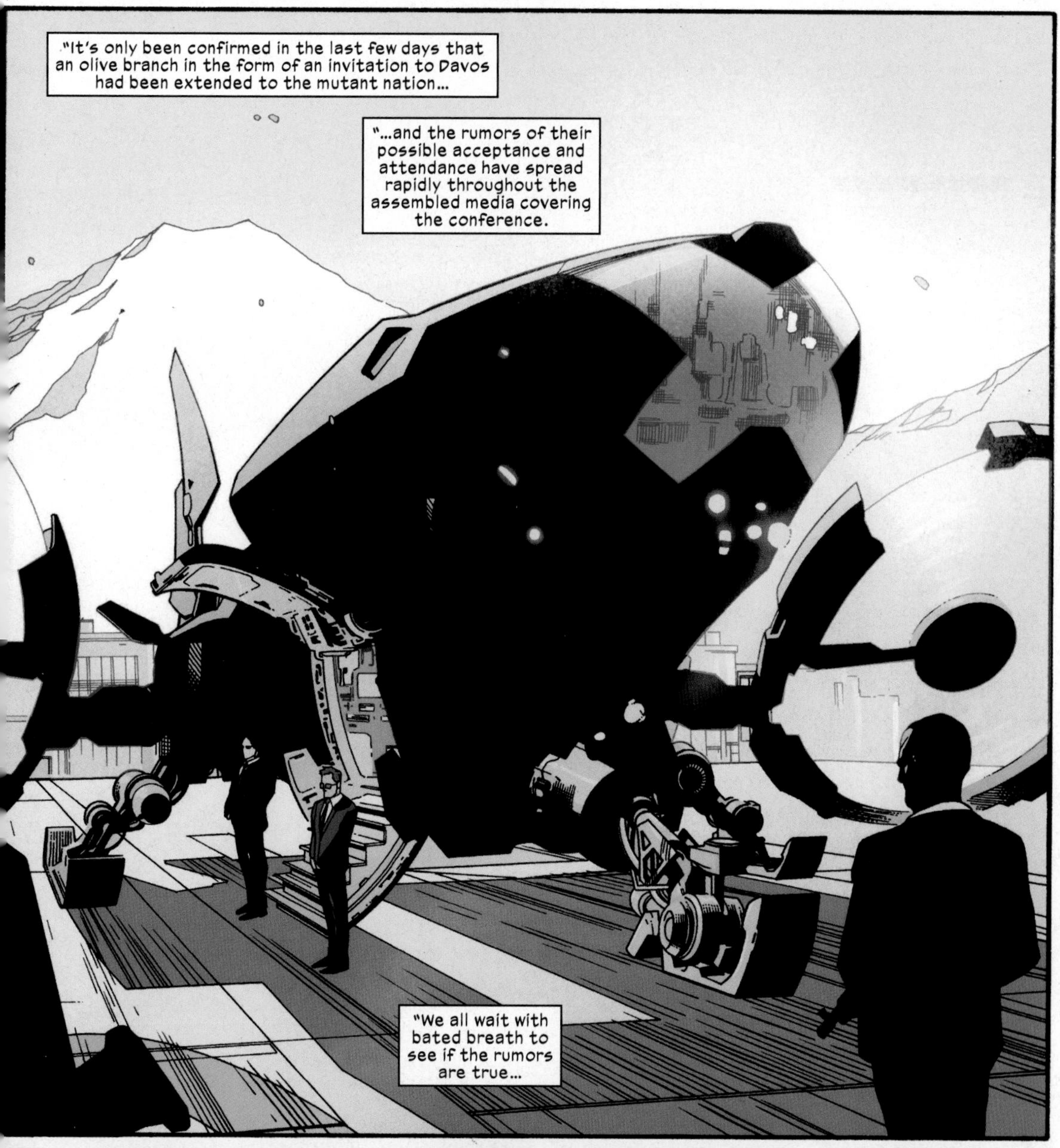
"It's only been confirmed in the last few days that an olive branch in the form of an invitation to Davos had been extended to the mutant nation...
"...and the rumors of their possible acceptance and attendance have spread rapidly throughout the assembled media covering the conference.
"We all wait with bated breath to see if the rumors are true...

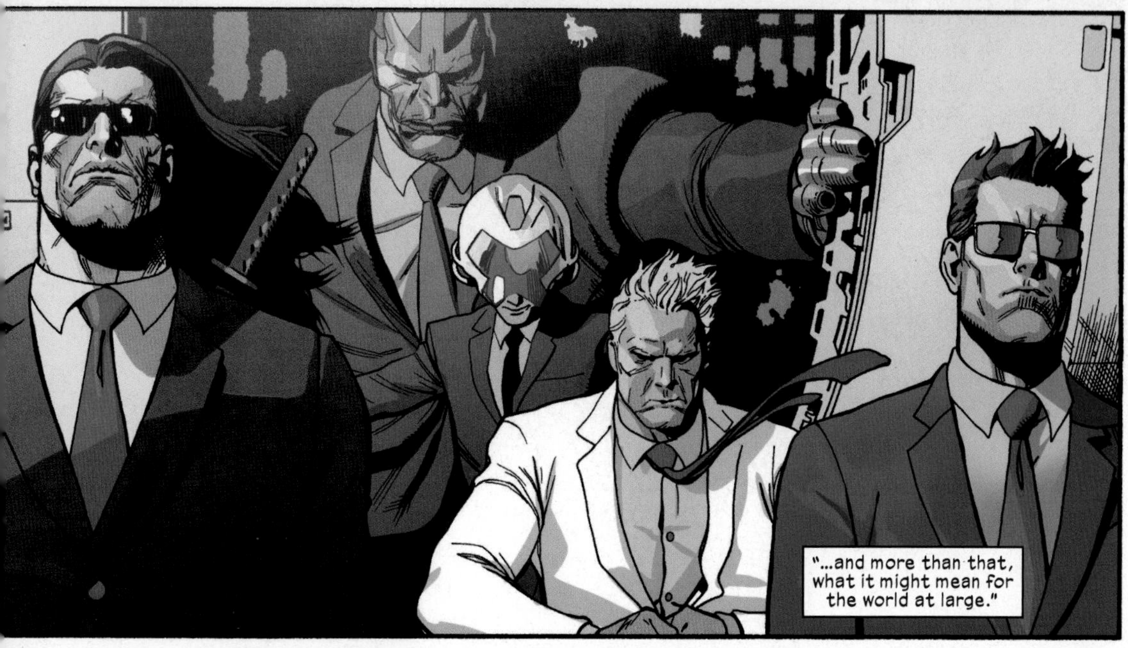
"...and more than that, what it might mean for the world at large."

[00_mutants_of_X]
[00_the_world__X]

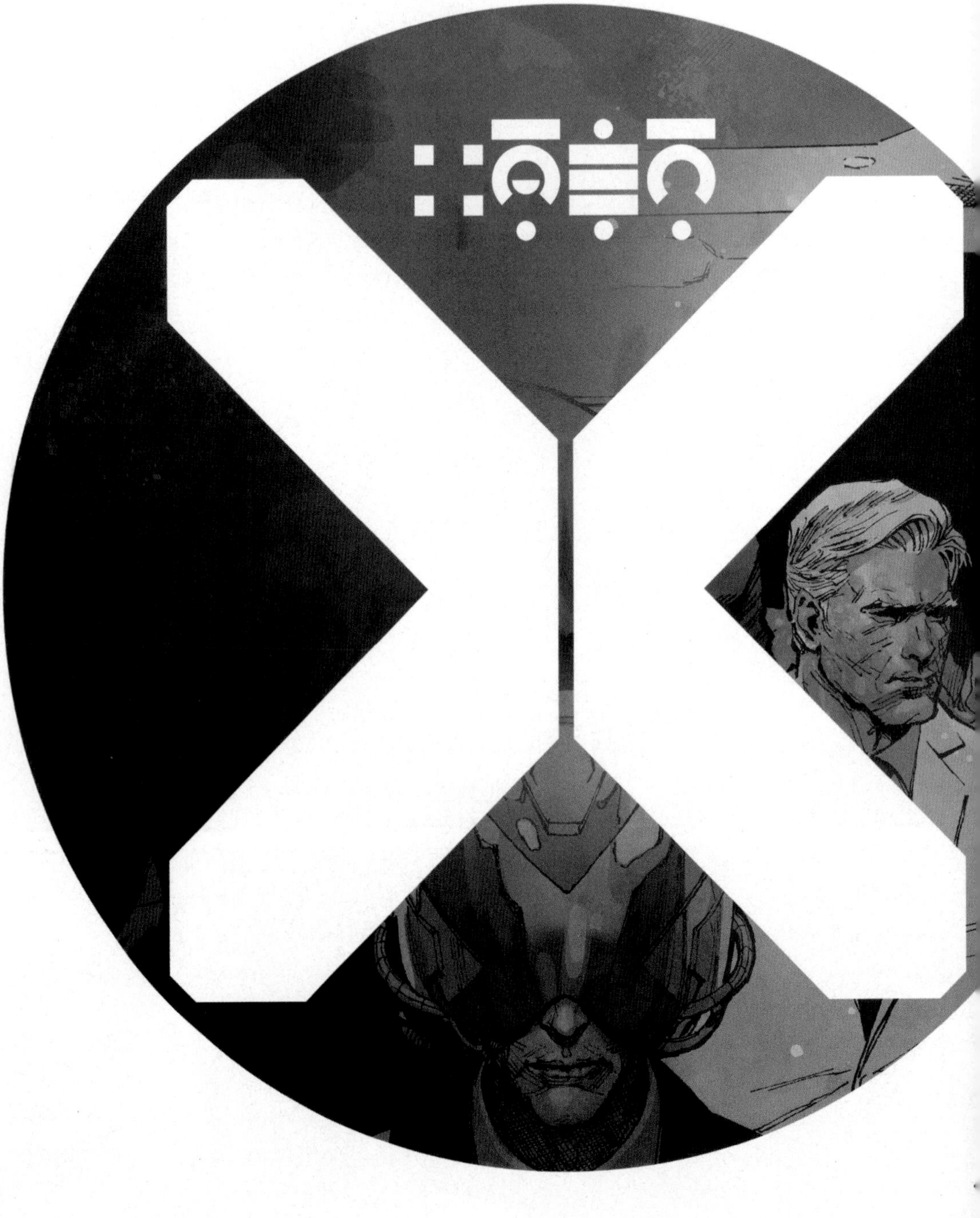

JONATHAN HICKMAN.............................[WRITER]
LEINIL FRANCIS YU ....[ARTIST]
GERRY ALANGUILAN & LEINIL FRANCIS YU..........[INKERS]
SUNNY GHO................................[COLOR ARTIST]
VC's CLAYTON COWLES.........................[LETTERER]
TOM MULLER..................................[DESIGN]

LEINIL FRANCIS YU & SUNNY GHO...........[COVER ARTISTS]

BELEN ORTEGA & JESUS ABURTOV....[VARIANT COVER ARTISTS]

NICK RUSSELL..............................[PRODUCTION]

ANNALISE BISSA.......................[ASSISTANT EDITOR]
JORDAN D. WHITE..............................[EDITOR]
C.B. CEBULSKI........................[EDITOR IN CHIEF]

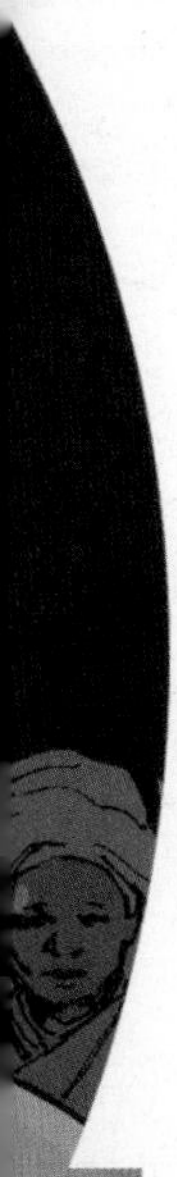

[04] X-MEN

[ISSUE FOUR].............GLOBAL ECONOMICS
X-MEN CREATED BY.................STAN LEE & JACK KIRBY

[00_mutants_of_X]
[00_the_world__X]

[00_00...0]
[00_00...4]

[00_unite_]
[00_____]

[00_____]

[00_____X]

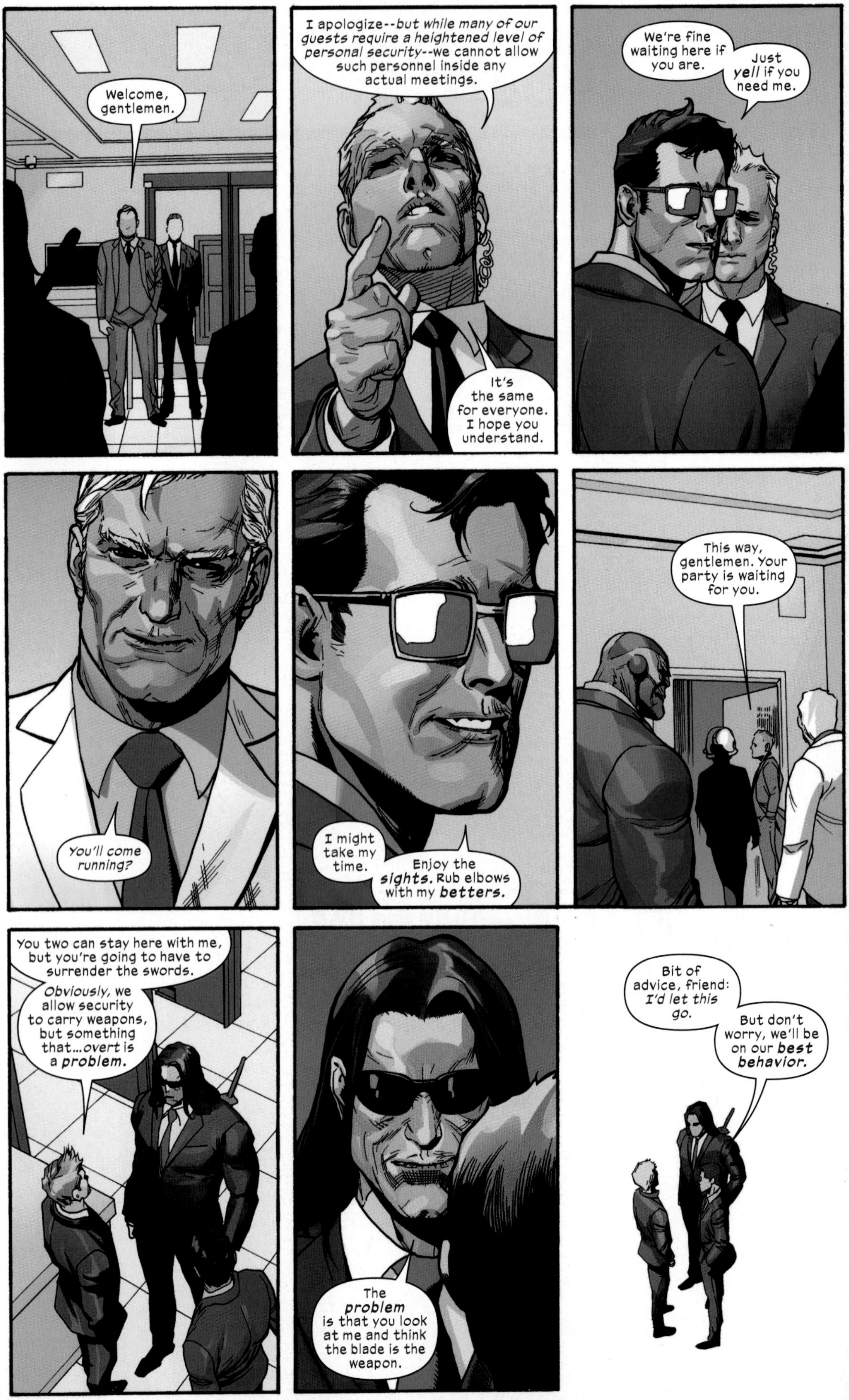
Welcome, gentlemen.
I apologize--*but while many of our guests require a heightened level of personal security*--we cannot allow such personnel inside any actual meetings.
It's the same for everyone. I hope you understand.
We're fine waiting here if you are.
Just *yell* if you need me.
You'll come running?
I might take my time.
Enjoy the ***sights.*** Rub elbows with my ***betters.***
This way, gentlemen. Your party is waiting for you.
You two can stay here with me, but you're going to have to surrender the swords.
Obviously, we allow security to carry weapons, but something that...*overt* is a ***problem.***
The ***problem*** is that you look at me and think the blade is the weapon.
Bit of advice, friend: *I'd let this go.*
But don't worry, we'll be on our ***best behavior.***

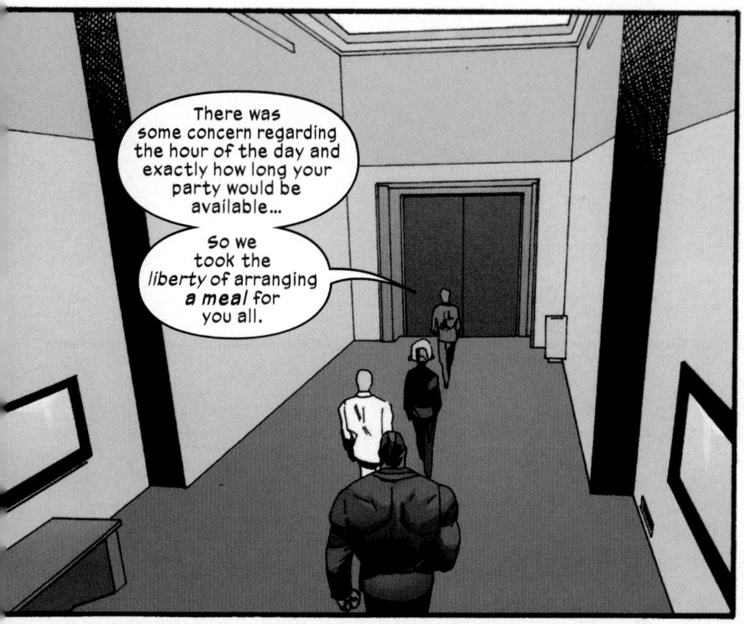
There was some concern regarding the hour of the day and exactly how long your party would be available...
So we took the *liberty* of arranging ***a meal*** for you all.

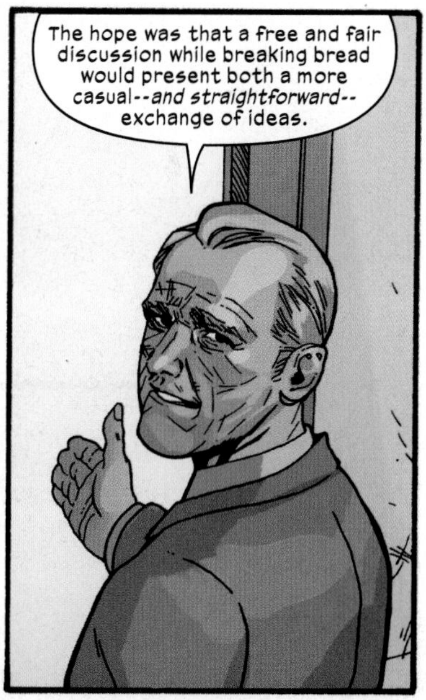
The hope was that a free and fair discussion while breaking bread would present both a more casual--*and straightforward*--exchange of ideas.

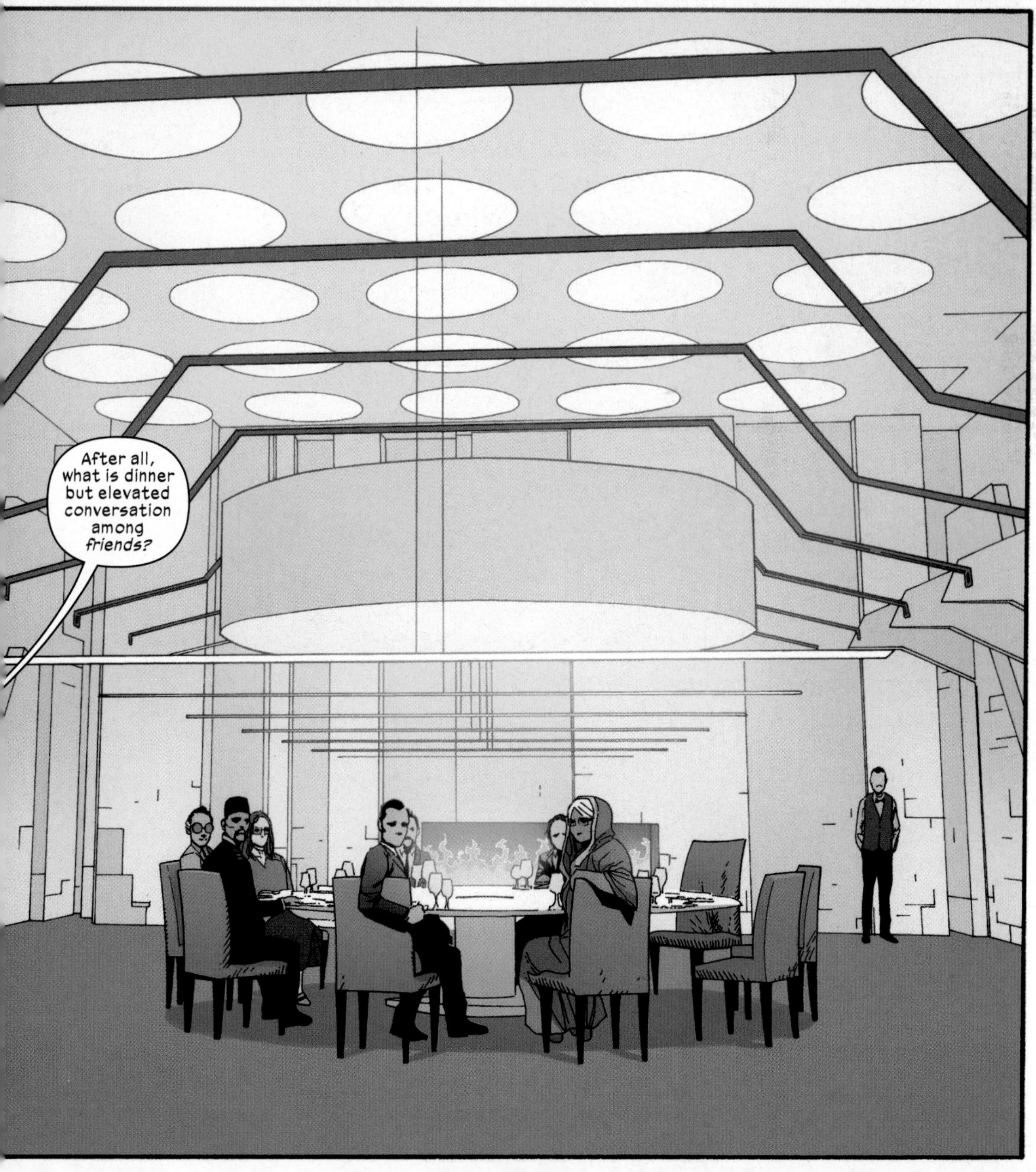
After all, what is dinner but elevated conversation among *friends?*

World Economic Forum
DINNER MENU

Watermelon Gazpacho
Infused with Habanero and Poblano Chiles

Shredded Kale,
Mushrooms, Bacon, Parmesan

+

Olive Wagyu
[Kagawa Prefecture]
Colbert Sauce

+

Brioche Tressée de Metz

IN ATTENDANCE:
—

KRAKOAN COUNCIL
```
Charles Xavier....................................Professor X
Erik Lehnsherr...................................Magneto
En Sabah Nur.....................................Apocalypse
```

POLITICAL REPRESENTATIVES
```
Hodari...........................................Wakandan Attaché
Ma Mingyu........................................Chinese Ambassador
Reilly Marshall..................................U.S. Ambassador
```

INTERNATIONAL GUESTS
```
Frederico João de Cézare.........................Brazil.........[Academic]
Daniela Gentile..................................Italy..........[Business]
Ludovic von Bergen...............................Switzerland.....[Business]
Banhi Gahlot.....................................India..........[Business]
```

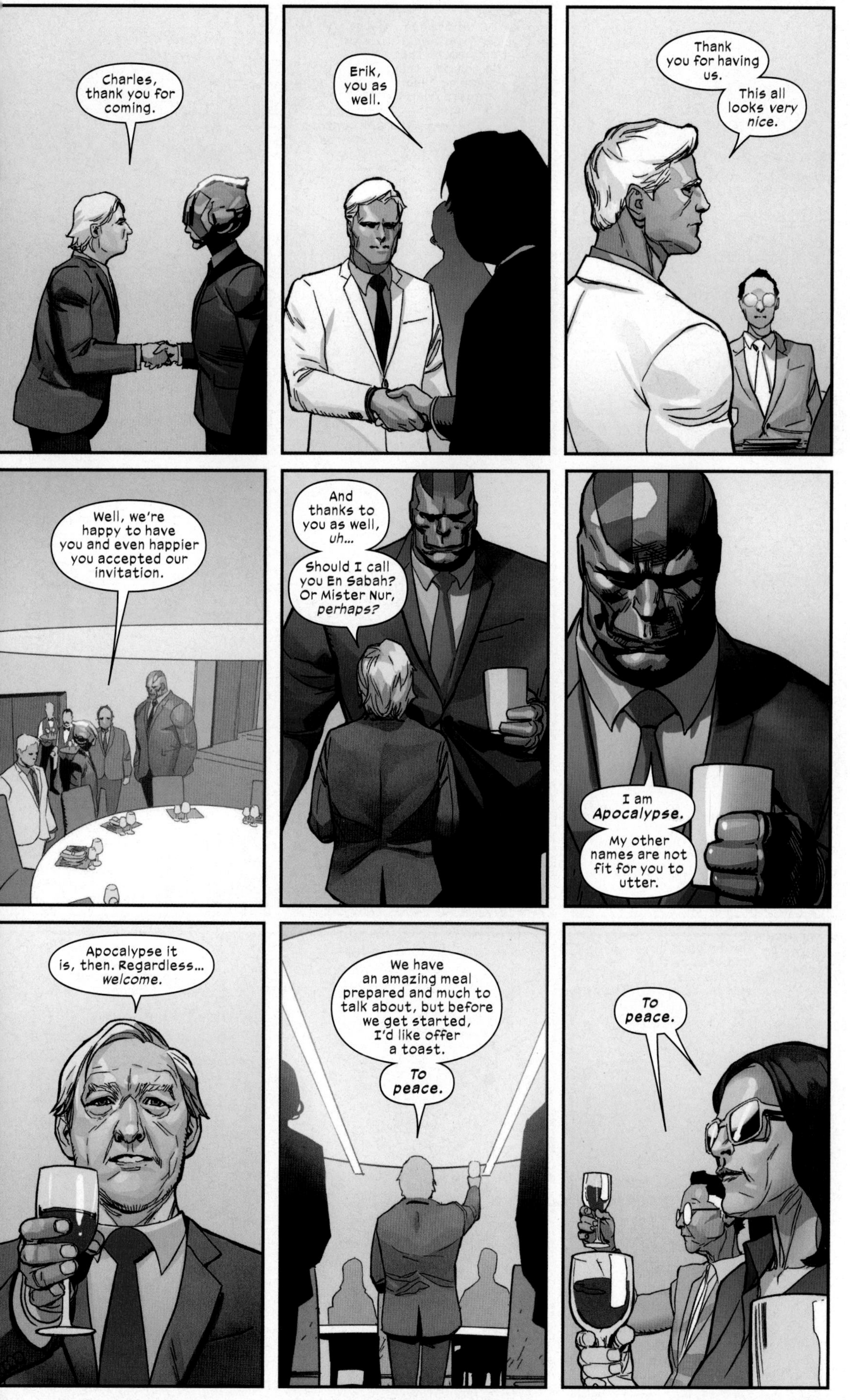
Charles, thank you for coming.
Erik, you as well.
Thank you for having us.
This all looks very nice.
Well, we're happy to have you and even happier you accepted our invitation.
And thanks to you as well, uh...
Should I call you En Sabah? Or Mister Nur, perhaps?
I am Apocalypse.
My other names are not fit for you to utter.
Apocalypse it is, then. Regardless... welcome.
We have an amazing meal prepared and much to talk about, but before we get started, I'd like offer a toast.
To peace.
To peace.

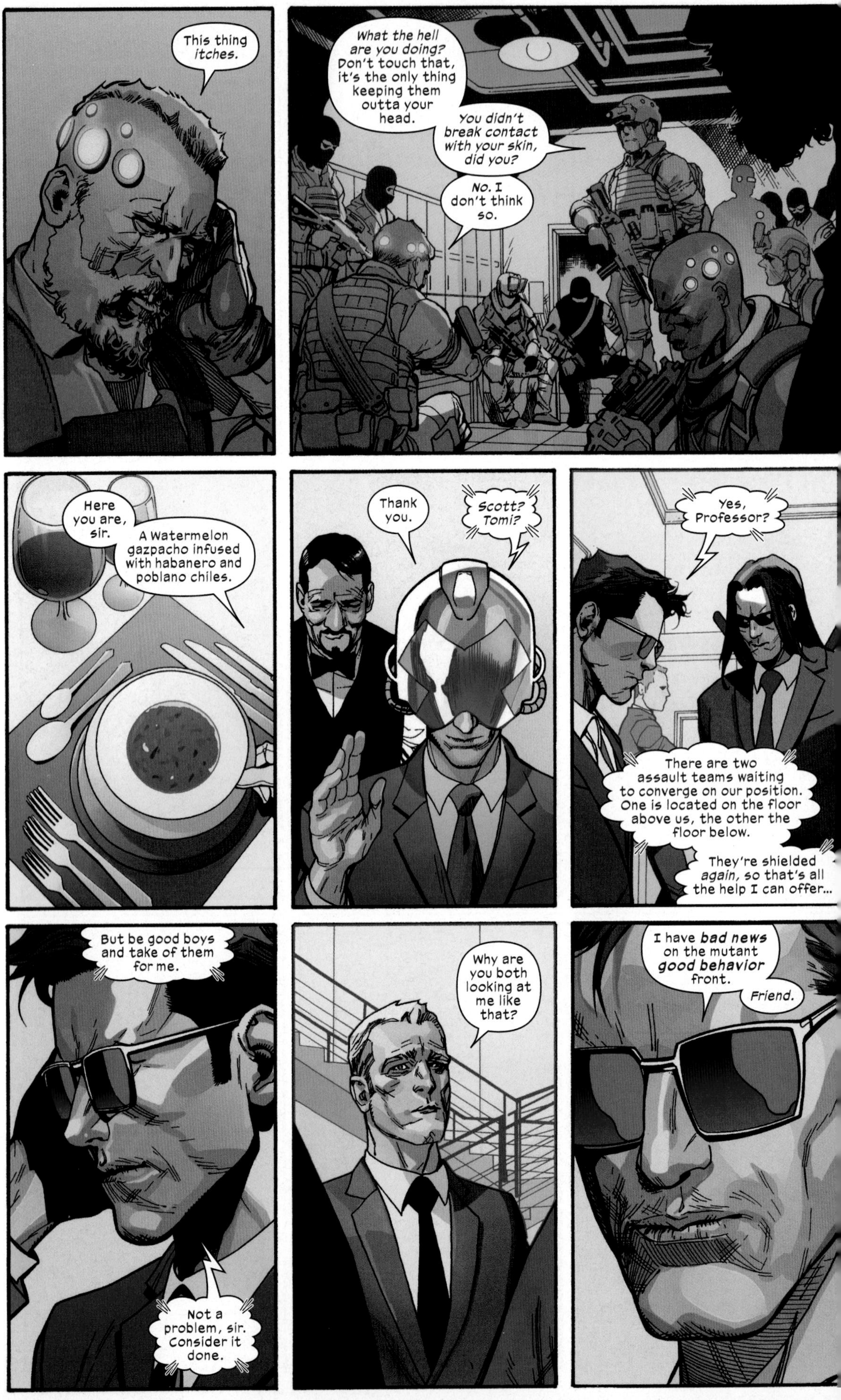
This thing *itches.*
What the hell are you doing? Don't touch that, it's the only thing keeping them outta your head.
You didn't break contact with your skin, did you?
No. I don't think so.
Here you are, sir.
A Watermelon gazpacho infused with habanero and poblano chiles.
Thank you.
Scott? Tomi?
Yes, Professor?
There are two assault teams waiting to converge on our position. One is located on the floor above us, the other the floor below.
They're shielded *again,* so that's all the help I can offer...
But be good boys and take of them for me.
Not a problem, sir. Consider it done.
Why are you both looking at me like that?
I have **bad news** on the mutant **good behavior** front.
Friend.

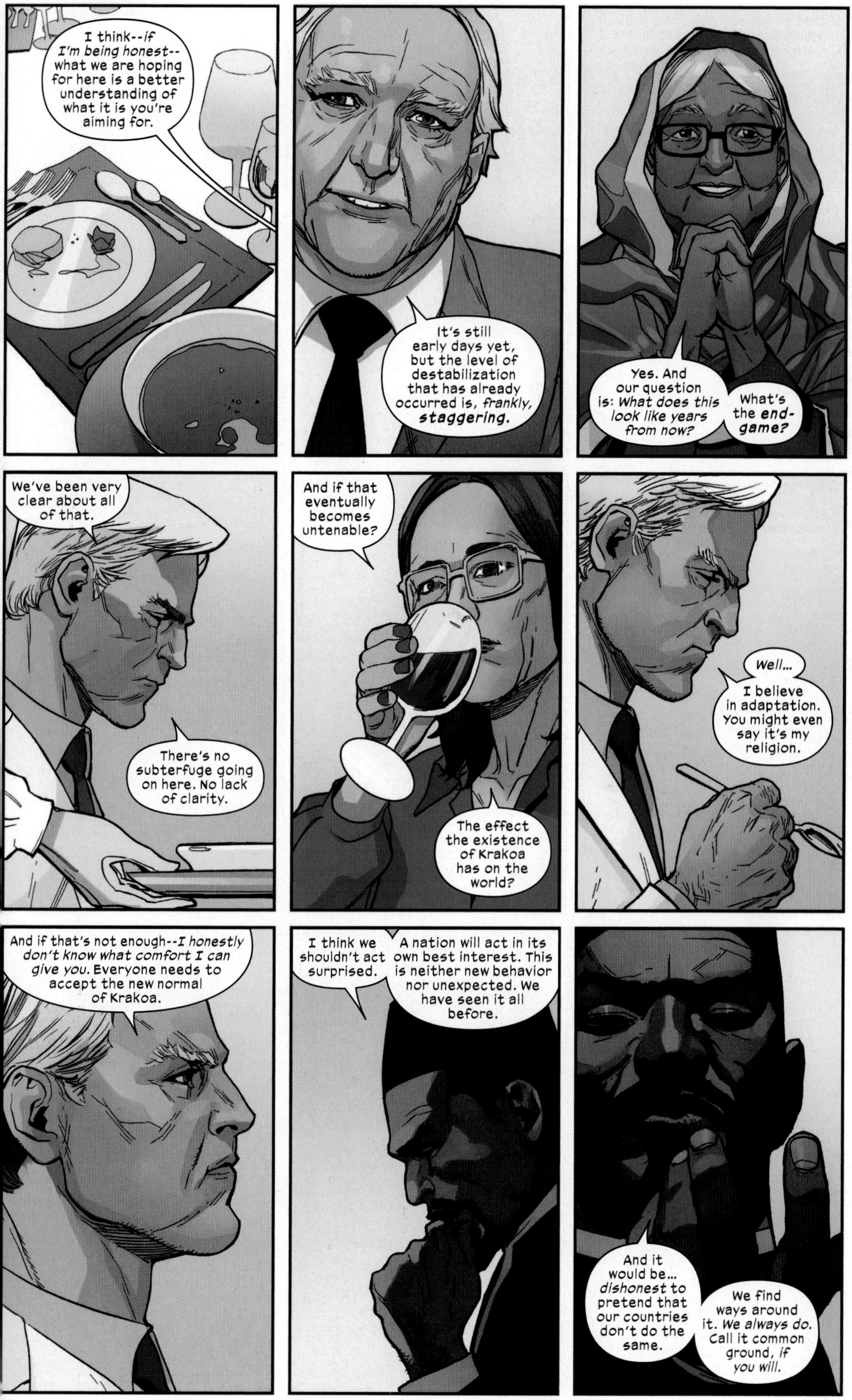

I think--*if I'm being honest*--what we are hoping for here is a better understanding of what it is you're aiming for.
It's still early days yet, but the level of destabilization that has already occurred is, *frankly*, ***staggering***.
Yes. And our question is: *What does this look like years from now?*
What's the ***end-game?***
We've been very clear about all of that.
There's no subterfuge going on here. No lack of clarity.
And if that eventually becomes untenable?
The effect the existence of Krakoa has on the world?
Well...
I believe in adaptation. You might even say it's my religion.
And if that's not enough--*I honestly don't know what comfort I can give you.* Everyone needs to accept the new normal of Krakoa.
I think we shouldn't act surprised.
A nation will act in its own best interest. This is neither new behavior nor unexpected. We have seen it all before.
And it would be... *dishonest* to pretend that our countries don't do the same.
We find ways around it. *We always do.* Call it common ground, *if you will.*

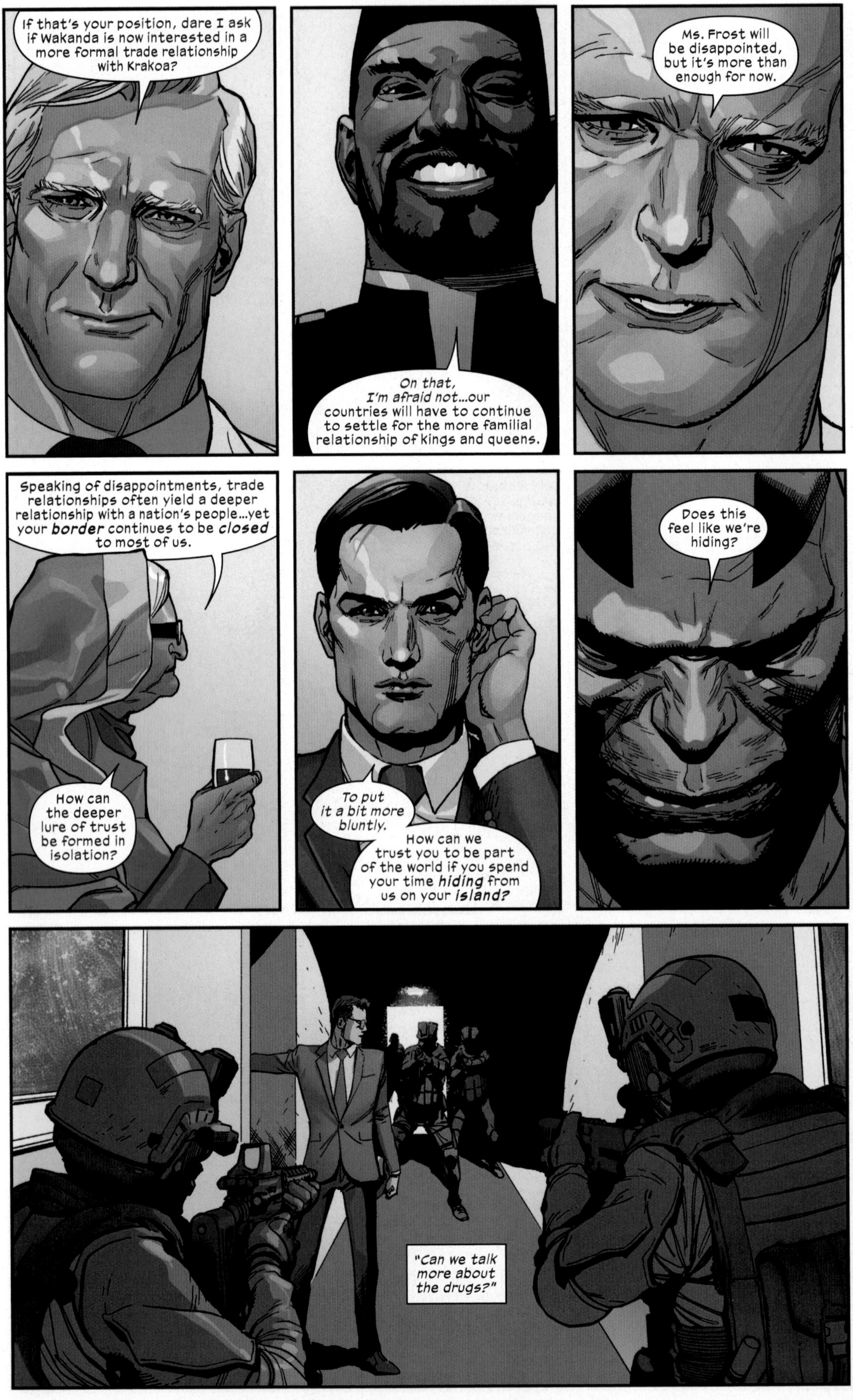
If that's your position, dare I ask if Wakanda is now interested in a more formal trade relationship with Krakoa?
On that, I'm afraid not...our countries will have to continue to settle for the more familial relationship of kings and queens.
Ms. Frost will be disappointed, but it's more than enough for now.
Speaking of disappointments, trade relationships often yield a deeper relationship with a nation's people...yet your *border* continues to be *closed* to most of us.
How can the deeper lure of trust be formed in isolation?
To put it a bit more bluntly.
How can we trust you to be part of the world if you spend your time *hiding* from us on your *island?*
Does this feel like we're hiding?
"Can we talk more about the drugs?"

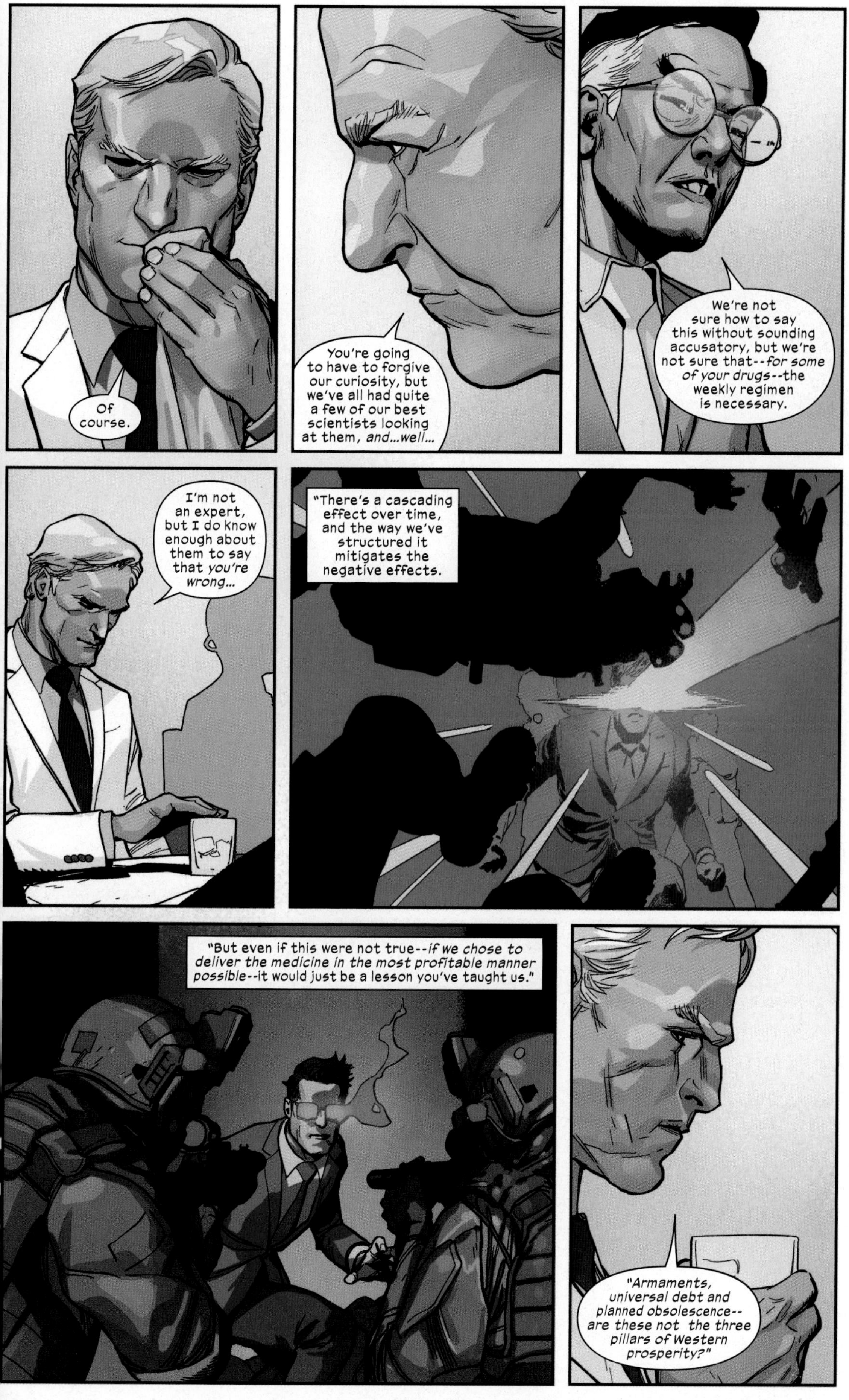
Of course.
You're going to have to forgive our curiosity, but we've all had quite a few of our best scientists looking at them, and...well...
We're not sure how to say this without sounding accusatory, but we're not sure that--for some of your drugs--the weekly regimen is necessary.
I'm not an expert, but I do know enough about them to say that you're wrong...
"There's a cascading effect over time, and the way we've structured it mitigates the negative effects.
"But even if this were not true--if we chose to deliver the medicine in the most profitable manner possible--it would just be a lesson you've taught us."
"Armaments, universal debt and planned obsolescence--are these not the three pillars of Western prosperity?"

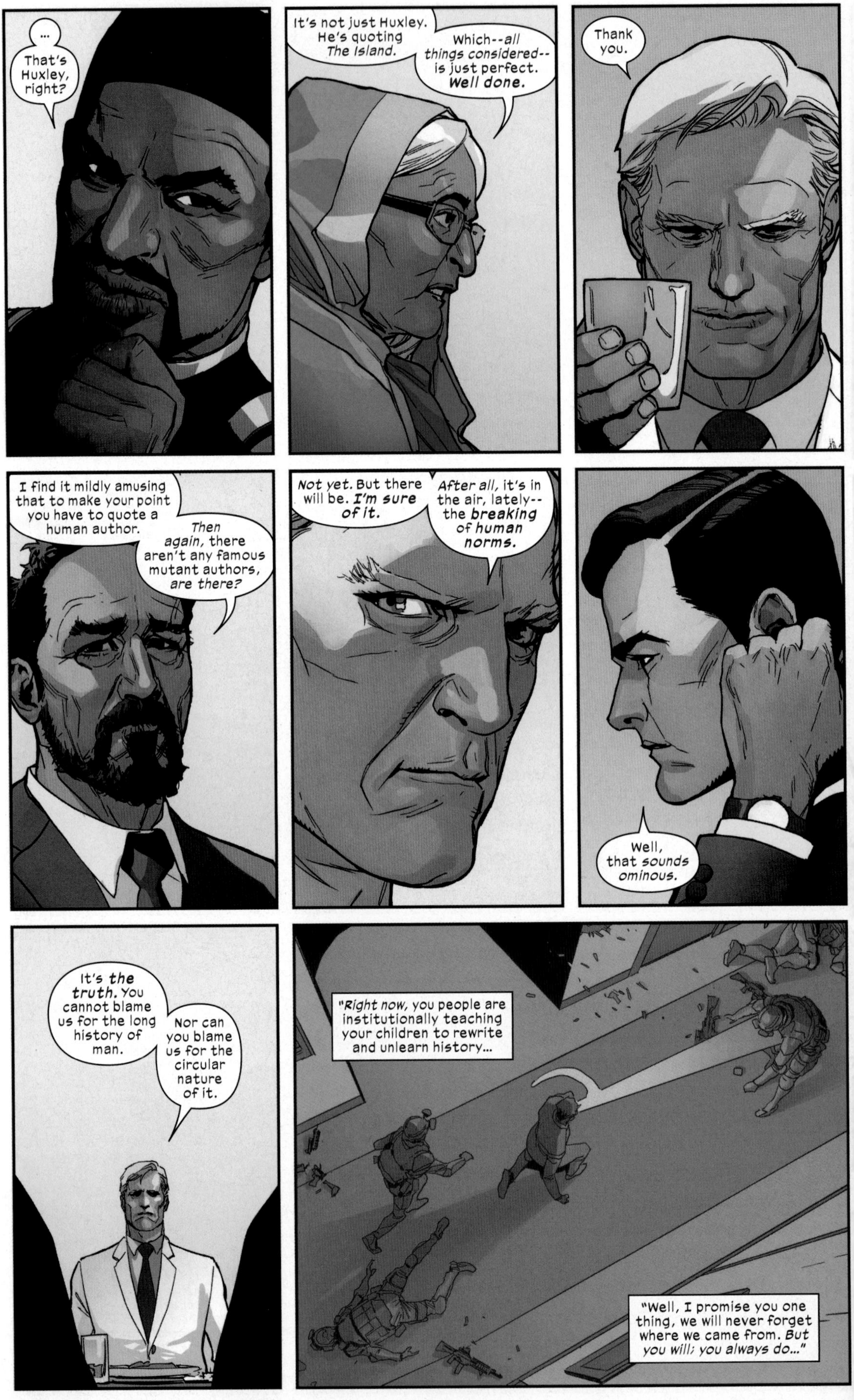

...
That's Huxley, right?
It's not just Huxley. He's quoting *The Island.*
Which--*all things considered*--is just perfect. **Well done.**
Thank you.
I find it mildly amusing that to make your point you have to quote a human author.
Then again, there aren't any famous mutant authors, *are there?*
Not yet. But there will be. ***I'm sure of it.***
After all, it's in the air, lately--the ***breaking*** of ***human norms.***
Well, that *sounds ominous.*
It's ***the truth.*** You cannot blame us for the long history of man.
Nor can you blame us for the circular nature of it.
"*Right now,* you people are institutionally teaching your children to rewrite and unlearn history...
"Well, I promise you one thing, we will never forget where we came from. *But you will; you always do...*"

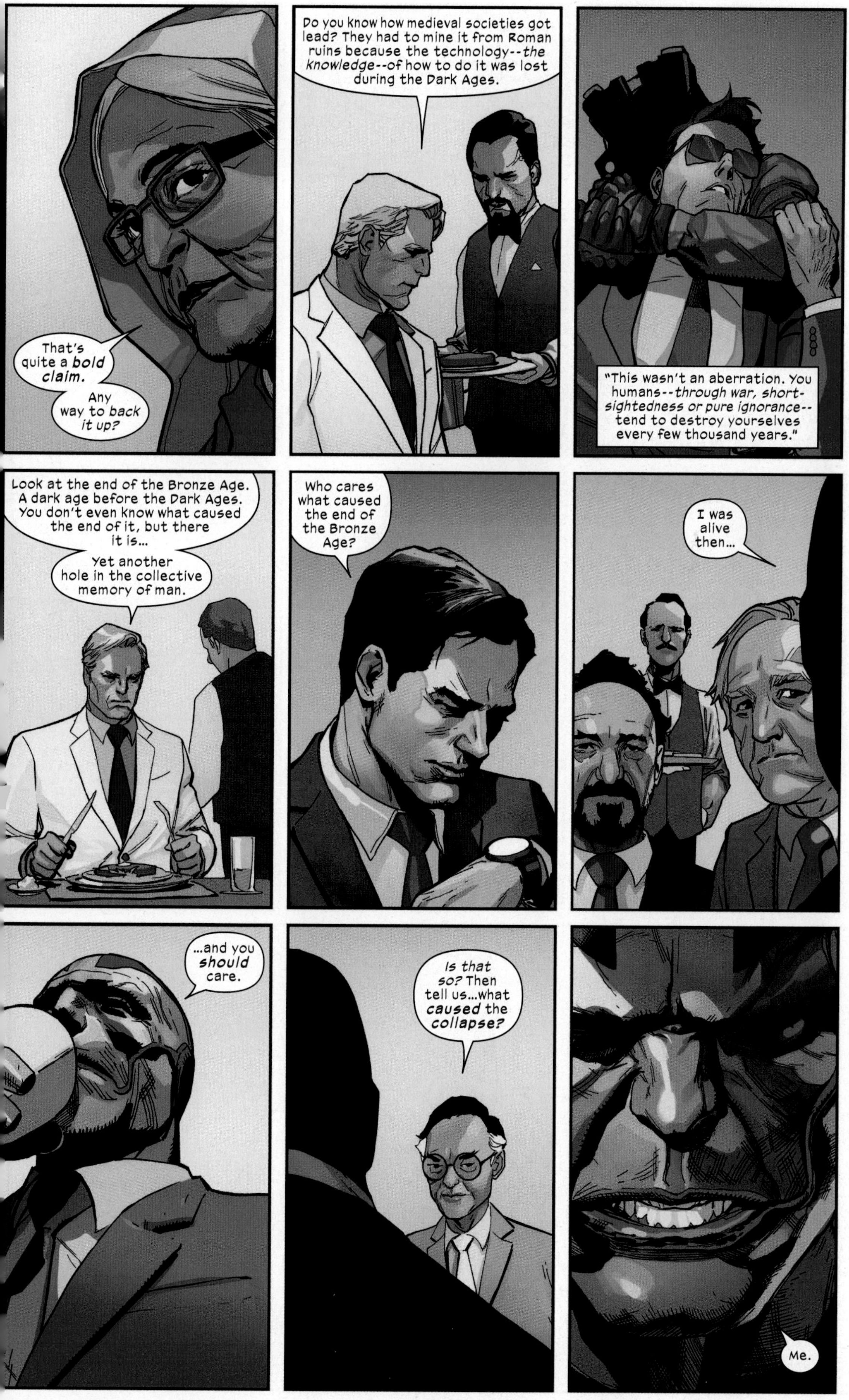
That's quite a bold claim.
Any way to back it up?
Do you know how medieval societies got lead? They had to mine it from Roman ruins because the technology--the knowledge--of how to do it was lost during the Dark Ages.
"This wasn't an aberration. You humans--through war, short-sightedness or pure ignorance--tend to destroy yourselves every few thousand years."
Look at the end of the Bronze Age. A dark age before the Dark Ages. You don't even know what caused the end of it, but there it is...
Yet another hole in the collective memory of man.
Who cares what caused the end of the Bronze Age?
I was alive then...
...and you should care.
Is that so? Then tell us...what caused the collapse?
Me.

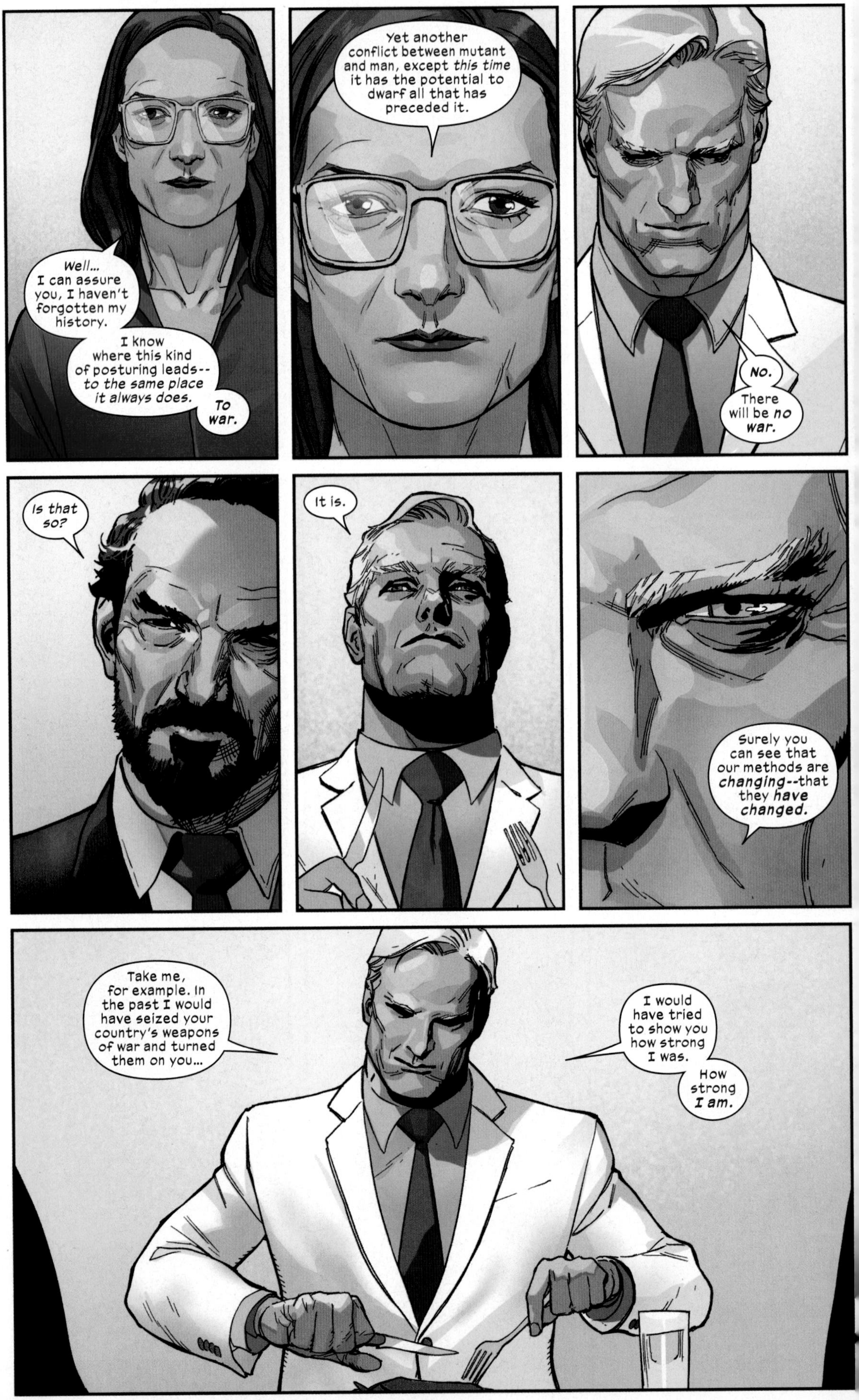

Well... I can assure you, I haven't forgotten my history.
I know where this kind of posturing leads-- *to the same place it always does.*
To war.
Yet another conflict between mutant and man, except *this time* it has the potential to dwarf all that has preceded it.
No.
There will be *no war.*
Is that so?
It is.
Surely you can see that our methods are *changing*--that they *have changed.*
Take me, for example. In the past I would have seized your country's weapons of war and turned them on you...
I would have tried to show you how strong I was.
How strong *I am.*

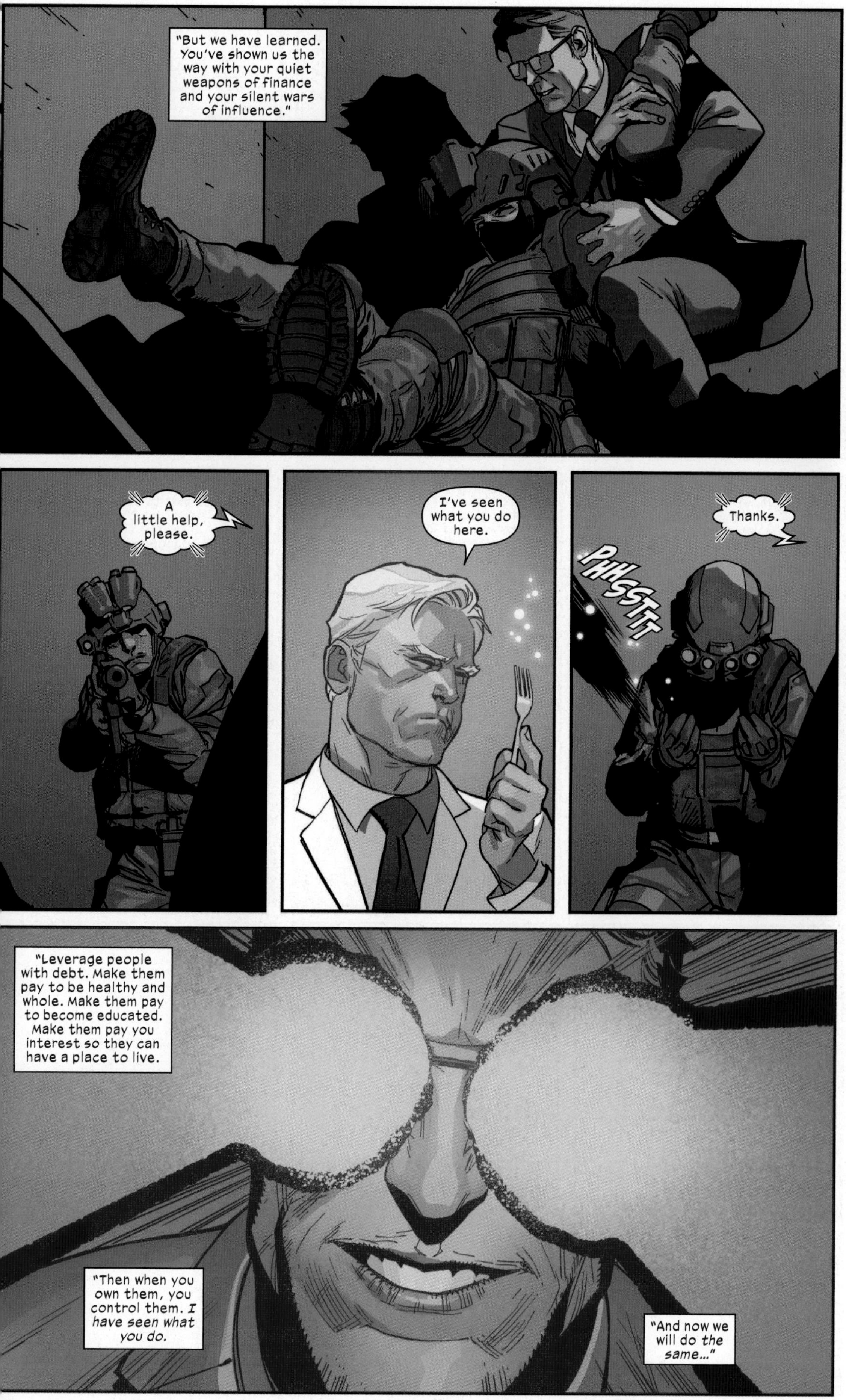
"But we have learned. You've shown us the way with your quiet weapons of finance and your silent wars of influence."
A little help, please.
I've seen what you do here.
Thanks.
PHHSSTTT
"Leverage people with debt. Make them pay to be healthy and whole. Make them pay to become educated. Make them pay you interest so they can have a place to live.
"Then when you own them, you control them. *I have seen what you do.*
"And now we will do *the same*..."

...but *better.*

Better versions of a better life. Better drugs for a longer, healthier existence.

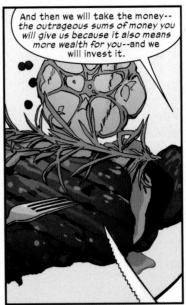

And then we will take the money-- the outrageous sums of money you will give us because it also means more wealth for you--and we will invest it.

We will buy your *banks.* We will buy your *schools.* We will buy your *media.*

We will buy *your politicians.*

And then, when we have bought all the rest, we will buy *you*-- because you have taught us that everything has a price.

And we are *happy to pay.*

Then, when we have this influence-- *we will use it.* We will make sure that the wrong sort of people--*and you know who*--no longer have any economic power.

We will not allow them inside our institutions, because it's important they do not have anywhere to peddle their dangerous, outdated ideas.

And that is how it will end. Like a fire with no oxygen.

Yes, of course, there will still be people who fear and hate us...they just simply won't be able to do anything about it any longer.

So as I said... There will be *no war.*

Oh, and by the way...

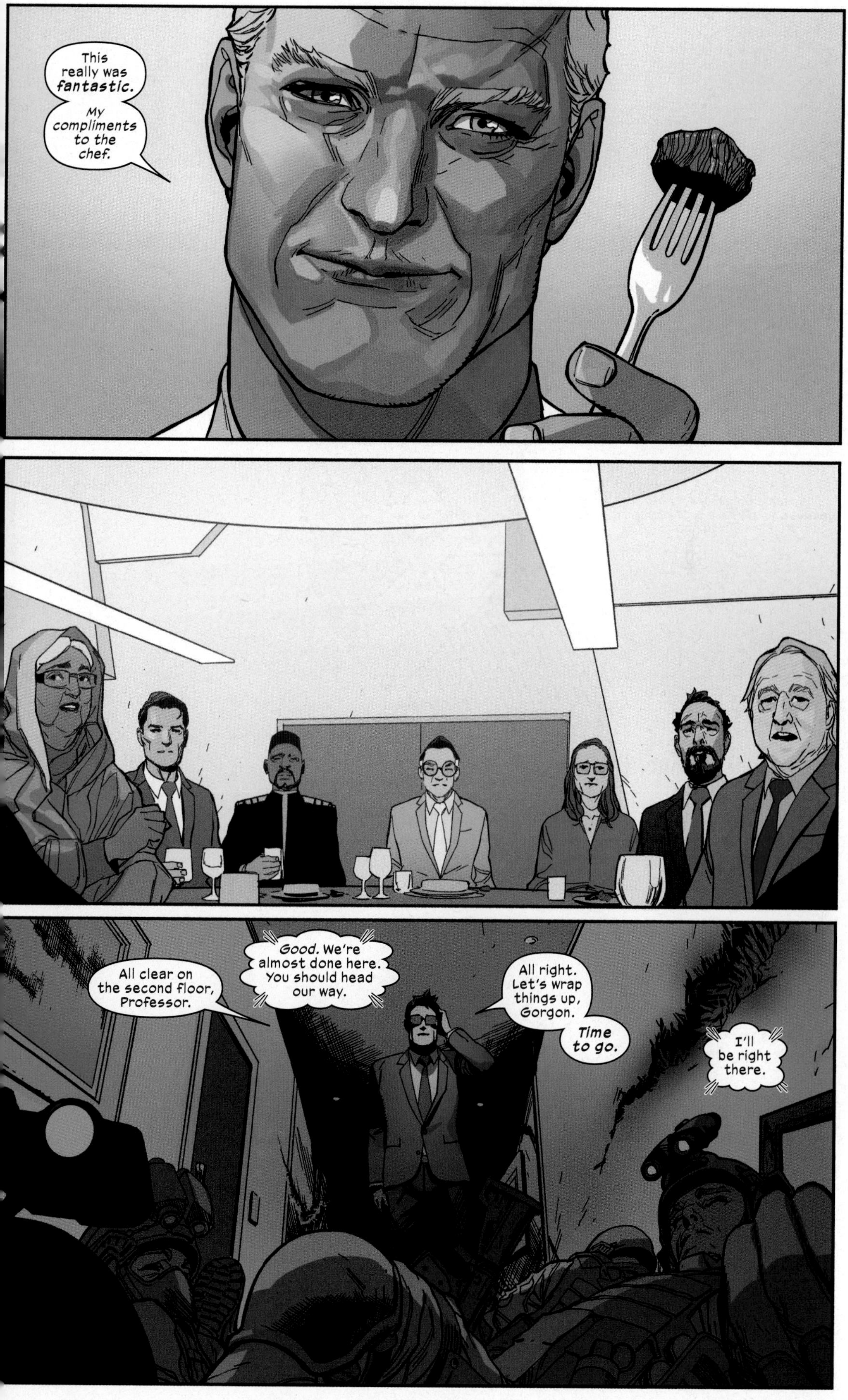
This really was fantastic.
My compliments to the chef.
All clear on the second floor, Professor.
Good. We're almost done here. You should head our way.
All right. Let's wrap things up, Gorgon.
Time to go.
I'll be right there.

KRAKOAN CAPTAINS

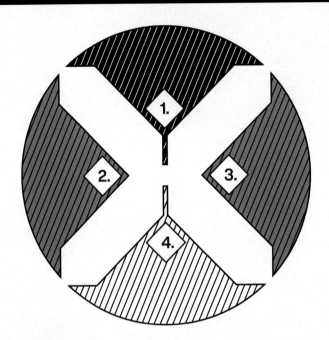

CAPTAIN HIERARCHY

[1]

CYCLOPS.........................MAGIK.......................
CAPTAIN COMMANDER..............CAPTAIN.....................
X-MEN..........................SEXTANT.....................

[2]

[3]

BISHOP.........................GORGON......................
CAPTAIN........................CAPTAIN.....................
HELLFIRE TRADING...............COUNCIL GUARD...............

[4]

GORGON

While the other three captains have broader, more extensive jurisdictions, Gorgon has a smaller, more specific one.* As one of the most experienced, and most lethal, mutants on Earth, he was chosen by the Captain Commander [after consultation with Wolverine] to act as the personal protector for members of the Quiet Council [especially when they leave Krakoa].

*After the events surrounding the assassination of Charles Xavier, if an Autumn council member plans to enter a hostile environment, the expectation is that Gorgon will accompany them.

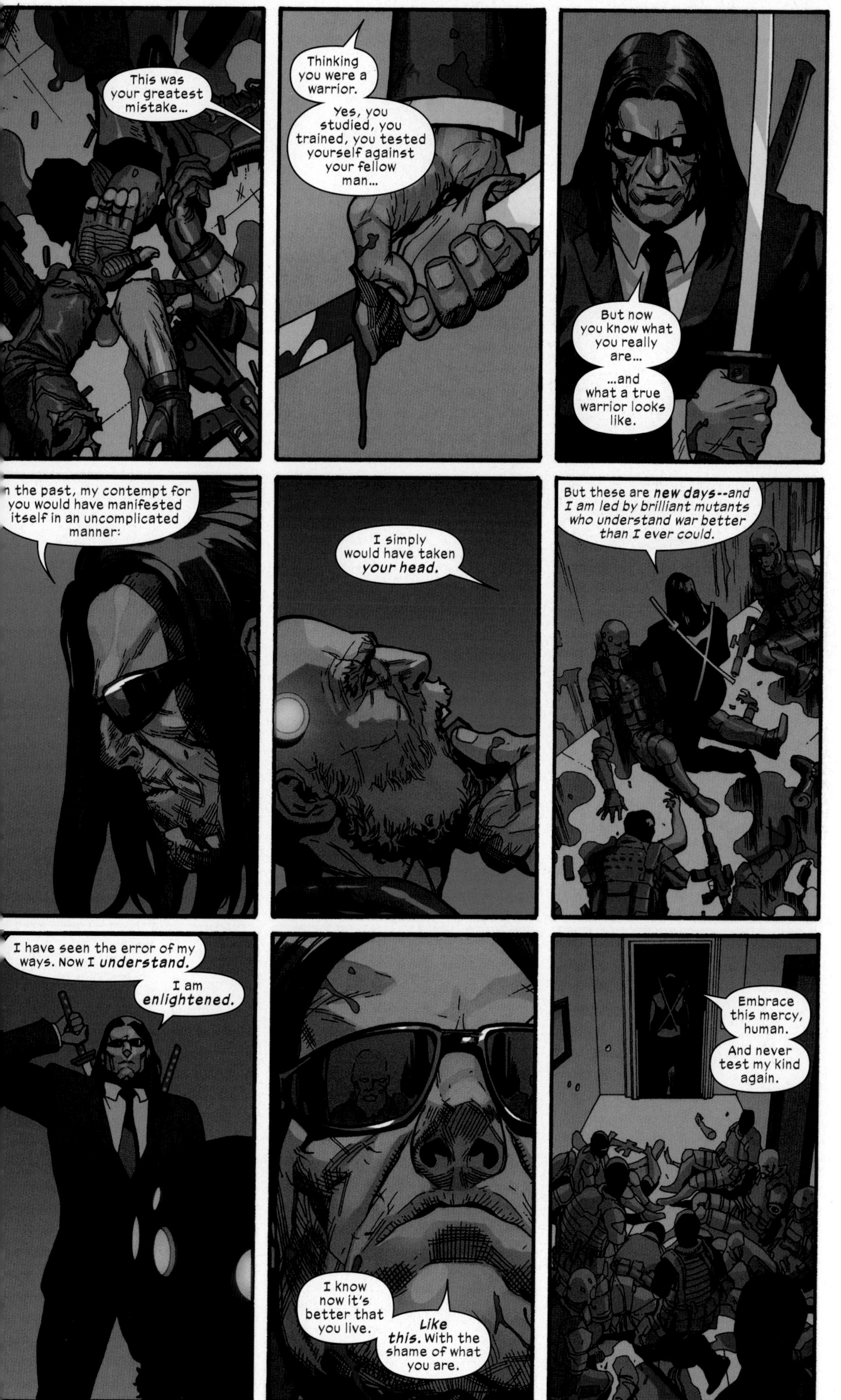
This was your greatest mistake...
Thinking you were a warrior.
Yes, you studied, you trained, you tested yourself against your fellow man...
But now you know what you really are...
...and what a true warrior looks like.
n the past, my contempt for you would have manifested itself in an uncomplicated manner:
I simply would have taken *your head.*
But these are *new days*--and *I am led by brilliant mutants who understand war better than I ever could.*
I have seen the error of my ways. Now I *understand.*
I am *enlightened.*
I know now it's better that you live.
Like this. With the shame of what you are.
Embrace this mercy, human.
And never test my kind again.

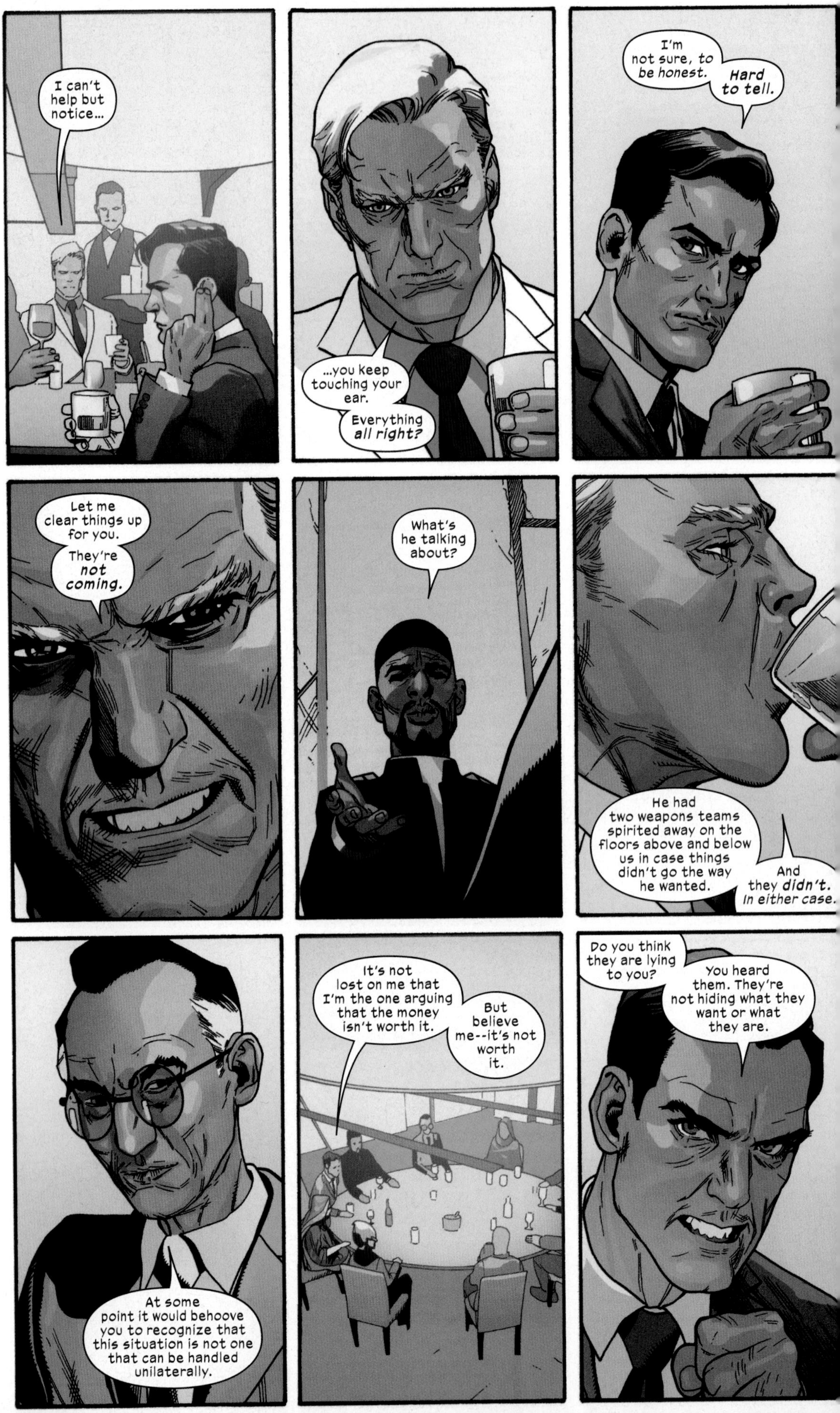
I can't help but notice...
...you keep touching your ear.
Everything all right?
I'm not sure, to be honest.
Hard to tell.
Let me clear things up for you.
They're not coming.
What's he talking about?
He had two weapons teams spirited away on the floors above and below us in case things didn't go the way he wanted.
And they didn't. In either case.
At some point it would behoove you to recognize that this situation is not one that can be handled unilaterally.
It's not lost on me that I'm the one arguing that the money isn't worth it.
But believe me--it's not worth it.
Do you think they are lying to you?
You heard them. They're not hiding what they want or what they are.

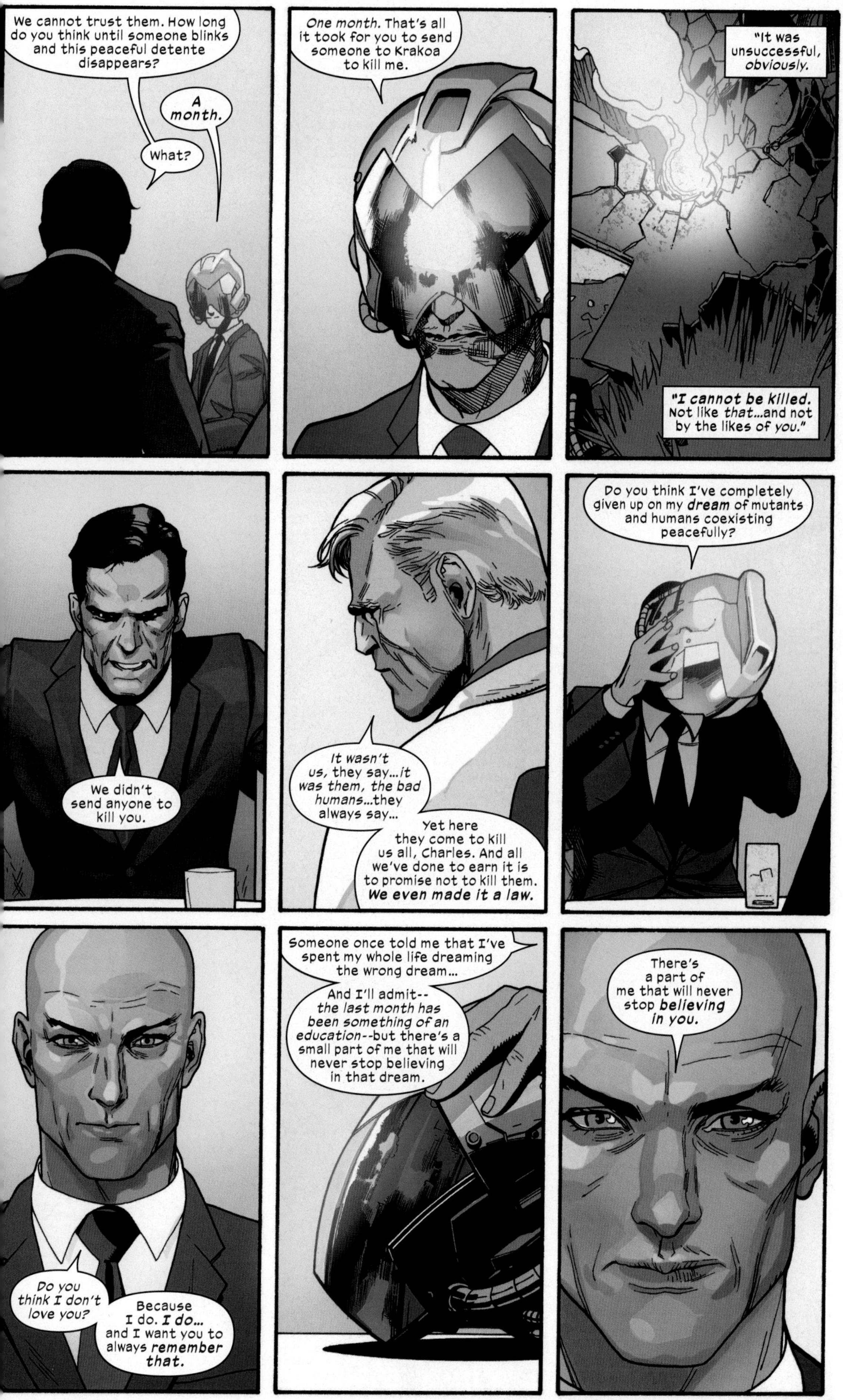
We cannot trust them. How long do you think until someone blinks and this peaceful detente disappears?
What?
A month.
One month. That's all it took for you to send someone to Krakoa to kill me.
"It was unsuccessful, obviously.
"I cannot be killed. Not like that...and not by the likes of you."
We didn't send anyone to kill you.
It wasn't us, they say...it was them, the bad humans...they always say...
Yet here they come to kill us all, Charles. And all we've done to earn it is to promise not to kill them. We even made it a law.
Do you think I've completely given up on my dream of mutants and humans coexisting peacefully?
Do you think I don't love you?
Because I do. I do... and I want you to always remember that.
Someone once told me that I've spent my whole life dreaming the wrong dream...
And I'll admit-- the last month has been something of an education--but there's a small part of me that will never stop believing in that dream.
There's a part of me that will never stop believing in you.

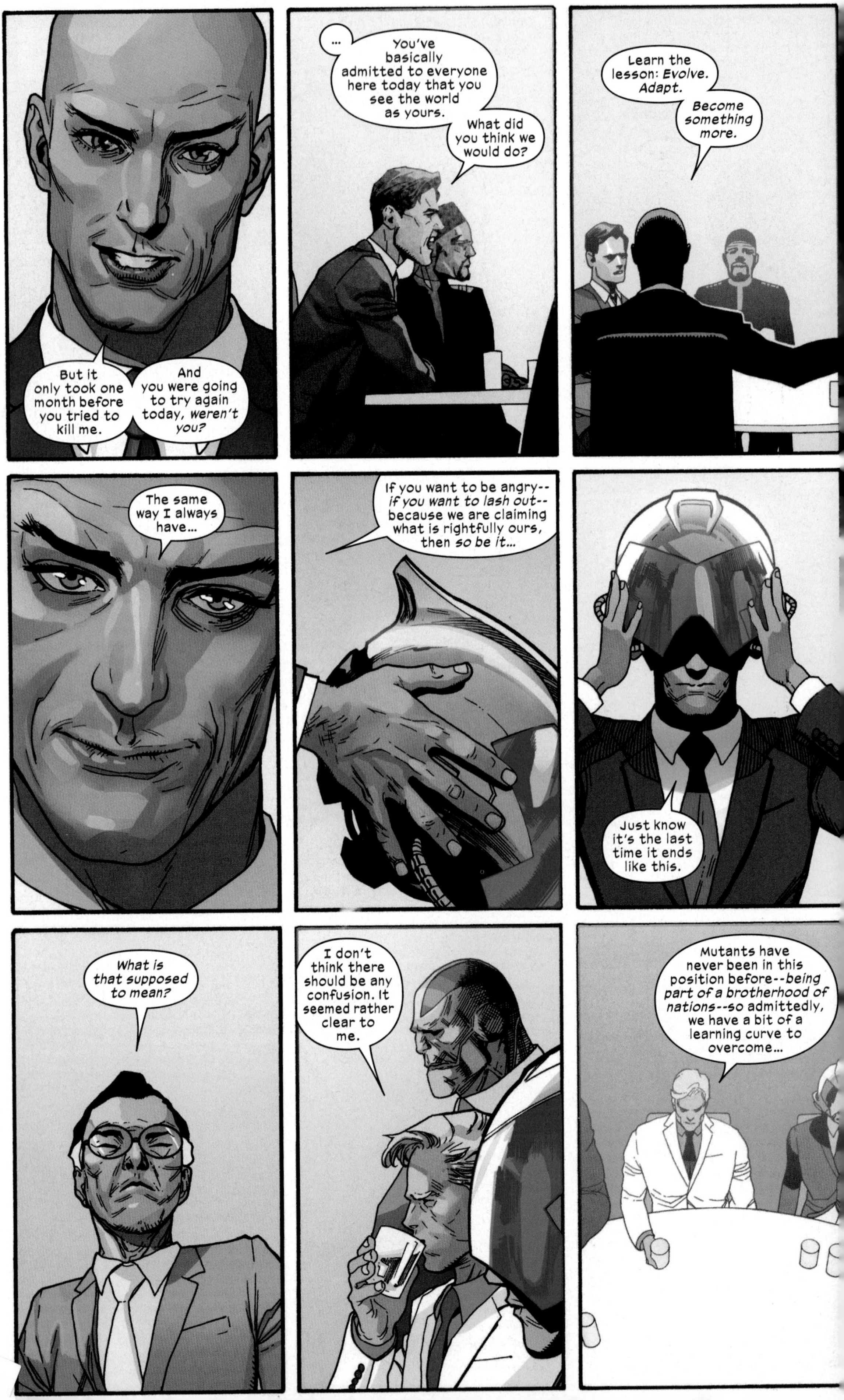

But it only took one month before you tried to kill me.
And you were going to try again today, *weren't you?*
...
You've basically admitted to everyone here today that you see the world as yours.
What did you think we would do?
Learn the lesson: *Evolve. Adapt.*
Become something more.
The same way I always have...
If you want to be angry-- *if you want to lash out--* because we are claiming what is rightfully ours, then *so be it...*
Just know it's the last time it ends like this.
What is that supposed to mean?
I don't think there should be any confusion. It seemed rather clear to me.
Mutants have never been in this position before--*being part of a brotherhood of nations*--so admittedly, we have a bit of a learning curve to overcome...

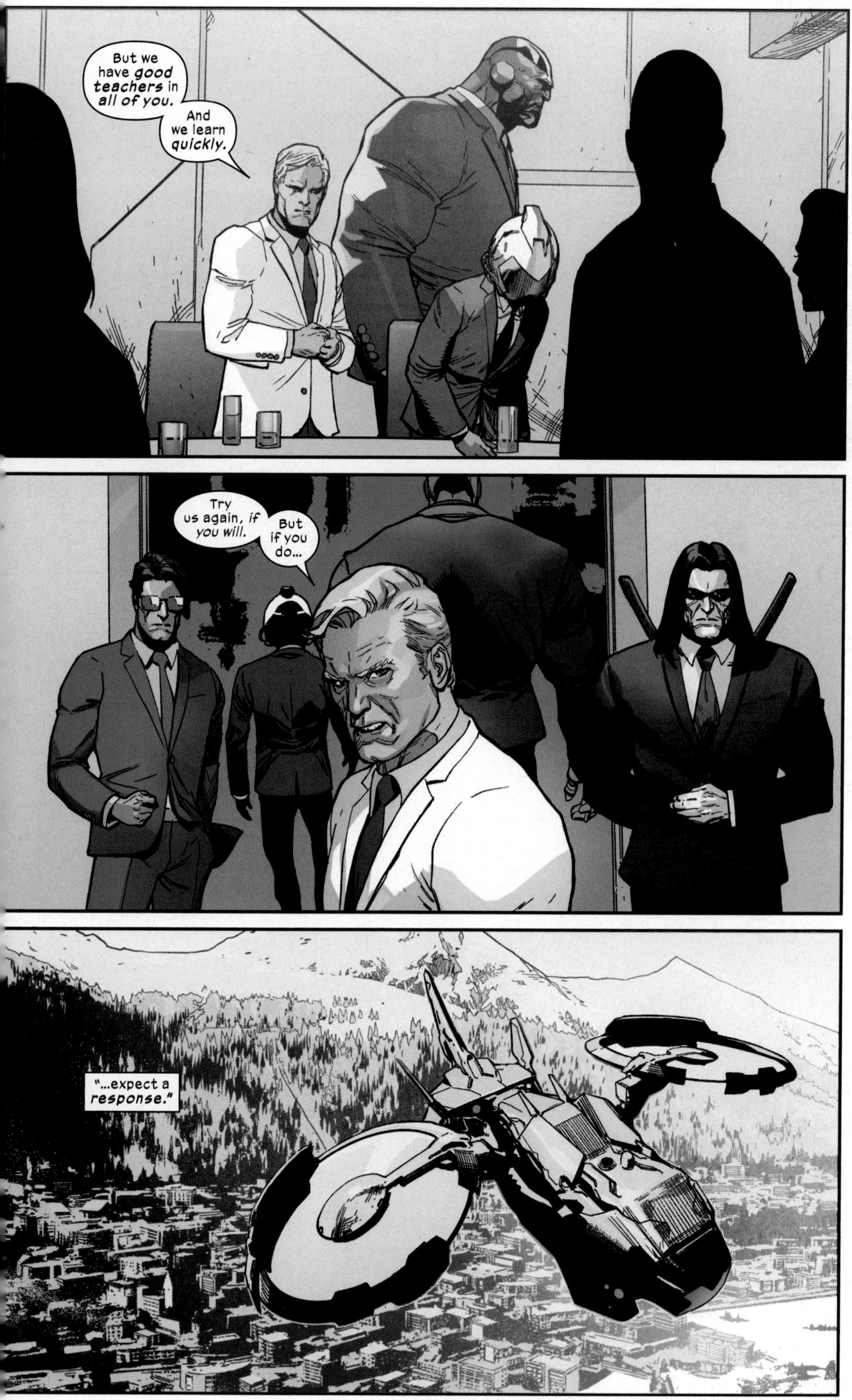
But we have good teachers in all of you.
And we learn quickly.
Try us again, if you will.
But if you do...
"...expect a response."